GOURMET CLASSICS

GOURMET CLASSICS

A cookbook containing a critical selection of some of the best and most authentic recipes.

Written
and
Revised
by
Andrew M. Shafer

Photography
by
Michael Gordon

PALM BOOKS

ACKNOWLEDGEMENTS

I would like to give special thanks to:
Viola Quanby, the inspiration for this book; Dorothy Gill, who gave me guidance when I needed it; Dorothy Bryant and Marcia Muller, both writers extraordinaire; Clarence Brown, for his friendship and help on this book; Michael Gordon, for his insights; Joseph Ware, for his generosity and good cheer; Christine Andermahr, for her dedication to the art of cooking; My friends, for their encouragement; and last but not least I would like to express my gratitude to my Family for having the ability to withstand my experiments. I love them all.

Jacket, Endpaper, and Book Design by
Andrew M. Shafer

Cover Photograph by
Michael Gordon

All inquiries should be addressed to:
Palm Books
2301 Sycamore Dr.
Dept. 34
Antioch, CA 94509

Library of Congress Cataloging in Publication Data
81-83811
Andrew M. Shafer
Gourmet Classics
Includes Index
1. Cookery, International 2. Cookery, French
1. Title: Gourmet Classics
TX
ISBN 0-9608036-0-2

Manufactured in the United States of America
10 9 8 7 6 5 4 3 2
First Edition

To Carol

CONTENTS

INTRODUCTION

My first gourmet dinner was like a revelation for me. I had no idea that food could taste this delicious. It is because of that experience that I began to search for the mysteries, as I saw them, of how these foods were prepared.

In my search, I found that practically everyone who made these specialties had a different idea of the way these foods should be prepared. So, I decided to focus on the classical preparation. I might have wandered a bit in my search, but I feel I have found the recipes that represent the regions I selected.

While looking for unique recipes, I discovered that many of them had not been recorded by their creators but were recorded as "Specialties of the House" in many of the fine, old restaurants. This is not to say that there aren't any specific individual creators of these dishes, for there are many. Included among them are *Brillat-Savarin* and *Carême,* who are two of the greatest chefs in modern history. I have not used any of their specific recipes because there have been volumes written on these two men, but I am quite certain they have had a considerable influence on the recipes I have included from France. France seems to be the central core of gastronomy, and with its history, France goes unchallenged by its dedication to the preparation of food.

The "Specialties of the House," as I mentioned, were many times the fame and fortune of these restaurants. It sometimes took as few as one recipe to popularize the establishment. Although many times it was the *Bill-of-Fare* or menu that made these places famous, these specialties were still unique in their effect on the success of an establishment.

I have included specialties like *Lobster Homard,* a dish prepared by *Léopold Mourier* of the Café de Paris in France. When he created his specialty, it was a little known dish that he proudly served. As time passed his popularity soared, and his menu became the talk of France.

In Vienna, Austria, a variety of specialties were developed at the Heumuble, an establishment that had originally begun as a cooking school. On its agenda were such specialties as *Apple Strudel, Weiner Schnitzel* and *Paprika Chicken,* which made the Heumuble a very popular place when it opened as a restaurant. By their endurance, these recipes from across the Atlantic have long outlived the Café de Paris and the Heumuble and have been added to the list of classics.

Besides these fine European restaurants, there were many great restaurants in America developing their own specialties. One of those early establishments was the old Bellevue in Philadelphia. Here, you could find the American Classic, "Pepper Pot." This recipe, that came out of the old Bellevue, was the model recipe for the best Hotel/Restaurants on the East Coast.

On the West Coast, you could find such original recipes as "Chicken in the Shell" in San Francisco at the Iron Horse, a restaurant that created some of the first, distinct Western specialties. And, in the Southern United States, the Creole kitchens were busy inventing classics like the famous *Gumbo* recipes.

I have also included a variety of similar recipes to give you a better understanding of the difference in preparation of food that will allow you to compare the way a chef, with little effort, could change the usual recipe into the unusual.

In gathering recipes, such as these, it is impossible to include every recipe in this cookbook that I would like to include; so, I would like to take this opportunity to apologize to those people whose region I have overlooked or just did not have room for at this time.

By giving these recipes, I realize the limitations in regard to the utensils, supplies, and the reasonable amount of time to be spent preparing meals. Recipes that would be simple for experienced cooks or chefs might overwhelm a person as to the preparation; therefore, all the recipes I have included have been simplified in such a way as to make them easily understood and a success. After you have learned the process of preparing these recipes, be creative, and who knows, you might create your own "classic."

A lesson I have learned from the *"Gourmet Chef"* is that they do the best they can with the products at hand. In other words, if a chef lives in an area that has good, fresh fish that is what his specialty will be based upon.

The sections I have indicated with a star (★) describe the recipes that I hope will give you some insights as to how the chefs pursued their art.

Enjoy.

LANGUAGE OF CUISINE

Acidulated Water — Water (normally 1 quart); in which 1 tablespoon of vinegar or 1 tablespoon of lemon juice has been added.

Baine-marie — A pan half-filled with hot water into which another pan is set—either to keep sauces warm or to cook certain dishes, such as: Custards and Egg sauces.

Blanching — The immersion of various ingredients in boiling water. This is done to reduce the pungency of some vegetables, such as onions and cabbage, or to make vegetables, fruits and nuts easier to peel, such as tomatoes, peaches and almonds

Bouillon — The stock or broth resulting from boiling meat or fish in water with vegetables and seasonings.

Chapon — A slice of French bread that has been rubbed with garlic. The Chapon is then placed in with the lettuce of a tossed salad to add flavor.

Clarify — To make a liquid clear.

Clarified Butter — Butter that has been heated to remove residue. Clarified butter keeps longer and does not burn as easily as unclarified butter.

Consommé — Bouillon that has been clarified. The bouillon is clarified with egg whites, diced vegetables and either lean ground beef or minced meat.

Court Bouillon — A prepared liquid for poaching fish.

Croquettes — Preparations of meats, vegetables, fruits or nuts coated with bread crumbs and then deep-fried.

Croustades — Preparations of bread or puff paste that have been filled with a meat or fruit mixture.

Dredge — To coat with flour or sugar.

en Julienne — Shredding or cutting food into strips approximately ⅛ inch wide and 2 to 3 inches long.

Fond or Fumet — Meat stock that has been refrigerated for later use in sauces.

Forcemeats or Stuffings A mixture of ingredients that is minced, chopped, spiced and combined to be cooked separately or used as a flavoring inside other foods.

Frying This is one of the most common ways to cook, but often the most abused. The easiest way to fry is with clarified butter at medium-low heat in a covered frying pan, allowing 10 to 15 minutes per side for most meats.

Glaze Viande or Meat Extract Do not confuse this with Drippings—the residue or essence of food left in the pan after frying or roasting. Glaze Viande can be bought as a condiment, but with little effort you can make your own by boiling down bouillion until it is dark brown and syrupy.

Marron A chestnut prepared for the use in desserts and pralines. To roast the chestnut for use in these dishes, slit the surface, place the chestnut in a pan with a little water and bake in a moderate oven 8 to 10 minutes.

Panada Bread Sauce. Prepared with bread, milk and spices.

Parboil To boil in salted water until partially cooked, usually 10 minutes.

Parfait A frozen dessert served in stemmed glasses.

Pâté A meat spread served as hors d'oeuvres or as a meat loaf with a pastry crust.

Poaching To cook gently in simmering liquid. Normally, the liquid is brought to a boil, the heat is reduced to simmer and the food is set in the liquid to poach.

Praline Nuts or fruits with a coating of sugar.

Puff Paste A flaky dough used in a variety of pastries, such as: Brioches (cakes, usually in the shape of a ball with a smaller ball pressed into the top), Tarts (flat, open pastry shells filled with various fruits), Patty shells (small pie-like enclosed shells to hold forcemeats), Bouchèes (small, open shells filled with forcemeats), Rissoles (a ball or roll of rich minced meat or fish, covered with pastry and deep fried) and Vol-au-Vents (a small covered pie of light puff paste with a raised border—after cooking, the lid is removed and it is filled with a ragoût of meat).

Ragoût Meat, fowl, or fish cut in pieces of the same size, browned in fat, sprinkled with flour and simmered in stock. Ragoût can be prepared with or without vegetables.

Roasting To cook meat by a concentrated heat either in the oven or on a spit. This method seals the outer surface of the meat and drives the juices inward—contributing to the cooking. Pot-roasting, unlike normal roasting, is cooking meat and/or vegetables by steam in a casserole with a tightly-fitting lid.

Roux A mixture of butter and flour used in thickening sauces, soups and gravies. For the best results make the roux separately and add the hot liquid.

Sauté To cook or brown meat or vegetables in very hot oil, butter or fat, turning the food frequently during cooking.

Scald To heat liquid just below the boiling point.

Stock A liquid used as a base for sauces, soups, ragoûts and braising (a process of cooking in an airtight pan, adding very little liquid). Stock is made by boiling meat, bones, vegetables and seasonings in water.

Suet Solid animal fat used in some cooking.

Timbales Small individual baked custards served in timbale cups. Timbale cups are small baking cups.

Truffle A food of the mushroom or fungi family that grows underground.

HORS D'OEUVRES

Hors d'Oeuvres offer plenty of scope for originality of treatment and should have a touch of artistry about them. Served as the first course of luncheon or dinner, they should be pleasing to the eye and stimulating to the appetite. Shrimps, caviar, anchovies, herring, smoked salmon, tuna fish and sardines are some of the most popular fish to select from. All vegetables lend themselves to hors d'oeuvre combinations when combined with either French or Mayonnaise Dressing. Stuffed eggs are always included in hors d'oeuvres. Thin slices of ham or salami may also be introduced as hors d'oeuvres. Antipasto, which is packed in oil and imported from Italy, is ready to serve.

Stuffed Celery

Separate a head of celery into stalks and select 6 of the medium-sized pieces to be filled with the following mixture: Mash ¼ of a pound of Roquefort cheese in small mixing bowl with 2 pats of butter, 1 tablespoon of freshly grated horseradish, (If fresh ingredients are not available, adjust recipe accordingly, generally only ½ of dried ingredients is necessary.), a dash of Worcestershire sauce and ⅓ teaspoon of paprika. Fill the celery stalks by squeezing mixture through a pastry tube. If a pastry tube is not available, make one out of heavy glazed paper (meat wrapping paper works well) and squeeze mixture through the small open end.

Ripe Olives, California Style

Black olives may be purchased in glass jars or cans. The quality is the same; either one is fine. Drain off the liquid. Into a pint-size jar, add 2 or 3 slices of lemon, 4 cloves of garlic, peeled and cut in halves, ½ cup of olive oil and the drained olives. Cover tightly and turn jar upside down a few times, so oil can cover olives. Set in the refrigerator to chill and let stand overnight.

Salted Almonds

Scald ½ pound of almonds with boiling water and let stand 2 minutes. Drain, plunge them into cold water and rub off the skins. Dry on a soft towel or napkin. Heat ⅓ cup of olive oil in a small saucepan. When hot, put in ¼ of the blanched almonds, and fry until lightly browned, stirring to obtain an even color. Remove with skimmer and drain on unglazed brown paper. Sprinkle with salt and proceed with the same method until all the almonds are browned.

Roasted Almonds

Blanch almonds in scalding water for 2 minutes. Rub off skins and slice. Roast the almond slices in hot oil for 5 minutes and dry on brown paper. Do not salt the almond slices. Serve them as an hors d'oeuvre or sprinkle them on salads.

Anchovies In Olive Oil

Purchase anchovies packed in salt and allow to soak for 1 hour in tarragon vinegar. Then pick them out of the vinegar (one at a time) and hold under the cold water faucet to wash off any small bits of bone or fin adhering to the fish. Place on a small dish and add just enough olive oil to moisten. Add a few capers.

Caviar On Toast

Slice bread ½ inch thick, cut into rounds with biscuit cutter and toast. Spread lightly with fresh butter and then with caviar, taking care not to have the caviar come down on the sides. Decorate the outer edge with a border of egg yolk—chopped fine. Serve with quartered lemon and chopped raw onion.

Grilled Sardines à la Seville

Select large sardines for this purpose. Drain off the oil and heat both sides of the sardine in a frying pan. Handle them carefully when turning them in the pan. Toast bread to a light brown and cut into rectangles the same size as the sardines. Dip one side of the toasted pieces in olive oil and spread each piece with Anchovy Paste (see Index) that has been mixed with a little finely minced parsley. Place

1 sardine on each piece of toast and place in moderate oven to heat. Serve with Lemon Butter (see Prepared Butters).

Anchovies On Toast

Drain off the oil from the anchovies. Chop them finely, and then pound to a paste; mix with a little finely chopped chives, chopped parsley, and chopped shallots and add a little of the oil to obtain a smooth mixture. Toast bread and cut in oblong shapes. Spread with the anchovy mixture and place 1 whole rolled anchovy in the center of each piece of toast. Return to the oven to heat and serve with lemon juice.

Shrimps, Mexican

Drop 1 pound of fresh shrimps in boiling, salted water and cook for 20 minutes. When cool, remove shells and set aside to chill. Peel 2 large ripe tomatoes and chop them fine. Also finely chop 1 heart of celery. Combine shrimps, chopped tomatoes and celery. Season highly with ¼ teaspoon cayenne pepper and ½ teaspoon salt. Add mayonnaise to moisten and mix well. Serve cold.

Bismarck Salad

Finely shred 1 small heart of lettuce and 1 stalk of celery. Grate ½ cup of raw carrot and thinly slice 1 herring. Combine all together and moisten with ⅓ cup of French Dressing (see Index) and 2 table-spoons of Chili sauce. Toss lightly until salad is thoroughly mixed with dressing. Lettuce and celery should be crisp and cold before cutting.

Canapé of Crabmeat

For 6 persons, purchase 1 pound of fresh crabmeat. Mix crabmeat with 2 cupfuls of Rich Cream Sauce (see Index on Sauces) and add 1 tablespoonful each of finely chopped green pepper and pimento. Season with salt, cayenne pepper and ½ teaspoon of curry powder.

With a biscuit cutter, make round pieces of toast about 3 inches in diameter and build the creamed crabmeat on the toast keeping the center high: sprinkle over with fresh grated Parmesan cheese, dot with butter and place in a hot oven for 10 minutes to brown.

Tomato and Sardine Appetizer

Mix together ¼ cup of olive oil, 2 tablespoons vinegar and ¼ teaspoon paprika. Remove scales and bones from 6 sardines and tear them into small pieces. Add sardines to oil mixture and pour over sliced ripe tomatoes, which have been arranged on crisp lettuce leaves.

Tomatoes, Falisse

Select large ripe tomatoes of uniform size. Cover with boiling water for one minute—drain, hold under cold water and carefully remove the tomato skin. Cut in halves, crosswise. Scoop out seeds and soft pulp and invert hollowed halves to drain while you prepare the Falisse mixture: Finely chop 2 hard-boiled eggs and 6 ripe olives and mix together. Then add 1 tablespoon of Anchovy Paste (see Index) and mix all together. Carefully spread a layer of this mixture in each tomato and place a cold poached egg on top. Cover each tomato with thin Horseradish Mayonnaise (as follows) and decorate the top with thin strips of smoked salmon.

Horseradish Mayonnaise

Thin 1 cup of mayonnaise with ⅓ cup of cream. Add 1 tablespoon of freshly grated horseradish.

Stuffed Tomatoes

Select 6 tomatoes of uniform size. Scald them with boiling hot water and immediately plunge them into cold water. With a very small, sharp knife remove the entire skin. Place them on a cutting board (stem end downward) and carefully cut a thin slice from the rounded end. Lay the slice to one side and scoop out the center of the tomato. Fill tomatoes with Crab Meat Ravigote (see Index) and place rounded slice on top to form a cap. Arrange tomatoes on a platter and pour a thin coating of mayonnaise over each one. Garnish with sprigs of parsley.

Fish Salad Aspic

Canned salmon, tuna fish or crabmeat may be used in this recipe. However, be sure the fish is carefully gone over to remove small bones or shell. Soak 1 level tablespoon of gelatin in ¼ cup cold water 5 minutes. Then add to it ¾ cup Hot Boiled Salad Dressing (see Index), also ½ cup chopped celery, ½ of a green pepper, finely chopped; 2 tablespoons chopped olives, ½ teaspoon salt, ¼ teaspoon paprika, a few grains cayenne pepper and 2 teaspoons vinegar. Mix thoroughly and turn into a wet fish mold to chill. Unmold, garnish with watercress and thinly sliced cucumbers, marinated in French Dressing (see Index). I specified a fish mold because the aspic will be more attractive when turned out, but if you haven't one, use any shape mold.

Mushroom Stems

Save the stems of the mushrooms for this appetizing dish. Scrape the stems and split them in halves if large and leave the small ones whole. Fry them in butter until cooked—set aside to cool. Now marinate them in French Dressing, and if one likes the flavor of garlic, I would suggest rubbing the bowl with a clove of garlic before making the French Dressing. Sprinkle finely chopped parsley over mushrooms. (See Index for Salad Dressing.)

Deviled Cheese Crisps
Stuffed Eggs
Black Olives, California Style
Fish Salad Aspic
Mushroom Bouchèes
Roasted Almonds
Canapé of Crabmeat

Stuffed Eggs, Rector

This is a very delicious, cold-egg dish, and while the original recipe calls for Pâté de Fois Gras (goose livers), for those who cannot obtain the goose livers, substitute a very good quality of liverwurst.

Cut six hard-boiled eggs in halves, lengthwise. Scrape the yolks into a mixing bowl; mash them, season with pepper, salt and add a little cream and about an equal amount of Pâté de Fois Gras (or liverwurst). When thoroughly mixed, refill the egg whites with the mixture and place each egg on a small piece of crisp lettuce. Cover with Russian Dressing and serve cold. (See Index for Dressing.)

Eggs, Clichy

Cook string beans (split lengthwise) in boiling, salted water until tender. Drain, when cool, marinate in French Dressing. Cover with thin slices of hard-boiled eggs (cut eggs with wire egg slicer) and pour Russian Dressing over all. (See Index for Salad Dressings.)

Stuffed Eggs

Cut hard-boiled eggs in halves, lengthwise. Scrape yolks into a bowl and work them to a paste with a little cream and finely minced parsley. Season to taste with salt, pepper and a few grains of cayenne. Fill egg whites with mixture and dot with mayonnaise.

Stuffed Eggs, Mornay

6 hard-boiled eggs
4 tablespoons cooked white meat of chicken
2 tablespoons truffles or mushrooms
4 tablespoons cream
Salt
Few grains cayenne
1½ cups Mornay Sauce

Cut hard-boiled eggs in halves, lengthwise. Remove yolks, mash with finely chopped chicken, chopped truffles, cream and season with salt and cayenne. Fill egg whites with yolk mixture and arrange them in small baking pan. Cover with Mornay Sauce and place in moderate oven until lightly browned. (See Index on Sauces.)

Eggs à la Russe

Cut hard-boiled eggs in halves, lengthwise. Scrape out the yolks and carefully fill the egg whites with caviar. Finely chop the egg yolks and use as a decoration by placing a border around caviar. Cross 2 thin strips of anchovies on top.

Deviled Cheese Crisps

Cream ¼ cup of butter with ½ teaspoon of mustard. Add 5 ounces of cheese spread and work it into the mustard butter until thoroughly blended and smooth. Cut bread in thin slices and spread with cheese mixture. Cut each slice into 4 strips and place in a hot oven to toast.

Cheese Snack

Make 1 cupful of Rich White Sauce (see Sauces) and add 1 cupful grated American cheese. When well mixed, add two egg yolks, beaten lightly, and remove from heat—then add the egg whites, beaten stiff. Cover oblong pieces of toast with this mixture and place under broiler to brown. Sprinkle with paprika and serve immediately.

Hot Slaw

Finely shred 3 cups of cabbage. Make a Hot Slaw Salad Dressing as follows: Mix together 2 level tablespoons flour, 2 level tablespoons sugar, ½ teaspoon salt and ½ teaspoon mustard. Add to dry ingredients: 2 egg yolks which have been beaten with ¼ cup vinegar, and ¾ cup milk. Cook in top of double boiler until thick, creamy and smooth. Then add 2 tablespoons of butter and beat until butter is blended in. Add the shredded cabbage and cook for 5 to 10 minutes. Season to taste with additional salt and serve while hot.

Cold Slaw, Mayonnaise Dressing

Mix together in a large bowl: 2 cups finely shredded cabbage, ½ cup shredded green pepper, 1 stalk of celery, finely sliced, and a slight grating of onion. Season with a few grains of cayenne pepper and moisten with ½ cup of mayonnaise. Toss until the vegetables have completely absorbed the dressing. Decorate the top with a dash of paprika.

Cold Slaw, Sour Cream Dressing

Season 3 cups finely shredded cabbage with ½ teaspoon salt, ¼ teaspoon celery salt and ¼ teaspoon paprika. Make Sour Cream Dressing as follows: Beat 1 cup cold sour cream until thick, add ⅓ cup vinegar, ⅓ cup sugar, ½ teaspoon salt and ¼ teaspoon paprika and continue to beat 2 or 3 minutes longer. Mix shredded cabbage with dressing and serve cold.

SOUPS

2

The French are noted for making many different kinds of substantial nourishing soups and at very little cost. Economy teaches them to utilize all the outer leaves and stalks of the vegetable kingdom for the soup pot. There is no waste from the average French kitchen. This is due to the Pot-au-Feu (pot at the fire), which is always ready to receive wholesome bits of food that might, otherwise, be thrown away. Even though there are many kinds of soup, the main thing to remember: They must be appetizing and of good flavor. Soup plates or cups should be heated before the hot soup is poured in as it is most important that hot soups be served HOT. The cold or jellied bouillons should be served COLD.

Consommé

3 lb. fowl
3 lb. knuckle of veal
2 lbs. bottom round and marrow bone
6 quarts cold water
3 sprigs parsley
2 sprigs marjoram
2 sprigs thyme
½ bay leaf
3 cloves
10 peppercorns
1 tablespoon salt
1 medium-sized onion, sliced
½ cup carrots, diced
½ cup celery and leaves, sliced

Purchase fowl but do not cut it up. Cut veal and beef into small pieces. Put whole fowl and veal in soup kettle. Cover with cold water and let stand while you prepare the beef. Scrape the marrow from bones into hot frying pan, add cut up beef and brown on all sides. Add browned beef and bones to soup kettle and bring very slowly to the boiling point. Reduce heat and simmer for 5 hours. Add vegetables and seasonings and simmer 2 hours longer. Strain, cool, remove fat and clear with white of egg before serving. Fowl may be used for chicken salad or sandwiches.

Consommé Alfredo

Into each plate of consommé, add 1 poached egg and sprinkle top with grated Parmesan cheese.

Consommé Royal

Into each plate of consommé, add 8 or 10 cubes of Egg Custard cut ¼ inch square. Egg Custard to be made as follows: Slightly beat the yolks of 3 eggs, add ⅓ cup consommé, few grains salt and few grains of nutmeg. Pour into small buttered cup, place in a pan of hot water and bake about 1 hour at 300° until firm. Remove from cup and slice custard into ¼ inch cubes.

Petite Marmite

Into each plate of consommé, add 2 pieces of beef, 2 pieces of veal and 1 piece of chicken wing. Slice a Club roll in ¼ inch pieces, toast, and add 3 or 4 pieces of toasted roll to each portion of soup. Sprinkle over with grated Parmesan cheese.

Brown Stock

5 lbs. shin of beef and marrow bone
3 to 5 quarts of cold water
2 sprigs marjoram
3 sprigs parsley
1 small bay leaf
⅓ cup sliced onion
½ cup diced carrot
½ cup diced celery and leaves
10 peppercorns
1 tablespoon salt

Cut meat into small pieces. Put ½ in the soup kettle, add cold water and let it stand while the remaining half is being prepared. Scrape marrow from bones and melt it in a large frying pan. When hot, add remaining half of meat and brown nicely on all sides. Add browned meat and bones to soup kettle and bring very slowly to the boiling point. Reduce heat to minimum and simmer for 5 hours. Add vegetables and seasonings and cook 2 hours longer. Strain, and keep in cool place until wanted.

White Stock

Purchase a veal knuckle weighing about 4 pounds. Wipe it with a damp cloth and place it in a saucepan with 5 pints of cold water, 1 tablespoon salt, 10 peppercorns, 3 stalks of celery and leaves, 1 onion, 1 sprig of parsley, 1 sliced carrot and 1 blade of mace. Bring very gradually to the boiling point as this method extracts the meat juices and essence from the bone. Cover saucepan tightly and simmer for 5 hours. Skim the stock occasionally to remove scum, which rises to the top. Strain through double thickness of cheesecloth, and now you have a clear "White Soup Stock." A 4 pound fowl may be substituted for the veal knuckle as white soup stock can be made from either chicken or veal.

Philadelphia Pepper Pot

Cut 4 slices of bacon into dice and fry to a golden brown. Add 1 onion, finely chopped, and 1 chopped green pepper and cook gently for 5 minutes. Then add 2 quarts of White Stock (see above) and 1 pound of tripe, which has been thoroughly washed and shredded. Season with ½ teaspoon salt, ½ teaspoon of coarsely ground pepper, (use small pepper mill or pound peppercorns until finely crushed), and bring to the boiling point. Then add 1 cup of small diced potatoes and simmer for 1 hour. Thicken with 2 tablespoons of flour, which has been creamed with 2 tablespoons of butter. Just before serving add ½ cup of heavy cream.

Pepper Pot

Here is the exact recipe as given by George Boldt:

"Boil 2 pounds of honeycomb tripe for 7 hours or longer. The more you boil tripe, the better it is. After it is cooked, remove from the heat and allow to cool off in the refrigerator until wanted. Boil a knuckle of veal slowly until it is thoroughly cooked, which will require about 3 hours. Remove the veal and into the juice in which the veal was cooked, place a sprig of parsley, 1 whole onion, 1 heaping cupful of diced raw potatoes and a Bouquet of Herbs (see Techniques). Also, add ½ cupful of dough balls about ½ inch in diameter. Let this simmer for about 1 hour to reduce to desired quantity. When it is almost cooked, add 1 tablespoonful of flour and stir it thoroughly. Season well with fresh-ground pepper from a pepper mill and add necessary salt. Remove the herbs and onion. Now chop the veal and tripe into very small pieces and add them to the pot."

★

Pepper Pot was served in the old Bellevue Hotel in Philadelphia. As a matter of fact, it was served in all the best hotels. This recipe was given by George Boldt, the chef at the Bellevue, and it was the model recipe.

I recommend that you give the tripe plenty of preliminary cooking. This tenderizes the tripe. The best way to prepare Pepper Pot is to give yourself 2 days for cooking. Fix the tripe the first day and let it set overnight and reheat it the next day.

Onion Soup Au Gratin

1 quart Beef Broth or Consommé (see Stock)
4 large onions
2 tablespoons butter
1 teaspoon Worcestershire sauce
½ teaspoon salt
⅛ teaspoon pepper
2 Club rolls (split and toasted)
Grated Parmesan cheese

Slice onions thin and brown in butter. Add more butter, if necessary, to keep them moist while cooking. When onions are tender, add the Beef Broth, Worcestershire sauce, salt and pepper. Bring to the boiling point, arrange the toasted rolls on top; sprinkle over with grated Parmesan cheese and place under broiler to melt and brown cheese. A marmite is the proper utensil to serve onion soup in; and if you decide to have onion soup often, then I would advise you to purchase one of these earthen dishes.

Russian Borsch

Select a duck for roasting. The duck should not be stuffed. Place it in a very hot oven for 10 to 15 minutes to brown, but do not cook it. Remove duck from oven and put it in a large soup pot with cold water to cover. Boil slowly for 2 to 3 hours. Now, remove the duck from stock and grate about 10 cooked beets into the stock. Season with salt and a little onion juice scraped from an onion. Allow to boil for several minutes then strain through a very fine sieve. Clarify with white of an egg. Like all soups, borsch must be served piping hot. A bowl of sour cream is passed at the table, and a small ladle full is dropped into each soup plate.

Cream of Mushroom Soup

½ pound mushrooms
4 cups White Stock (see Stock)
3 tablespoons butter
2 tablespoons flour
½ cup cream
Lemon rind

Wash mushrooms. Chop or slice them into small pieces. Cook them 20 minutes with White Stock. Strain stock into another saucepan, rub mushrooms through a sieve into the stock. Reheat, thicken with butter and flour creamed together. Stir until perfectly smooth, then add cream and season with salt and pepper. Rub the soup plates or cups with lemon rind as this will impart a delightful flavor.

Ox-Tail Soup

Purchase 1 ox tail and slice it in pieces ½ inch thick. Wash the pieces

and drain on a clean towel—season with salt and pepper and dredge with flour. Fry the pieces of ox tail in fat, turning and browning all sides, add 3 pints of Beef Stock (see Stock, Brown) to the pan and simmer for 1 hour. Then add ½ cup diced carrots, ½ cup sliced or diced turnip, ½ cup chopped onion and ½ cup diced celery. Cook 15 or 20 minutes longer until vegetables are tender, season with salt and a few grains of cayenne pepper, 1 teaspoon strained lemon juice, and 1 teaspoon of Worcestershire sauce. If there is sherry in the house, add 1 tablespoonful to the soup just before serving.

Mulligatawny Soup

Mulligatawny soup is not difficult to make, and every well stocked pantry should contain the ingredients for it. It is especially appetizing during the cold weather, so let your imagination soar beyond the commonplace and have this delicious soup more often:

1 onion; 1 carrot; ½ cupful diced celery and tops; a sprig of parsley; blade of mace; 2 cloves; 1 apple or a stalk of rhubarb; 1 teaspoonful meat extract; ½ cupful fat; ½ cupful flour; 1 dessertspoonful of curry powder; 1 quart of stock (White or Brown, see Stock); salt; and 1 teaspoonful lemon juice. Wash, peel and cut the vegetables and apple into dice, melt the fat and fry the vegetables until brown—stirring them often. Add the flour and curry powder and fry for several minutes, remove from the heat and add the stock gradually, mixing the flour smoothly before adding all the stock. Bring to a boil, stirring all the time. Now add the apple, meat extract and a little salt. Simmer gently ¾ hour in the covered pan, stirring occasionally. When the vegetables are soft, the soup is finished cooking; so remove from heat and add the lemon juice and more salt, if necessary. If the soup is too thick, thin out with a little stock.

Chicken Gumbo

6 cups Chicken Stock (see Stock)
½ cup sliced okra
½ cup diced chicken (white meat only)
1 cup canned tomatoes
¼ cup diced cooken ham
¼ cup cooked rice
Salt and pepper

Slice okra in ¼ inch slices; add to Chicken Stock and cook 20 minutes. Add tomato pulp, which has been cut up and seeds removed, diced white meat, diced cooked ham and rice. Bring to a boil. Add seasonings to taste and serve.

★

Chicken Gumbo Oven Rice

Gumbo is essentially a Creole dish. The Creole is a descendant of French and Spanish parents, and they have developed a style of cuisine that has the praise of their ancestors. With their love of seasonings, the combination of the delicate French preparation and the Spanish taste for strong spices, the Creole have created a flavor that I'm sure you will enjoy.

This recipe came from the chef of the Rector Restaurant, a New York restaurant that was famous in the 1930's. Here is a description of him preparing the dish:

First, he went to the old French Market and bought a large tender chicken. He cleaned and cut up the chicken as if preparing it for fricassee. After sprinkling a liberal amount of salt and pepper on the disjointed chicken, he cut 2 large slices of lean ham into dice. He chopped 1 large onion, 3 sprigs of parsley and 1 sprig of thyme, very fine. Next, he dropped 2 tablespoons of butter—or 1 tablespoon of lard—into a very deep stewing pot. When the butter or lard was hot, he put in the chicken and the ham, covered the pot closely and allowed it to fry for about 8 minutes. He added the chopped onion, parsley and thyme and kept stirring to prevent burning. After this was nicely browned, he added 2 quarts of oyster water and another 2 quarts of boiling water. The oyster water was not added until it was thoroughly heated. He then added 1 bay leaf, chopped fine. One bay leaf was exactly the right amount to balance the scales of gastronomy. He cut a pepper pod in half, removed the seeds and dropped in half of the pod.

Remember to remove the seeds from the pepper pod; only the red-pepper will suffice. The chef dropped in only half of the pepper, the other half is then halved again before it disappears in the deep stewing pot. This almost completes the gumbo, which was set back on the stove to simmer for 1 hour longer. At exactly 3 minutes before it was to be served, the lid was removed from the pot and 3 dozen large, fresh oysters were added. The chef allowed the gumbo to remain on the stove 3 minutes, and then he took the pot away from the heat. He, meanwhile, prepared the serving tureens in a bain-marie, hotwater bath.

He was now ready to add the Sassafrass filé. (Sassafrass filé, now called Gumbo filé, was a powder made by the Choctaw Indians from the tender leaves of the sassafrass. The Creole saw the culinary possibilities of pulverized sassafrass and used it to develop their Gumbo recipes.) He added the filé by dropping 2 tablespoonfuls of the filé into the boiling-hot gumbo, taking great care to drop a pinch at a time and stirring very thoroughly with the other hand. No time was lost in pouring the gumbo into the hot tureens, for once he had added the filé, the gumbo could never be warmed over again. He served it with rice, which had been boiling at the same time the gumbo was being prepared. The rice was served separately in its own individual dish. 2 spoonfuls of rice was about the right amount for each dish of gumbo.

The Chef's rice:

He picked the rice clean and washed it in cold water, rubbing the rice between his hands to remove all the dust. He then poured off the old water and added fresh, repeating this process 3 times. He allowed a quart of water to come to a boil, adding 1 teaspoonful of salt. He did not throw in the rice until the water was vigorously boiling. This prevented the rice from jellying in a mass. After it had boiled 20 minutes, the chef drained off the water, then placed the rice in an oven so that the heat in the dry oven would absorb all the moisture in the rice. At the end of 10 minutes the rice was puffed and flaky, each kernel being distinct and beautiful. This type of rice was served with chicken, fish, vegetables and all Creole gravies.

Rhode Island Clam Chowder

4 cups clams and liquor
4 cups diced potato
½ cup diced salt pork
1 chopped onion (medium-size)
2 cups boiling water
1 cup tomato pulp
¼ teaspoon soda

1½ cups scalded milk
2 tablespoons butter
½ cup cream
Salt and pepper
Few Caraway seeds (Optional)

Wash clams, remove hard part and chop finely. Parboil potatoes and drain. Cook chopped onion and salt pork over low heat for 15 minutes. Arrange clams, parboiled potatoes, cooked salt pork and onion in layers in saucepan. Cover with 2 cups boiling water, reserved strained clam liquor and cook until potatoes are tender. Then add tomato pulp, soda, milk, butter and cream. Add seasonings and serve with oyster crackers.

New England Fish Chowder

Fresh haddock or cod can be used in this recipe. Since both these fish are easily obtained the year around, you can have this delightful chowder any time you desire it. Purchase 3 or 4 pounds of haddock or cod. Remove skin and bone and cut into 1-inch square pieces. Pare and thinly slice 4 or 5 medium-sized potatoes and place them in cold water until you are ready to use them in the chowder. Cut 2 slices of salt pork into dice and slowly fry in saucepan until all the fat is extracted. Remove diced pork and add 1 large sliced onion and fry slowly for 5 minutes. Then place a layer of fish in the saucepan and lay the sliced potatoes on top. Season with very little salt and pepper and add enough cold water to cover. Bring slowly to boiling point and SIMMER until potatoes are cooked. Make a roux—of 2 tablespoons of butter and 2 tablespoons of flour and gradually add 3 cups of milk to it. Add thickened milk to fish and potatoes and bring to the boiling point. Remove from heat and add a few chowder crackers. Serve immediately.

Bisque of Clam

2 quarts clams (in shell)
½ cup cold water
2½ cups hot water
3 tablespoons butter
3 tablespoons flour

1 cup cream
¼ teaspoon salt
Few grains paprika

Wash clams in several changes of water to remove sand. Put in saucepan, add cold water, cover tightly and steam until shells are opened. Strain liquor through cheesecloth, add hot water. Melt butter, blend in flour and gradually add hot clam liquor. Bring to boiling point and cook gently for 15 minutes. Stir in hot cream, add salt. Serve in cups or plates and sprinkle a few grains of paprika on each portion.

Bisque of Salmon

2 cups cooked salmon
1 cup canned tomatoes
1 small onion, finely chopped
1 tablespoon chopped parsley
2 cups water
⅛ teaspoon baking soda
5 tablespoons butter
4 tablespoons flour
3 cups milk
Salt and pepper

Drain oil from can of salmon, place in saucepan with tomatoes, onion, parsley and water. Simmer slowly 20 minutes. Add baking soda. Thicken with butter, flour and milk blended together. Season to taste with salt and pepper. Strain into hot soup plates.

Sacher Fish Soup
★
Back Huhn
Salat Sacher
Sachertorte

The following recipes were given by Madame Sacher of the famous Sacher Restaurant in Vienna. She ran the entire business, doing all the marketing, overlooking the dining room and supervising the kitchen. Like other good Viennese restaurants, her chefs were all women.

She began her menu with Sacher Fish Soup:

"Take 1 parsnip, 1 celery root, 2 onions and cut fine. Make a thickening of browned butter and flour, put your cut vegetable into it and fry for a few minutes. Add vinegar, a little claret wine, some clear Stock (see Stock, Fish), peppercorns, 1 laurel leaf, 1 slice of toasted rye bread, chopped parsley, chopped green celery, chopped thyme, the head, bones and all the meat of the carp is added, and boil all this for 1 hour. The roe of the carp is boiled in salted water, to which vinegar is added according to taste. The soup is then passed through a sieve with a very fine mesh, after which the roe is put into the stock. Serve with croutons of toasted bread fried in butter."

The Austrian chef utilizes the head and bones of carp to get the essence, in exactly the same manner that a knuckle of beef is boiled to extract the stock. Her soup was followed with chicken. The chicken was Back Huhn, which means chicken fried in bread crumbs:

Cut a small chicken in quarters, and skin. Roll in flour. Then dip the floured chicken into a Light Egg Batter (see Batter). After this, roll in bread crumbs and fry slowly in lard.

With the Back Huhn, she served asparagus, that was just plain asparagus mixed with bread crumbs and butter.

Next, was Salat Sacher, a vegetable salad in the Sacherian manner:

The vegetables are cut in small cubes and consist of carrots, potatoes, red beets, hearts of artichokes and very small pearl onions. The dressing is mayonnaise and cream, with a little sugar blended into it. This is not a raw salad, as all the vegetables are cooked thoroughly. It is served on small leaves of lettuce.

For dessert, she served her exclusive, Sachertorte, or tartlet, which was a piece of cake dipped in apricot marmalade and covered with chocolate icing.

Soups Without Stock

These delicious soups have become very popular over the years. They are perhaps best known as creamed soups, which means that they are made from a vegetable base and combined with milk, butter and flour. They are nutritious and appetizing.

Split Pea Soup

2 cups split peas
2 quarts cold water
1 small onion, finely chopped
½ small bay leaf
2 cups milk
4 tablespoons butter
1 teaspoon salt
Few grains pepper
Finely chopped mint (Optional)

Wash peas and soak in water with onion and bay leaf overnight. Next morning, cook gently for 2 to 3 hours until peas are soft enough to sieve. Rub through a coarse sieve; add milk, butter, salt and pepper. Reheat. Sprinkle each portion with finely chopped mint.

Tomato Bouillon

3 cups strained tomato juice
½ small bay leaf
1 small onion, finely sliced
2 whole cloves
1 tablespoon butter
Few grains pepper
Few grains celery salt
Whipped cream

Cook tomato juice, bayleaf, onion and clove to boiling point and let simmer for 5 minutes. Strain; add butter and seasonings and top each cup with a spoonful of whipped cream.

Beet Soup

2 bunches new beets
½ cup chopped celery
1 teaspoon salt
2 cups cold water
1 cup milk
½ cup cream
2 tablespoons butter
1 tablespoon flour

Scrub beets until perfectly clean. Grate them into a saucepan and add chopped celery, salt and cold water. Boil gently for 10 or 12 minutes. Force through a sieve, add milk and cream. Reheat, and thicken with butter and flour creamed together.

Venetian Bean Soup ★ Venetian Chicken

Chef Alfredo demonstrated a fair example of the culinary by his simple recipes that he prepared at his canal restaurant, the Taverna La Venice in Venice, Italy.

He specialized in Venetian Bean Soup and Chicken with Tomato Sauce:

Take some beans and wash them in running water. Add oil, butter and chopped bacon according to taste. Then add some raw minced ham and cover the beans with water. Allow it to boil slowly for 3 or 4 hours.

Venetian Chicken with Tomato Sauce:

Slice a few onions and brown them in butter. Place a breast of chicken in the pan and add a couple of sliced fresh tomatoes. Allow this to cook for about 15 minutes. If you want to make it hot, add some peperoni, which is equivalent to cayenne pepper, and 1 whole peperoni is enough.

Cream of Lima Bean

2 cups dried lima beans
6 cups cold water
½ small bay leaf
1 small onion
4 tablespoons butter
2 tablespoons flour
2 cups milk
1 cup cream
1 teaspoon salt
⅛ teaspoon pepper

Wash beans and soak overnight in cold water. In the morning, add bay leaf and onion and bring to boiling point. Boil gently for 1 to 1½ hours. Rub through a sieve, add milk, cream, and seasonings. Bring to boiling point and thicken with butter and flour creamed together.

Purée of Tomato Soup

Open a quart can of tomatoes and pour contents into a saucepan. Add 2 cups of water, 1 scant tablespoon sugar. 1 small bay leaf, 10 peppercorns, 4 whole cloves and 1 slice of onion. Bring to a boil, cover saucepan and simmer slowly for 20 minutes. Strain and season with 1 scant teaspoon salt. Melt 3 tablespoons butter and blend in 3 tablespoons flour until perfectly smooth. Then gradually add the strained tomato liquid to the butter and flour and bring to a boil. Serve with croutons.

Purée of Pea Soup

Pick over 1 pint of dried peas and soak overnight in cold water. Drain and put them in a saucepan with 2½ quarts of cold water, ½ onion, a few celery leaves and ¼ pound of salt pork. A small ham bone may be used, instead of the salt pork. Bring slowly to a boil and simmer until peas are soft enough to rub through a sieve—about 3 or 4 hours. Rub peas through a sieve and add the purée to 3 tablespoons butter that has been melted and blended with 3 tablespoons of flour. Season with salt and pepper and dilute to proper consistency with milk. Always add a few fresh green peas to a Purée of Pea Soup.

Mongole Soup

Mongole Soup is made from equal portions of Purée of Tomato and Purée of Pea (see above). Carrots, white turnips and leeks are cut en Julienne (see Glossary) and added as a garnish.

Cut carrots, white turnips and leeks in Julienne slices and cook in boiling, salted water until tender, also cook a few green peas (fresh) in a separate saucepan. The peas will take a little longer to cook, so start them in advance of the vegetables en Julienne. Combine equal portions of Purée of Tomato with Purée of Pea and as Mongole Soup is to be served rather thick it may be necessary to thicken with Roux (see Glossary). The method, of course, is to add the Mongole Soup gradually to the Roux and stir until perfectly smooth. Bring to a boil and add the cooked vegetables.

Potato Soup

4 medium-sized potatoes
4 cups milk
1 small onion, sliced
3 tablespoons butter
2 tablespoons flour
1 teaspoon salt
⅛ teaspoon pepper
Few grains cayenne
Finely chopped parsley

Wash and pare potatoes. Cut into small pieces and cook in boiling, salted water 20 minutes or until potatoes are soft. Scald milk with sliced onion, remove onion, and add milk to potatoes which have been rubbed through a potato ricer. Season with salt, pepper and cayenne. Thicken with butter and flour creamed together. Let boil 2 minutes. Pour into a hot soup tureen and sprinkle finely chopped parsley on top.

Cream of Onion

4 cups milk
2 cups sliced white onions
2 tablespoons butter
2 tablespoons flour
Few grains cayenne
Salt

Cook sliced onions in milk 25 or 30 minutes. Strain and rub through a sieve. Thicken with butter and flour blended together. Add seasoning.

Cream of Corn

2 cups milk
1 slice onion
1 can corn

2 cups water
2 tablespoons butter
2 tablespoons flour
½ tablespoon salt
⅛ teaspoon pepper

Scald onion with milk. Add water to corn and simmer 20 minutes. Rub corn through a coarse sieve. Remove onion from milk. Add milk to sieved corn. Thicken with butter and flour creamed together. Add seasonings.

Jellied Chicken Consommé

2 level tablespoons gelatin
½ cup cold water
1 quart Chicken Consommé (see Stock)
Salt and pepper

Soak gelatin in cold water 5 minutes, add hot consommé and season. Pour into a mold which has been rinsed in cold water. Chill. Unmold, beat slightly and serve in cold bouillon cups.

Jellied Tomato Bouillon

2 level tablespoons gelatin
½ cup cold water
2 cups strained tomato juice
Slight grated onion to taste
2 cups White Stock, clarified (see Stock)
Piece of lemon rind
Few grains of cayenne

Soak gelatin in cold water 5 minutes. Heat tomato juice, White Stock, lemon rind and add seasonings to taste. Season highly as chilled or frozen mixtures require more seasonings than when served hot. Add soaked gelatin to hot stock and stir until dissolved. Strain, turn into wet mold and chill. Unmold, beat slightly and serve in cold bouillon cups.

Jellied Madrilene

2 level tablespoons gelatin
½ cup cold water

1 cup Brown Stock (see Stock)
Slight grating of onion
3 cups strained tomato juice
Few grains cayenne
Salt and pepper

Soak gelatin in cold water 5 minutes. Heat Brown Stock and tomato juice. Add seasonings to taste. Add soaked gelatin to hot stock and stir until dissolved, strain, turn into wet mold and chill. Unmold, beat slightly and serve in cold bouillon cups.

Minestroné à la Genovese

3 potatoes, diced
¼ head cabbage, shredded
1 pt. string beans, cut 1 inch long
1 cup dry beans, soaked overnight
1 cup fresh or canned peas
½ pound noodles, rice or spaghetti
4 or 5 qts. water
1 tablespoon salt

Add salt to water and when boiling add string beans. Let boil 10 minutes, then add balance of ingredients and let cook until all are tender. If the soup thickens too much, add more water; if too thin, take enough water out to make the right consistency; this is to be done before adding the Pesto:

Pesto

3 tablespoons butter
3 tablespoons olive oil
3 tablespoons grated Parmesan cheese
2 tablespoons parsley, finely chopped
1 small clove of garlic, finely chopped
Salt and pepper to taste
¼ cup cream

Cream butter; add all ingredients, leaving cream to be added last. Stir Pesto into soup and let boil 5 minutes. Serve with additional grated Parmesan cheese. Minestroné is much better the second day or if allowed to cool and reheated. For a variation of this soup, replace the parsley in the Pesto with basil.

SHELLFISH

3

Cocktail Sauce for Shellfish

¾ cup tomato catsup
¼ cup grated horseradish
¼ teaspoon salt
2 tablespoons strained lemon juice
10 drops Tabasco sauce
1 Tablespoon Worcestershire sauce

Mix ingredients together—add desired shellfish and serve in small cocktail glasses.

Oyster Cocktail

Serve 6 oysters on the half shell to each portion. Arrange them on a bed of finely chopped ice. Garnish each plate with 1 sprig parsley and 1 piece of lemon.

Clam Cocktail

Follow directions for oyster cocktail.

Oysters Casino

Perhaps, one of the tastiest oyster dishes I know of is Oysters Casino, which is particularly nice for luncheon or late supper.

Select large fresh oysters for this recipe. Arrange oysters on the half shell in a shallow baking pan. Season with salt, cayenne pepper and a little paprika. On each oyster place a piece of sliced bacon that is about the size of the oyster, 1 pinch of finely chopped green pepper, 1 pinch of chopped pimento and a few bits of fresh butter. Now, broil under moderate heat (350°) until cooked. Bacon will cook first, so when both sides are broiled, remove to a hot dish while oysters cook a little longer. About 10 minutes should cook the oysters and

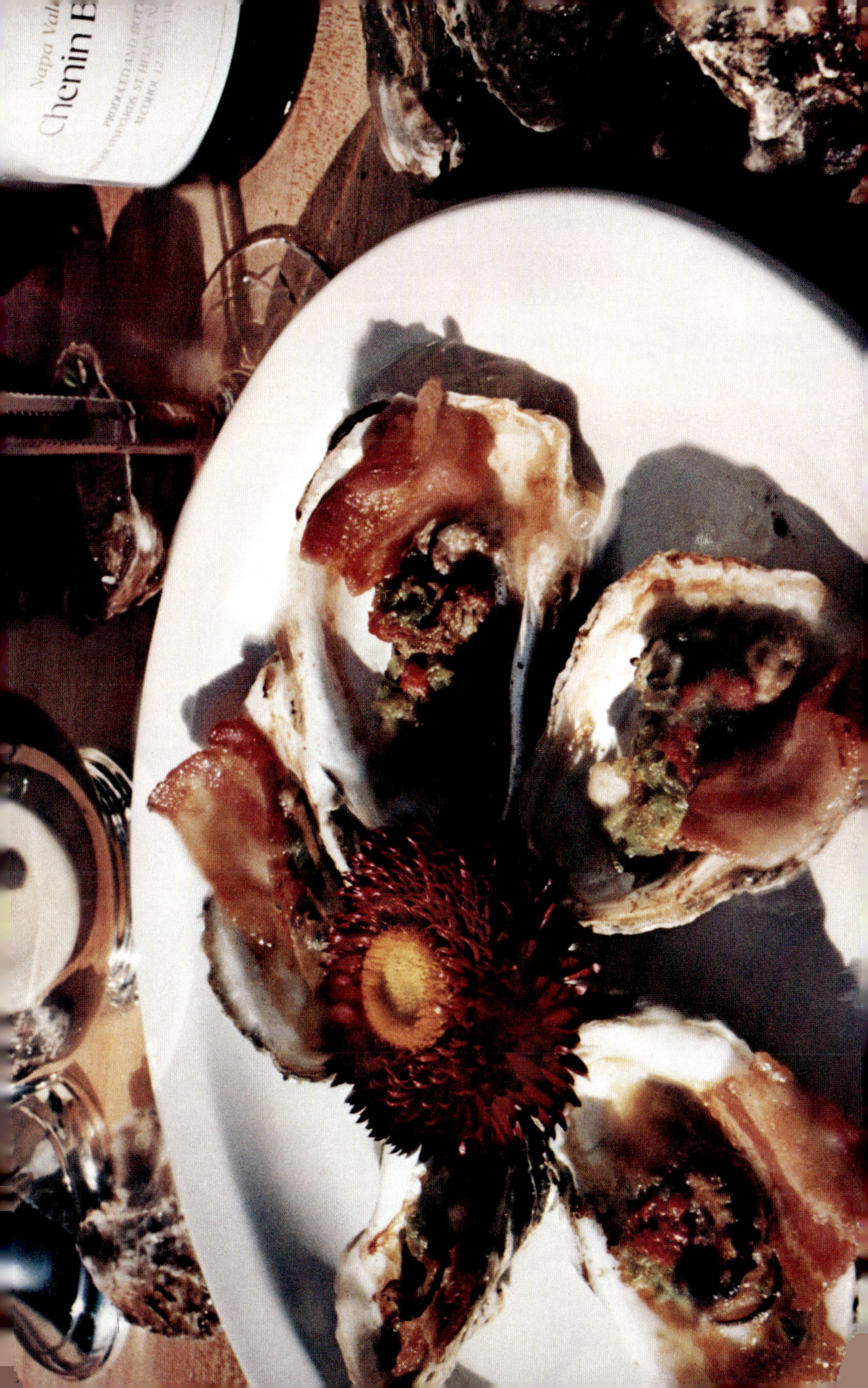

peppers. Keep oysters moist by adding a little butter or oyster liquor while cooking. Serve in the shells and garnish each oyster with the small piece of broiled bacon and a tiny sprig of parsley.

Deviled Oysters

Make a thick sauce of 3 tablespoons of melted butter blended with 3 tablespoons of flour in a saucepan and gradually add ¾ cup milk. Remove from heat and add 1 slightly beaten egg yolk, ¼ teaspoon salt, a few grains of cayenne, 1 teaspoon dry mustard, 1 teaspoon finely chopped parsley and 1 teaspoon lemon juice. To the sauce, add 1 pint of oysters that have been drained from their liquor and slightly chopped. Fill large buttered oyster shells with the mixture and cover over with buttered crumbs. Bake 15 minutes in a hot oven.

Oyster Stew

Allow 8 medium-sized oysters for each portion. Place them in a small saucepan with ¼ cup strained oyster liquor. Season with salt and a pinch of cayenne, and bring to a quick boil. Cover, boil 1 minute. Skim top and add 1 cup hot milk and ½ cup cream. Bring to a boil, remove immediately from heat as this keeps the milk from separating. Add 1 tablespoon fresh butter and pour it into a soup tureen. Sprinkle top with paprika and serve with oyster crackers.

Oysters, Pan Roast

Poach the oysters in a saucepan in their own liquor, 5 minutes. Season with salt and cayenne pepper and bring to a quick boil. Boil 1 minute, add several small pieces of butter and cook 1 minute longer. Arrange oysters on freshly made toast and add a few drops of Worcestershire sauce to oyster liquor and pour over oysters. Sprinkle top with finely chopped parsley.

Fried Oysters, Rector

Allow 6 or 8 medium-sized oysters for each portion. Drain, reserve liquor, season with salt and a few grains of cayenne. Roll in cracker meal and dip in egg that has been beaten with 2 tablespoons strained oyster liquor, 1 teaspoon Worcestershire sauce and ½ teaspoon English mustard. Then roll in bread crumbs mixed with an equal quantity of finely shredded crabmeat. Fry in clarified butter until nicely browned. Arrange on a hot platter and garnish with parsley and quartered lemon.

Broiled Oysters, Celery Sauce

Follow directions for Fried Oysters, Rector. Garnish with Celery Sauce and triangles of fresh toast. (See Index for Celery Sauce.)

Baked Oysters, Longchamps

Cook 4 chopped shallots in butter until lightly browned. Add 12 medium-sized oysters and moisten with 2 tablespoons of sherry. Cook gently for 5 minutes, (medium-low). Sprinkle with 1 teaspoon of finely chopped parsley and season with a little salt and a few grains of cayenne. Add ½ cup Cream Sauce (see Index) and ¼ cup finely chopped mushrooms, and pour into a buttered baking dish. Sprinkle top with bread crumbs and dot with small pieces of butter. Place in moderate oven until nicely browned.

Baked Oysters, Rector

Purchase 12 medium-sized oysters to be opened on the half shell. Season with paprika and sprinkle a pinch a grated horseradish over each one. To ½ cup bread crumbs, add 2 tablespoons grated Swiss cheese. Mix thoroughly and cover each oyster with prepared crumbs. Dot with butter and bake in a moderate oven until nicely browned. Garnish with sprigs of parsley and quartered lemon.

Oysters Poulette

Poach 12 oysters in their own liquor 5 minutes. Remove oysters with skimmer to hot serving dish. Add ½ cup Cream Sauce (see Index) to oyster liquor and reduce by cooking over moderate heat for several minutes. Season with salt, a few grains of cayenne pepper and a few grains of nutmeg. Thicken with 2 egg yolks, slightly beaten with 1 tablespoon of cream. Bring to a boil, remove from heat, add 1 tablespoon of butter and 1 teaspoon of strained lemon juice. Add ¼ cup sliced mushrooms and pour sauce over poached oysters.

Oysters à la Poulette

★

This recipe was given by a chef, who was first employed at the Poodle Dog—one of the first French restaurants in San Francisco—as a waiter. His name was Pierre, and he and his partners soon opened their own restaurant called the Pup, which was located on Stockton and Market. Pierre then sold out his interest shortly after, and launched the Tortoni, which became famous for its Table d'Hôte dinners. His specialties were fish cooked in wine, frog legs and Oysters à la Poulette, which he prepared in the following manner:

He beat 1 cup butter and 3 tablespoons flour together until it was velvety and white. He then added about a teaspoon of salt, a dash of pepper and 1 teaspoon of lemon juice. He slowly poured 1 pint of good Chicken Stock (see Index) over this mixture and allowed it to simmer for about 10 or 12 minutes. Sometimes he substituted veal stock, but this was entirely up to the patrons. He whipped the yolks of 3 eggs in a saucepan, meanwhile, drenching them gradually with the cooked sauce until all of the sauce was mixed with the yolks. This was then poured into a double boiler. The mixture was stirred for about 2 minutes. Then, 2 dozen of the largest California oysters were put into the double boiler and were allowed to cook until the edges of the oysters curled up. It was served hot.

Broiled Oysters on Toast

Select large oysters and place on towel to dry. Season lightly with salt, pepper and a few grains of cayenne. Dip in flour and place in shallow pan for broiling. Dot each oyster with butter and cook under moderate heat until browned. Keep oysters moist by basting with the melted butter. When cooked, place 5 oysters on a strip of toast (cut the toast to hold just 5 oysters). Add a piece of butter to the pan that the oysters were cooked in as the essence of the oysters is still in the pan, and by adding a piece of butter and mixing it well, a delicious sauce is made. Pour a little sauce over each portion and garnish with parsley and lemon.

Oysters Sauté

During the winter months, oysters are at their best. They are fat and plump and have a delicious flavor.

Select small oysters for this recipe . . . about 2 dozen. Lift them out of the oyster liquor and dry on a towel. Season with salt, pepper and a few grains of cayenne. Dip each oyster in flour and brown on both sides in hot butter in a chafing dish. When the oysters are cooked, lay them on freshly made thin toast. To the butter that remains in the chafing dish, add 1 teaspoon of Worcestershire sauce and an additional piece of butter . . . mix these two ingredients well and pour over the oysters which have been arranged on the toast. Lastly, sprinkle a little finely chopped parsley over them and serve.

Oyster and Scallop Fricassee

If the scallops are small, they need not be cut; otherwise, cut them in halves or quarters. To 1 cup of scallops, add 1 dozen oysters . . . bring to a boil in the strained oyster liquor and allow to boil for 3 minutes. Remove oysters and scallops from liquor and add thin cream to the liquor to make 2 cupfuls. In another saucepan, melt 2 tablespoons of butter and blend in 1 tablespoon of flour. Mix until perfectly smooth. Now, pour the hot liquid gradually into the blended butter and flour . . . stirring and mixing until it is smooth. Season with salt, pepper and a few grains of cayenne. Add the oysters and scallops, also ½ cup thinly sliced, canned mushrooms and 1 egg yolk that has been beaten with 1 tablespoon of cream. Serve with toast.

Oyster Forcemeat

The ingredients for this British novelty are 18 oysters, ½ pint of bread crumbs, 1 egg, 1 ounce of suet, 1 teaspoonful of dried mixed herbs, salt, pepper and a pinch of nutmeg.

The method of preparation is, first, to cut the oysters into quarters. Mix them with the bread crumbs, herbs and seasoning and the suet which has been finely shredded. Beat the egg and bind the mixture with it. If it proves to be too dry, add another egg or a little milk.

The oyster forcemeat is used as stuffing for roast or boiled turkey, chicken or capon. This forcemeat used as stuffing can also be made to stuff fresh haddock and boned joints of veal.

Soft Shell Clams, Babcock Sauce

Wash 2 quarts of clams thoroughly to remove all sand. Put them into a saucepan, add ½ cup of cold water, cover saucepan, and remove from heat when shells open. Remove clams to hot towel while you make the sauce: Melt 3 tablespoons of butter, blend in 1 tablespoon of flour, ½ teaspoon English mustard and gradually add 1 cup of clam liquor which has been strained through a double thickness of cheesecloth. Bring to a boil and add ½ teaspoon freshly ground black pepper. Freshly ground black pepper is the secret of Babcock Sauce. Grind whole black peppercorns in a small pepper mill until you have the desired quantity. Sauce should be heavily flecked with pepper.

Cherrystone Clams, Casino

Prepare same as Oysters Casino.

Soft Shell Clams, Mexicano

12 medium clams
1 tablespoon butter
¼ teaspoon salt
Few grains cayenne
2 shallots, finely chopped
½ green pepper, finely chopped
1 large fresh tomato, peeled and chopped
1 teaspoon Worcestershire sauce

Wash clams, open shells, remove clams and save liquor. Melt butter in saucepan, add clams and cook several minutes. Add seasonings, shallots, green pepper and tomato. Add reserved clam liquor and Worcestershire sauce and bring to boiling point. Serve.

Clam Fritters

12 raw clams (medium-sized)
2 tablespoons flour
1 teaspoon finely chopped chives
1 teaspoon baking powder (scant)
2 tablespoons fresh bread crumbs
¼ teaspoon salt
1 egg
⅛ teaspoon pepper
Few grains nutmeg

Mince clams. Put them in a mixing bowl and add the dry ingredients, sifted together. Add chives, breadcrumbs and slightly beaten egg and mix well. Drop by spoonfuls into deep hot oil or fat and cook until nicely browned. Drain and garnish with parsley and quartered lemon.

Crab Meat au Gratin

To 1 pound of crab meat, add 2 cups of Rich Cream Sauce (see Index), which has been seasoned with 1 tablespoon Worcestershire sauce. Add pepper and salt to taste and pour mixture into a buttered gratin dish. Sprinkle top with grated Parmesan cheese and bread crumbs. Dot top with several bits of butter and place in moderate oven to brown.

Crab Meat, Rector

Melt 2 tablespoons of fresh butter in a frying pan. When hot, add 1 pound of crab meat, which has been carefully picked and all bits of shell removed. Season with salt, cayenne pepper and moisten with 3 tablespoons of white wine and let cook about 5 minutes. Remove crab meat with a skimmer to a buttered gratin dish and garnish with about 20 oyster crabs and 8 or 10 mushrooms, which have been sliced and fried in butter 2 minutes. Add 1 cup of cream to wine remaining in pan and bring to a boil. Thicken with 1 tablespoon of butter and 1 tablespoon of flour creamed together. Stir in 1 heaping tablespoon of grated Parmesan cheese and pour sauce over crab meat. Dot top with several small bits of butter and place in moderate oven to brown.

Crab Meat, Maryland

Season 1 pound of crab meat with a little salt and a few grains of cayenne pepper. Melt 2 tablespoons of butter in a frying pan and when hot, add the crab meat and 3 tablespoons of sherry wine and cook for 5 minutes, then add 1 cup cream and bring to a boil. Thicken with Terrapin Butter (see Index). Serve with triangles of toast.

Crab Meat, Creole

Cut 1 green pepper, 1 medium-sized onion and a thin slice of ham into Julienne slices (about 2 inches long and ⅛ inch wide). Cook gently in butter until onions and green pepper are soft . . . about 10 minutes. Then add 3 ripe tomatoes, which have been peeled and cut into small pieces (remove as many tomato seeds as possible), 6 mushrooms thinly sliced, and 1 clove of crushed garlic. Moisten with 3 tablespoons white wine and 4 tablespoons of stock and cook 10 minutes longer. Add 1 pound of crab meat, season with salt and a few grains of cayenne and mix all ingredients together. Serve with small timbales of boiled rice.

Crab Meat Cocktail

Carefully pick over the crab meat and remove bits of shell. Into each cocktail glass, put 2 tablespoons of Cocktail Sauce; fill glass to brim with crab meat and cover with Cocktail Sauce. (See index for Seafood Cocktail Sauce.)

Crab Meat Salad

To 1 cup of cold boiled crab meat, add ½ cup finely diced celery and 1 large ripe tomato which has been peeled, seeds removed, and cut into small pieces. Season with salt and a few grains of cayenne pepper. Add ½ cup of mayonnaise, mix thoroughly and serve on crisp lettuce leaves.

Stuffed Deviled Crab, Rector

When purchasing crab meat, ask your dealer to give you 6 empty crab shells. 1 pound of crab meat will be sufficient for 6 crab shells. The first procedure is to wash the empty crab shells in boiling water and turn them upside down to dry. For 1 pound of crab meat, make 2 cups of Cream Sauce as follows: Melt 2 tablespoons of butter, add 2 tablespoons flour, and when blended together, gradually add 2 cups of thin cream. Stir constantly, bring to the boiling point and cook for 5 minutes. Add salt to taste, a few grains of cayenne pepper, 1 teaspoon of dry mustard, 1 teaspoon Worcestershire sauce and the yolks of 2 eggs. Remove from the heat, add the pound of crab meat (pick it over carefully removing any bits of shell), and ½ cup of chopped cooked mushrooms. Mix all together and let cool. When cool enough to handle, fill the empty crab shell with the mixture building it up rather high and rounded. Sprinkle with bread crumbs and dot with small bits of butter. Place in the oven to bake until the crumbs are browned. If crab shells are not to be obtained, use fancy scalloped dishes to bake in.

Stuffed Hard Shell Crabs, Indienne

Follow above recipe. In place of mustard, substitute 1 tablespoon of curry powder. Mix curry powder with flour and butter when making Cream Sauce.

Curried Crab Meat au Gratin

Pick over 1 pound of crab meat to remove bits of shell. Melt 2 tablespoons butter, blend in 2 tablespoons flour and 1 tablespoon curry powder; gradually add 1½ cup of thin cream, stirring constantly until sauce reaches boiling point. Add crab meat to curried sauce and pour into a buttered gratin dish. Sprinkle top with bread crumbs, grated Parmesan cheese and dot with small bits of butter. Place in a moderate oven to brown.

Broiled Soft Shell Crabs, Ravigote Butter

Dress and wash the crabs for broiling. Rub each one with butter and broil under moderate heat. Baste with butter while broiling and sprinkle lightly with salt. When both sides are broiled, remove to hot platter and serve with Ravigote Butter, as follows:

Ravigote Butter

½ oz. green tarragon
½ oz. green chives
½ oz. parsley
1 oz. shallot, finely chopped and blanched
1 oz. chervil

Wash the tarragon, chives, parsley and chervil. Blanch finely chopped shallots by pouring boiling water over them and draining immediately. Pound all together in a mortar until thoroughly macerated. Then work in ¼ pound of fresh butter and color with a little spinach juice.

Crab Meat Dewey

Pick over 1 pound of crab meat to remove bits of shell. Melt 2 tablespoons butter and blend in 2 tablespoons flour and gradually add ½ cup Chicken Stock (see Stock) and 2 cups of thin cream. Bring to a boil and cook for several minutes. Season with salt and a few grains of cayenne and stir in 2 egg yolks. Mix the sauce until perfectly smooth and add the crab meat and 1 cup of thinly sliced, cooked mushrooms. Hold over the heat until hot but do not allow to boil again. Just before serving add a piece of butter and 2 tablespoons of sherry. Serve with toast.

Curried Crab Meat

Pick over 1 pound of fresh crab meat to remove bits of shell. Melt 2 tablespoons butter, blend in 2 tablespoons flour and 1 tablespoon curry powder; gradually add 2 cups of thin cream, stirring constantly until sauce reaches boiling point. Add crab meat to curried sauce, season to taste with salt and hold over low heat until thoroughly heated. Serve with fresh toast.

Crab Meat à la Mornay

Carefully pick over the crab meat and remove all bits of shell. For 2 cups of crab meat, make the following quantity of sauce: Melt 2 tablespoons of butter, blend in 2 scant tablespoons of flour and gradually add 2 cups of scalded cream. Stir constantly, bring to the boiling point and let boil for 2 or 3 minutes. Place the saucepan containing the cream sauce in a very hot oven. When a brown crust has formed on the top, remove from oven and carefully remove and discard the browned crust. Have ready ¼ cup grated Parmesan cheese, ¼ cup grated Gruyère cheese and ⅛ pound sweet butter. Now hold a small wire whisk in your right hand and whip the sauce continually while adding small bits of butter alternating with both kinds of cheese until the cheese and butter have been used up. It is important to add the cheese and butter to the cream sauce immediately as it comes out of the oven because the intense heat of the sauce must melt not only the butter but also the two kinds of cheese. The whipping must be done rapidly; otherwise, the ingredients will not blend. Now season with a little salt and a few grains of cayenne pepper and strain through a very fine sieve. Arrange crab meat in a shallow casserole and pour the Mornay Sauce over it. Place under the broiler until it becomes a golden brown.

Crab Meat Ravigote (Cold)

For 6 persons soak 1 pound of fresh crab meat in vinegar for 15 minutes. Now squeeze the vinegar from the crab meat and season with salt, pepper and paprika and place it in a large mixing bowl with 1 cup of mayonnaise, 1 tablespoon finely chopped gherkins and 1 teaspoon chopped parsley. Mix thoroughly and fill 6 empty crab shells with the mixture, and decorate with a thin coating of mayonnaise and 2 thin strips of pimiento crossed on top.

Lobster Americaine

A female lobster is preferable because of the roe. Cut the uncooked lobster (weighing about 2½ pounds) in crosswise sections in 1½ inch pieces. Cut the claws in halves. The lobster meat is not to be removed from the shell, but carefully remove the roe. Put about 6 tablespoons of olive oil in a large saucepan, and when oil is very hot, add the sections of lobster (in the shell), 2 tablespoons brandy and 1 cup of fish Consommé (see Stock). Cover pan and cook for 20 minutes, occasionally turning the pieces of lobster. In the meantime, prepare the following: 2 small carrots, chopped fine; 1 clove of garlic, chopped; 1 small onion, chopped fine; 4 medium-sized tomatoes, cut in quarters; and the roe of the lobster, chopped fine. Add chopped vegatables and roe to lobster along with a pinch of thyme, ½ bay leaf and 1 cup of Tomato Sauce (see Sauce). Cook all together for 15 or 20 minutes. Enrich the sauce with 1 teaspoon beef extract and a piece of fresh butter. Last but not least, add a small glass of sherry (about 2 oz.). Because of sauce, serve in deep plates and sprinkle over with finely chopped parsley.

Lobster à la Newburg

This delightful dish was named in honor of a bon vivant, whose name was Wenburg. Being of a modest nature, he spelled the first syllable of his name backwards; hence, the name became "Newburg." Here are two recipes for preparing Lobster Newburg. The first one comes from the Rector's, a New York restaurant, the second was served in the well known Prunier restaurant in Paris, France.

Select an uncooked (preferably live) lobster weighing about 2 pounds and plunge it into boiling, salted water to cook for 20 minutes. Remove from water, and when cool, cut and break open the shell and remove the lobster meat and cut it into pieces about the size of a small walnut. Now melt 2 tablespoons of fresh butter and cook the pieces of lobster in it for several minutes. Then season with salt and a few grains of cayenne pepper and 2 tablespoons of sherry wine. Cook 1 minute and add ½ cup heavy cream and 2 egg yolks, slightly beaten. Do not allow to boil after yolks have been added. Serve with triangles of fresh toast.

Lobster Newburg (Prunier)

The method of Prunier is very delicious—simply because all the essence of the lobster goes into the sauce. The American recipe calls for cold boiled lobster but the French cut up a live lobster and sauté the pieces in the shell.

Cut a lobster into pieces an inch long, brown in butter, season with salt, pepper and moisten with madeira or sherry . . . about 2 tablespoons. If possible, add 1 chopped truffle while cooking. Let it cook for 20 minutes keeping it covered while cooking. Take the pieces of lobster from the shell and place them in a warm dish while you make the sauce in the pan in which the lobster was cooked. Remember the essence of the lobster is in the pan, so add ½ cup heavy cream to it and heat, but do not let it boil. Add another tablespoon of sherry wine and thicken with the 2 egg yolks, slightly beaten. Pour the sauce over the lobster and serve.

Lobster en Brochette

Remove the lobster meat from a cold boiled lobster and cut into pieces about 1 inch square. Cut some sliced bacon into 1-inch pieces. Now take a skewer about 10 inches long and fill it with alternate pieces of bacon and lobster. Place a medium-sized mushroom on the end of the skewer. Roll in bread crumbs and broil until bacon and mushrooms are cooked. Turn and baste during the broiling with some melted butter and bacon drippings. Serve 1 skewer to a portion.

Lobster Croquettes, Sauce Tartare

Make a thick white sauce by melting 2 tablespoons butter, blend in 2 tablespoons flour and gradually add 1 cup of milk. Bring to a boil and stir until perfectly smooth. Remove from heat and season with ½ teaspoon salt and a few grains of pepper. Have ready 2 cups of chopped lobster meat seasoned with ½ teaspoon of salt, a few grains of cayenne, a few gratings of nutmeg, 1 teaspoon finely chopped parsley and 1 teaspoon strained lemon juice. When white sauce is cool, add it to seasoned lobster meat and shape into small croquettes, roll in crumbs, dip in beaten egg, and again roll in crumbs. Fry in deep hot fat and drain on paper. The egg, used for crumbing, should be beaten in a deep plate and diluted with 2 tablespoons of cold water. Serve with the following sauce:

Sauce Tartare

To ½ cup of mayonnaise, add 3 pickled gherkins, finely chopped, ½ teaspoon finely chopped shallots, ½ teaspoon fresh tarragon, finely chopped and ½ teaspoon parsley, finely chopped. Thin with 1 tablespoon vinegar to which has been added a few grains of cayenne and a pinch of mustard. Mix thoroughly and serve in sauce boat.

Broiled Lobster

Select a lobster weighing about 2 pounds. Split the lobster for broiling and remove the intestinal vein. Arrange the split lobster on the broiler pan (cut side upward), sprinkle with a few grains of paprika and spread with butter. Cook under moderate heat for 20 minutes, basting occasionally with melted butter. Remove broiler pan and lightly cover lobster meat with buttered bread crumbs. Return to oven broiler until nicely browned. Serve with melted butter and quartered lemon.

Lobster Thermidor

Split a cold boiled lobster, lengthwise. Remove meat and chop in very small pieces. Prepare a cream sauce as follows: Melt 1 tablespoon of butter, blend in 1 tablespoon flour and gradually add ¾ cup cream, stirring constantly until sauce reaches boiling point. Let boil 2 minutes, add 1 teaspoon English mustard, ¼ teaspoon salt and a few grains of cayenne. Add chopped lobster meat to sauce, also add ¼ cup of finely chopped, cooked mushrooms and mix well. Fill empty lobster shells with mixture building it up rather high. Sprinkle over with grated Parmesan cheese and place under moderate broiler to brown.

Lobster Homard

Cut the lobster into 2 parts, lengthwise, and roast in an oven, baste with olive oil. After it is roasted, take the meat out of the shells and cut it into small cubes. Make a Sauce Mornay (see Sauces), and add to the Mornay some English mustard, a little White Stock (see Stock) and "fines herbes" (parsley, chervil, tarragon, and chives). Place a little bed of the sauce in each shell and then replace the meat, packing it in loosely. Over all, spread the balance of the Sauce Mornay. Then sprinkle with grated Parmesan cheese and broil until the top turns golden brown.

★

Chicken à l'Archiduc Crêpes Suzette

Lobster Homard, or Lobster Thermidor, as it was called, was served at the Café de Paris. This dish was originated by Léopold Mourier, the proprietor and Chief Chef of the restaurant. Mourier took over the Café de Paris about 1878, and it soon became renowned all over Europe for its fine food. Lobster Homard seemed to be the favorite dish with the early American explorers of Paris. Another one of the specialties at the Café de Paris was Poularde à l'Archiduc, which is sautéed chicken:

Cut the chicken in 4 to 6 pieces and sauté in a saucepan with butter, and then glaze with white Bordeaux wine and a little port. The sauce which is in the pan should be thickened with 1 cupful of cream mixed with the yolks of 4 eggs. Remove the chicken, and with a wooden spoon, stir the sauce gently. Pour the sauce over the chicken and serve.

Another recipe, which helped to popularize the Café de Paris, was Crêpes Suzette:

Beat 1 litre of flour—a fraction more than 1 quart—with 9 egg yolks, 1 whole egg, a small glass of cognac, a few dashes of orange juice, salt, sugar and melted butter. Spread a very thin layer of this mixture in a buttered frying pan or use a crêpe maker and allow it to brown on either side. The results will be thin pancakes. Spread the following mixture over the crêpes: To 3 tablespoons melted butter, add the grated peel from 1 orange and 1 lemon, 5 tablespoons of powdered sugar, 2 tablespoons orange juice and 2 tablespoons fine champagne (adjust your mixture accordingly to the quantity of crêpes). The crêpes are then folded, placed in a chafing dish, lightly covered with cognac or liqueur and ignited. They are then served very hot from the chafing dish.

Lobster Gratinée

Slice the lobster lengthwise, down the middle. Remove the flesh and chop it into small pieces. Make a Sauce Béchamel (see Sauces), adding Gruyère cheese. Mix the lobster meat with the sauce and then stuff into the 2 half-shells. Powder with grated cheese and brown in the oven.

★

The recipe here for Lobster Gratinée and the recipe for Boiled Chicken St. Simeon (see Poultry) were generously given by Chef Jules of the Hotel St. Simeon, located in Honfleur, which is on the Gold Coast of France. It has been said that, "A seat at a St. Simeon table for lunch was about as economical as a seat at the New York Stock Exchange."

Lobster Farci

Plunge a small live lobster into boiling, salted water, cover pan and cook for 15 minutes. Drain, and when cool, split lobster shell, lengthwise. Remove claws from shell. Remove meat from shell and claws and cut into small dice. Melt 1 tablespoon butter in a frying pan and add 2 shallots finely chopped and cook for 2 minutes. Sprinkle 1 tablespoon of flour into pan and gradually add 1 cup of Chicken Stock (see Stock). Bring to a boil and add the diced lobster meat and ½ finely diced mushrooms and let cook for 5 minutes. Season with salt and pepper. Thicken with 2 slightly beaten egg yolks—diluted with 2 tablespoons cream and cook for 1 minute. When cool, stuff lobster shells with mixture and sprinkle top with bread crumbs and dot with bits of butter. Place in moderate oven until browned. Serve garnished with parsley and quartered lemon.

Lobster W. W.

Split fresh chicken lobsters, lengthwise. Carefully remove green lobster fat. Remove meat from claws and shell and dip lobster meat in melted butter and roll in bread crumbs. Season lobster fat with a little salt, a few finely chopped chives and add enough soft bread crumbs to form into small cakes. Fry cakes and lobster meat in clarified butter until nicely browned. Arrange on a hot platter and spread with Maitre d'Hotel Butter (see Prepared Butters).

Lobster Cutlets, Tomato Sauce

Split a cold boiled lobster, lengthwise. Remove meat and season with salt and pepper. Slice meat into cutlets. Dip lightly in flour, then, in beaten egg and roll in bread crumbs. Fry in clarified butter until nicely browned. Have ready a thick well-seasoned Tomato Sauce. Pour it in a hot platter and arrange the cutlets on top of the sauce. (See Index for Sauce.)

Broiled Live Lobster, Maitre D'Hotel

Select a small lobster for broiling. Split it and rub the shell with oil and place on broiler to cook under moderate heat for 20 minutes, having split part explosed to heat. Keep lobster meat moist by basting with melted butter during the broiling. Remove to hot platter and spread meat with Maitre D'Hotel Butter. (See Prepared Butters.)

Broiled Deviled Lobster

Split a lobster for broiling. Spread meat with soft butter and broil under moderate heat for 10 or 12 minutes. Then spread deviled preparation over lobster meat, sprinkle with bread crumbs, dot with small bits of butter and return to broiler until nicely browned. Serve garnished with parsley, quartered lemon and melted butter. Deviled Preparation: Dissolve 1 teaspoon of English mustard in 1 teaspoon of Worcestershire sauce. Dilute with 2 tablespoons catsup and 1 tablespoon melted butter. This quantity is enough to spread on 1 lobster.

Lobster Bonnefoy

Cut a 2-pound fresh lobster in crosswise sections. Remove meat, which should be about the size of a walnut. Season with salt and cayenne pepper. Melt 1 tablespoon of butter in a frying pan, and when hot, add the lobster meat and cook for 2 minutes over high heat. Reduce heat and add 3 finely chopped shallots and cook for 2 minutes longer. Then add ¼ cup thinly sliced mushrooms, 4 tablespoons white wine, ½ cup Brown Sauce and ½ cup Tomato Sauce. (See Index for Sauces.) Cover pan and cook for 10 to 12 minutes. Remove from heat and add 1 teaspoon finely chopped parsley, 1 teaspoon finely chopped tarragon and ½ teaspoon finely chopped chives.

Lobster Creole

Remove meat from a boiled lobster and cut it into small pieces. Season with salt and cayenne and fry in butter until lightly browned. Then add 4 tablespoons of white wine, ½ cup Creole Sauce and 4 tablespoons of Chicken Stock. (See Index for Sauce and Stock.) Let cook for 5 or 6 minutes. Make a border of boiled rice on a platter and pour the Lobster Creole in the middle. Sprinkle top with finely chopped parsley.

Lobster Cocktail

Cut cold boiled lobster into medium-sized pieces. Arrange in glasses and follow directions given in Shrimp Cocktail. (See Index for Cocktail.)

Lobster and Shrimp Cocktail

By mixing equal portions of cold, boiled lobster and cold, boiled shrimps and combining in glasses with Cocktail Sauce, you get a delightful Shellfish Cocktail. (See Index for Cocktail Sauce.)

Shrimp Cocktail

Wash shrimps in cold water. Drain, plunge into boiling, salted water and cook 20 minutes. When cool, remove shells and set in the refrigerator to chill. Put 1 tablespoon of Cocktail Sauce in bottom of each glass. Add 3 shrimps, another tablespoon of sauce, fill glass to brim with shrimps and cover with Cocktail Sauce. (See Index for Sauce.) Serve with quartered lemon.

Shrimp Salad, French Dressing

To 1 cup of cold, boiled shrimps add ½ cup finely diced celery and 1 teaspoon grated onion. Marinate in ½ cup of French Dressing and serve on a bed of crisp lettuce leaves. (See Index for Dressing.)

Shrimps, Creole

Remove the shells from 1 pound of green shrimps. Melt 2 tablespoons of butter in a frying pan. When hot, add the shrimp and cook over medium-high heat for 2 minutes. Then add 4 tablespoons white wine and 1 cup of Creole Sauce. (See Index for Sauce.) Let simmer 5 minutes longer. Season to taste with salt and pepper and serve in a border of plain boiled rice.

Curried Shrimps

Remove the shells from 1 pound of cooked shrimps. Melt 2 tablespoons of butter in a frying pan. When hot, add the shrimps and cook over medium-high heat for 2 minutes. Season with salt and a few grains of cayenne. Then add 2 cups of Velouté Sauce (See Index for Sauce) and 1 tablespoon of curry powder mixed with 2 tablespoons of White stock. (See Index for Stock.) Let boil 5 minutes. Thicken with 2 egg yolks, slightly beaten with 1 tablespoon of cream. Remove from heat and just before serving, stir in 1 tablespoon of fresh butter. Serve with plain boiled rice.

Scallops à la Stites

Cook in butter without browning, 4 chopped shallots. Add 1 pound of scallops, 4 tablespoons white wine and cook for 5 minutes. Remove scallops with skimmer and chop finely. Also chop 8 or 10 cooked mushrooms. Return chopped scallops and mushrooms to pan and add 1 cup of Cream Sacue. (See Index on Sauces.) Bring to a boil. Boil for 2 minutes, add 2 egg yolks, slightly beaten with 1 tablespoon of cream. Season to taste and fill buttered scallop shells with mixture. Sprinkle top with bread crumbs and grated Parmesan cheese. Dot with small bits of butter and place in moderate oven to brown.

Scallops en Brochette

Fill small skewers with alternate pieces of scallop and small pieces of sliced bacon which has been partially broiled. When skewers are filled, place a small mushroom on the end. Dip each skewer in melted butter and roll in bread crumbs. Broil under moderate heat until nicely browned . . . baste occasionally with melted butter. Arrange skewers on a hot platter and garnish with sprigs of parsley.

Minced Scallops au Gratin

The large scallops, known as the deep sea scallops, will be just the kind for this recipe. If you have scallop shells, so much the better; otherwise use the small dishes that are copies after the shell.

Pour ½ cup of White Broth (see Stock) into a saucepan with 1 pound of scallops. Bring to a boil and remove from the heat. Drain the scallops (save the liquor) and mince them very finely. Now, cook in butter 1 heaping tablespoon of chopped shallots and cook over low heat, so they will not turn brown. The shallot is a small bulb belonging to the onion family. When shallots are cooked, sprinkle some flour into the pan and gradually add enough of the reserved liquor to make a sauce that will hold together. Heat to boiling point and add the minced scallops and 1 tablespoon of finley chopped parsley. Season to taste with salt and cayenne pepper. Fill well-buttered scallop shells with this preparation, building it, in such a way that it will be rounded on the top. Sprinkle over with bread crumbs and dot with small pieces of butter. Place in a hot oven to brown and serve, garnished with parsley.

Scallops, Orly

Place 1 pound of scallops in a mixing bowl. Sprinkle lightly with salt, pepper and a few grains of nutmeg. Add the strained juice of 1 lemon, 2 tablespoons of olive oil and ½ teaspoon of finely chopped shallots. Mix all together and stand in a cool place to marinate for 1 hour. Drain, roll in cracker dust and fry in deep hot fat until a golden brown. Garnish with fried parsley and serve with Tomato Sauce. (See Index for Sauce.)

Oyster Crabs, Sauce Béarnaise

1 pint oyster crabs
4 tablespoons brandy
2 tablespoons butter
¼ teaspoon salt
½ teaspoon paprika

Wash and drain oyster crabs. Put them in a saucepan with brandy, butter and seasonings. Ignite brandy and let burn 2 minutes. Extinguish flame by covering saucepan. Pour into hot serving dish and garnish with tiny crescents of Puff Paste (see Index). Serve with the following sauce:

Sauce Béarnaise

6 shallots
Few branches fresh tarragon
12 whole black peppers
1 cup vinegar
4 egg yolks

½ cup melted butter
Fresh finely chopped tarragon
Fresh finely chopped parsley

Add finely chopped shallots, tarragon branches and crushed peppercorns to vinegar and boil in uncovered saucepan until vinegar is reduced to ¼ original amount. Strain, gradually add slightly beaten egg yolks, and cook in double boiler until mixture thickens. Stir constantly with wire whisk and gradually add melted butter. When thoroughly blended and thick, remove from heat and add ½ teaspoon finely chopped tarragon and ½ teaspoon finely chopped parsely.

Fried Oyster Crabs, Sauce Tartare

Wash oyster crabs, drain, and dry on a towel. Roll lightly in flour, put them in a frying basket and cook in deep hot fat. Test the temperature of fat by browning a 1-inch cube of bread in 40 or 50 seconds. Drain crabs and serve them in croustades (small cup-like pastries—see Puff Paste) on a folded napkin. Serve the sauce separately:

Sauce Tartare

½ cup mayonnaise
½ teaspoon finely chopped parsley
½ teaspoon finely chopped chervil
½ teaspoon finely chopped tarragon
½ teaspoon finely chopped chives
½ teaspoon finely chopped shallots
½ teaspoon finely chopped capers
1 teaspoon chopped sour pickle

Mix finely chopped ingredients into mayonnaise. Set in a cool place until needed.

Oyster Crabs à la Newburg

1 pint oyster crabs
2 tablespoons butter
2 tablespoons sherry
Salt, pepper

Few grains cayenne
1 cup cream
2 egg yolks
2 tablespoons cream
1 tablespoon brandy

Wash and drain oyster crabs. Melt butter in a saucepan and place oyster crabs in to cook for 2 minutes. Season with a little salt, pepper and a few grains of cayenne. Moisten with sherry wine and stir in the cream. Bring to a boil and thicken with egg yolks which have been diluted with 2 tablespoons cream and brandy. Serve with freshly made toast cut in diamond or triangle shape.

Scampi

Remove the transparent shell in the same manner that you shuck a shrimp. A Light Egg Batter (see Batter) is prepared and the scampi is dipped gently into it. Then, the scampi is dipped in flour. A deep pot of boiling olive oil is made ready, and the scampi is placed in to fry. The scampi will sink to the bottom of the hot oil and rise to the top when it is golden brown.

Scampi are also cooked in boiling water that has been flavored with vinegar. When they are cooked this way, they are served cold with mayonnaise or tartar sauce. When the scampi are served hot, they can be garnished with Tomato Sauce. (See Index for Sauce.)

★

This individual recipe was handed down from the Cavaliere Roberto Salin, chef of the Royal Danieli in Venice. The Venetian chef cooks in a manner different from the chefs of other Italian cities. Where the Neapolitan cook prepares his asparagus with butter and grated cheese, the Milanese chef bakes his in the yolks of eggs and cheese, the Venetian simply boils his asparagus in water. You could say that this is the height of culinary simplicity. The chef then serves it with a sauce of vinegar and oil, which he mixes at the table under the guests' supervision. All Venetian cuisine is on the same plain lines.

The simplicity of modern Venetian food is due to the inheritance of countless sieges, which the Venetian endured during the wars of the Mediterranean cities and the Turkish invasions.

Terrapin

To prepare the terrapin for these recipes, you must first plunge the terrapin into boiling water. This is done for the purpose of loosening the skin. Keep terrapin in boiling water for 5 minutes. Remove, and rub off the skin with a rough towel. Place the terrapin in a saucepan on a board to cool. When cool, clip off the talons on the flippers, cut off tail and remove top and bottom shell. Carefully remove meat, liver and eggs (if any). Cut the meat into 1-inch pieces and cut the liver into small pieces; lay all the meat in a saucepan and cover with Chicken Stock (see Index for Stock). Season with a little salt and pepper, bring to boiling point, reduce heat and SIMMER for 10 minutes. Skim top while cooking.

Terrapin à la Maryland

To 2 cups of prepared terrapin, add 2 tablespoons of brandy and boil for 2 minutes. Thicken with 3 hard-boiled egg yolks, which have been mashed and creamed with 2 tablespoons butter and rubbed through fine seive. Cook 5 minutes longer. Season with salt and a few grains of cayenne . . . just before serving add 3 tablespoons sherry.

★

The Maryland Club of Baltimore was famous for their terrapin recipe. The basic recipe was compiled by Emil Hederer, the chef at the club. Emil Hederer at one time worked with George Boldt, the originator of Pepper Pot, at the Bellevue in Philadelphia. Emil Hederer was credited with cheffing in many of the fine restaurants, including: The Waldorf-Astoria, The Holland House and the Rector Restaurant in New York.

This is the original recipe for Terrapin à la Maryland as given by Emil Hederer:

"Plunge 4 terrapin in boiling water. This is done for the purpose of loosening the skin. Remove the terrapin and rub off the skins with a rough towel. Clip the talons on the flippers. Allow the terrapin to cool, and then clean them, which means, of course, removing the top and bottom shells. Cut the terrapin meat into small pieces. Place this meat in a saucepan and pour in about 2 quarts of good soup Stock (see Stock) and a pint of sherry. Cover the pan and allow to simmer over slow heat until the stock is fairly well reduced. Season with cayenne pepper and salt. Add ½ pint of very rich cream and stir in a small piece of sweet butter about the size of an egg."

Terrapin Baltimore

Drain 2 cups of prepared terrapin meat, reserve broth. Melt 2 tablespoons of butter in a saucepan, and when it becomes a light brown, add the terrapin meat and cook for 3 minutes. Then add the reserved broth and 3 tablespoons sherry. Stir in ⅓ teaspoon of beef extract to enrich sauce and cook 5 minutes longer. Remove from heat, add 1 tablespoon of butter and 2 tablespoons brandy. Season with a little salt and a few grains of cayenne.

Frog Legs, Poulette

Wash 1 pound of frog legs and dry carefully with a towel. Fry them in butter over low heat until lightly browned. Season with salt and pepper, moisten with 4 tablespoons white wine and 4 tablespoons Chicken Stock (see Stock). Cover pan and let cook for 5 or 6 minutes. Remove frog legs to serving dish, reduce stock in pan by cooking over high heat for 2 minutes, add 1 tablespoon of creamed butter (half butter and flour creamed together) and stir in gradually 1 cup of cream. Bring to a boil and thicken with 2 egg yolks, slightly beaten with 2 tablespoons of cream. Add ½ cup sliced mushrooms, which have cooked in butter 5 minutes. Pour hot sauce over frog legs and serve.

Frog Legs, Sauté Meunière

Frog legs are more delicious than ever. Years ago the small ones were in much more demand, but now the market offers a large size that are just as tender and of better quality.

Wash the frog legs carefully and lay on a clean towel to dry. Season with salt and pepper, dip in flour and fry in hot butter until a golden brown. Remove to hot platter. Then add a piece of butter to frying pan, and when it is lightly browned, remove from heat and pour over frog legs. For those who like the flavor of garlic, rub the platter with an opened clove of garlic before placing the frog legs on it. Garnish with quartered lemon.

FISH

4

Court Bouillon

It is most important to prepare a Court Bouillon for fish, which is to be boiled. Court Bouillon is in reality a Fish Broth, lightly seasoned with herbs, the purpose of which is to enhance the flavor of the boiled fish.

4 quarts water
½ cup vinegar
3 or 4 fish heads (flounder, bass or blackfish)
1 tablespoon salt
½ teaspoon whole peppercorns
1 small bay leaf
6 cloves
1 cup sliced onions
1 cup sliced carrots
1 cup diced celery & leaves
1 small bunch parsley

Put all ingredients in a saucepan and bring to a boil. Reduce the heat and simmer for 30 minutes. The mixture is now ready for the fish.

Fillet of Sole, Mornay

Carefully drop the fillets into Court Bouillon (see above). Poach the fillets at simmering point for 10 minutes. Drain, trim off uneven edges and arrange fillets crosswise on a silver platter (or one which can stand oven heat) and cover with Sauce Mornay made as follows: Prepare 3 cups of Rich Cream Sauce (see Sauces) in a saucepan and place it in a very hot oven until a brown crust has formed over the top. Remove pan from oven, discard brown crust, have ready on the side: ¼ cup grated Parmesan cheese, ¼ cup grated Gruyère cheese and ¼ pound of sweet butter. Hold a small wire whip in your right hand and whip the sauce while adding small bits of butter and alternating with both kinds of cheese until all the butter and cheese are added to Cream Sauce immediately as it comes out of the oven.

The intense heat of the Cream Sauce must melt not only the butter but the two kinds of cheese. The whipping must be done rapidly; otherwise, the butter, cheese and Cream Sauce will not blend smoothly. Now season with a little salt and a few grains of cayenne pepper and strain through a fine sieve. Cover poached fillets with

Mornay Sauce and place under broiler heat until lightly browned.

Fillet of Sole, Marguery

Remove 8 fillets from 2 flounders. Place bone, skin and heads in a stewpan. Add 1 pound of cut of fish (flounder, red snapper or cod), ½ cup sliced carrots, ½ leek, 2 sprigs of parsley, 10 peppercorns, ½ bay leaf and 1 quart of cold water. Bring to boiling point and simmer until the stock is reduced to 1 pint. Strain, pour stock over fillets which have been seasoned with salt and a few grains of cayenne and arranged in a buttered baking pan. Cover fillets with buttered brown paper and place in a moderate oven to poach for 15 or 20 minutes. Carefully lift fillets out of pan and arrange them on a hot platter (do not overlap or put one fillet on top of another). Strain stock into a small saucepan and reduce it by boiling to 1 cup, remove from heat and add 4 tablespoons of dry white wine. Thicken sauce with 3 egg yolks which have been slightly beaten, and add bit by bit, ¼ pound of fresh butter, stirring constantly until the sauce is perfectly smooth. Then add 1 teaspoon finely chopped parsley. Pour sauce over fillets that have been garnished with 1 dozen small steamed oysters and 1 dozen small boiled shrimps. Place platter under moderate broiler until lightly browned.

★

Filet Mignon Hederer

This recipe was obtained from the Café Marguery in Paris and given here by George Rector, the chef and owner of the Rector Restaurant in New York. He had apprenticed under the chef of the Café de Paris, and then under the chef of the Café Marguery where he learned the basic recipe of the sauce. He spent sixty days experimenting with the sauce. When he felt that he had perfected it, he had to prepare the sauce for a jury of seven master chefs in order to quality himself as a chef. They tasted the sauce and rendered a verdict with a vote of "Perfect."

George Rector was then sent to the Paris de Champs-Élysées as a visiting cook. The occasion was to assist in the preparation of a dinner in honor of King Oscar of Sweden. George Rector was to prepare his specialty; instead the King sent word to the kitchen that his favorite was Filet Mignon Hederer. Rector knew the recipe well and was permitted to assist another chef in the cooking. Here is the recipe exactly as they wrote it that day:

"Carefully trim a tenderloin of beef. Cut in small steaks and fry in butter. Lay on each one the soft part of stewed oysters. Garnish with blanched marrow. Serve with sauce Bordelaise and cèpes, adding a pinch of finely chopped parsley." (Cèpes are an edible variety of mushroom.)

For this dinner, George Rector was decorated by the French Government with the Cordon Blue and made an honorary member of the Société des Cuisiniers de Paris. He was the only American to be honored at that time.

Fillet of Sole, Tartare Sauce

Dip fillets in flour, next in beaten egg, and then in bread or cracker crumbs. Deep-fry at 375° until a golden brown. Test oil before dropping in the fillets—if it browns a piece of bread in 40 or 50 seconds, it is the right temperature to cook fillets. Garnish with lemons and sprigs of parsley. Serve sauce in individual lettuce leaves or sauce boat. (See Index for Tartare Sauce.)

Fillet of Sole, Sauté Meunière

If sole is not available, use the flounder, which closely resembles the taste of sole. Season fillets with salt and pepper and dip lightly in flour. Fry in clarified butter until a golden brown. Remove to hot platter and squeeze a little lemon juice over them. Add 2 tablespoons of butter to frying pan, and when it turns brown, remove it from heat and pour it over fillets.

Sole Maison

Butter an oval-shaped pan and put in thyme and laurel, a sprig of parsley, and season with salt and pepper from the pepper mill. Lay the sole in the pan. Pour an essence of Fish Consommé (see Stock) over the sole, just enough to cover the fish entirely. The Fish Consommé or Fond, as it is called in France, is obtained by boiling the bones and heads of fish after they have been filleted. The liquid essence from this process becomes the Fond. It is the secret of the dish, and there is no substitute for it.

Then, cover the sole in the pan and cook on medium-low heat. When the dish is about to come to a boil, set the pan to one side and allow the fish to cook for a minute off the heat. The idea is to let the fish cook without boiling. Pour the sauce out of the pan and reduce it separately in another pan over high heat. Then move this pan over to one side of the stove, and add small lumps of butter. Keep stirring with a whip and adding butter until you think you have a sufficient quantity of sauce. Strain through a very fine sieve or piece of cheesecloth. If necessary, place your sole on a platter to reheat in the oven. When the sole is ready to be served, pour the completed sauce over it.

★

Sole Maison was created at the L'IIotellerie Guillaume le ConQucrant—the Inn of William the Conqueror at Honfleur in the French province of Normandy. The Inn was considered to be the most famous of all the Inns throughout the world.

This Inn was built by or under the command of William the Conqueror on a favorable spot overlooking the River Dives. It was here the epicurian confronted the gourmet, because it was the fountainhead of restaurateurs.

It had gained its fame as a modern inn under the agile guidance of Madame Leremois, a woman with impeccable taste.

Black Bass, Portuguese

Purchase a medium-sized black bass...one weighing about 2 pounds. Rub fish with olive oil and season with salt and pepper. Place it in a greased baking dish, cover with 1 tablespoon of chopped onion and add 4 tablespoons of white wine. Bake in a moderate oven 20 to 25 minutes, basting occasionally with the wine. Remove fish from oven, cover with 1 cup of Creole Sauce (See Index for Sauce) sprinkle bread crumbs over top, dot with small bits of butter and return to oven until browned. Serve with Parsley Potatoes. (See

Potatoes.)

Baked Fillets of Black Bass

Remove fillets from a medium-sized black bass. Season with salt and pepper, arrange them in a shallow, buttered casserole, add 4 tablespoons white wine, cover with buttered brown paper, and place in a hot oven to cook for 10 or 12 minutes. Remove fillets to hot platter. Reduce liquor in casserole by cooking over a high heat for several minutes. Remove casserole from heat and add 3 slightly beaten egg yolks and 2 tablespoons of butter added bit by bit. Beat with a wire whip until sauce is thoroughly smooth and blended. Season to taste, strain, and pour sauce over the fillets.

Boiled Black Bass, Hollandaise Sauce

Clean a 3-pound black bass. Place it on rack of fish kettle and lower it into kettle containing boiling Court Bouillon (see Index), reduce heat to simmer. Simmer 15 minutes, remove fish, drain, arrange on hot platter, garnish with small Hollandaise Potatoes and serve Hollandaise Sauce separately. (See Index for Hollandaise Sauce and Hollandaise Potatoes.)

Steamed Black Bass, Parlsey Sauce

Clean a medium-sized black bass. Cook for 15 minutes by steaming over boiling water. (A fry basket makes an ideal receptacle to hold fish which is to be cooked over boiling water.) Remove the skin and place the fish on a hot platter. Garnish with small Parsley Potatoes and serve sauce separately. (See Index for Parsley Sauce and Parsley Potatoes.)

Broiled Striped Bass, Montauk

Dress the striped bass for broiling (opened to lay flat on broiler). If large ones are selected, split them. Season with salt and pepper and dip in oil. Broil under moderate heat until nicely browned. Remove to hot platter, spread fish with 2 tablespoons of Anchovy Butter and garnish with broiled scallops, broiled oysters and broiled mushrooms. (See Prepared Butters.)

Baked Fillets of Striped Bass

Follow recipe contained in Baked Fillets of Black Bass.

Sea Bass, Sauté Meunière

The small sea bass, those weighing about 1 pound, should be used in this recipe. Cut off fins and tail but leave the head on. Wash, then dry on a towel and dip each fish lightly in flour. Fry in clarified butter until nicely browned, allowing about 6 or 8 minutes for each side to cook. Remove fish to hot platter, squeeze some lemon juice over them, and sprinkle with finely chopped parsley. Add 2 tablespoons of butter to pan in which fish were cooked, and when the butter turns brown, remove it from heat and pour it over the fish.

Fillet of Sea Bass, Marguery

Follow directions contained in Fillet of Sole, Marguery, using sea bass fillets instead of flounder fillets. Serve with Sauce Marguery (see Index).

Fillet of Sea Bass, Mornay

Follow directions contained in Fillet of Sole, Mornay, using sea bass fillets instead of fillet of sole. Serve with Sauce Mornay (see Index).

Fried Halibut, Rector

Purchase halibut steaks weighing about ¾ pound apiece. Season with salt and pepper and dip them in 1 cup of cold Villeroi Sauce until thoroughly coated. Roll in bread crumbs and fry in clarified butter until nicely browned. Serve with a well-seasoned Tomato Sauce.

(See Index for Sauces.)

Steamed Halibut, Babcock Sauce

Steam a 3-pound piece of halibut by cooking over boiling water 35 to 40 minutes. Remove fish to hot platter and carefully peel off the skin. Garnish with Parisian Potatoes and serve with Babcock Sauce. (See Index for Babcock Sauce and Potatoes.)

Broiled Halibut Steak, Maitre d'Hotel

Purchase halibut steaks weighing about ¾ pound apiece. Season with salt and pepper and rub them with soft butter. Place on greased rack of broiler and broil under moderate heat until nicely browned, allowing about 8 or 10 minutes to each side. Remove steaks to hot platter and spread with Maitre d'Hotel Butter. (See Prepared Butters.)

Boiled Halibut, Sauce Mousseline

Cook a 3-pound piece of halibut in boiling Court Bouillon (see Index) 35 to 40 minutes. Have Court Bouillon boiling when fish is dropped in—bring again to boiling point, reduce heat and hold at simmering point until fish is cooked. Drain, remove skin, arrange fish on hot platter and garnish with Parisian Potatoes and a few sprigs of parsley. Serve sauce separately. (See Index for Mousseline Sauce and Parisian Potatoes.)

Baked Halibut Steak, au Gratin, Creole

Lay the halibut steak in a greased, shallow baking pan. Sear in hot oven for 10 minutes, then dot with 2 tablespoons of butter and season with a little salt and pepper. Add about 4 tablespoons of broth or water to the pan and continue baking for 20 minutes. Then sprinkle entire top surface with bread crumbs and grated Parmesan cheese; dot with butter and return to oven to brown. Remove to hot platter and garnish with Creole Sauce. (See Index for Creole Sauce.)

Baked Bluefish, Savory Stuffing

Prepare the Bluefish for baking. Wash, then dry and season with salt. Make a stuffing of 2 cups of bread crumbs, 1/8 teaspoon summer savory, 1/2 teaspoon whole sage, 1/4 cup chopped onion, salt and pepper to taste. Mix ingredients well and moisten with 3 tablespoons melted butter and add just enough water to make the stuffing moist but not wet. Fill fish with stuffing and sew the edges together. Lay the fish in a greased baking pan, dust lightly with flour, salt and pepper and place 3 or 4 slices of salt pork in the pan. Bake in a moderately hot oven, allowing 15 minutes to the pound. Baste every 10 minutes with the salt pork drippings. Serve with Creole Sauce. (See Index for Sauce). Mackerel, haddock or a scrod (a small cod) may be used in this recipe.

Broiled Bluefish, Maitre d'Hotel

Purchase a medium-sized bluefish; split and bone for broiling. Sprinkle with salt and pepper and dip in oil. Lay it skin side down on broiler and cook under moderate heat until nicely browned. (It is only necessary to broil the fish on open side.) Remove to hot platter and spread fish with Maitre d'Hotel Butter. (See Prepared Butters.)

Baked Bluefish, Italienne

Select a fish weighing about 4 pounds. Clean, wash and trim fins and tail. Season with salt and pepper and lay it in a buttered baking pan. Add 4 tablespoons white wine and 2 tablespoons of water and place it in a moderate oven 20 minutes, basting occasionally during that time. Remove from oven, pour 1 1/2 cups of Sauce Italienne over fish, return to oven and cook 20 minutes longer. (See Index for Sauce Italienne.)

Baked Bluefish, Creole

Clean a 4-pound bluefish, rub with oil and season with salt and pepper. Lay it in a buttered baking pan, add 1/2 cup tomato juice and sprinkle 1 tablespoon of finely chopped onion over fish. Place in moderate oven to bake for 30 minutes, basting occasionally during that time. Remove from oven, pour 1 cup of Creole Sauce over fish, sprinkle top with bread crumbs, dot with small bits of butter and return to oven until nicely browned—about 10 minutes. (See Index for Creole Sauce.)

Fillets of Pompano, Biscayne

Cut fillets from a pompano. Season with salt and pepper and dip lightly in flour. Fry in clarified butter until lightly browned. Remove fillets to a hot platter, and squeeze a little lemon juice over them. Add 2 tablespoons of butter to frying pan, and just as it turns brown, add 2 tablespoons finely shredded blanched almonds. Remove from heat immediately and pour over fish.

Boiled Pompano, Sauce Normande

Clean a 3-pound pompano. Place it on rack of fish kettle and lower it into a pan containing boiling Court Bouillon (see Index). Simmer 15 to 20 minutes. Drain, remove skin, arrange fish on hot platter, garnish with Parisian Potatoes (see Potatoes) and serve sauce separately. (See Index for Sauce Normande.)

Boiled Pompano, Babcock Sauce

Clean a 3-pound pompano. Place it on rack of fish kettle and lower it into kettle containing boiling Court Bouillon (see Index). Simmer 15 to 20 minutes. Drain, remove skins, arrange fish on hot platter, garnish with Hollandiase Potatoes (see Potatoes) and sprigs of parsley. Serve sauce separately. (See Index for Babcock Sauce.)

Bouillabaisse

★

This is a Creole dish, and like all good Creole dishes, it has a legend, which goes something like this:

Two fishermen from Marseilles were arguing in a rowboat as to the best method of cooking sturgeon and perch. As you may or may not know, the bouillabaisse consists of cooking two kinds of fish together. The fishermen agreed to settle their dispute by actually going through the practical test of cooking. The first failed. His efforts wound up with a concoction that was hardly fit for human consumption. The second succeeded. The fortunate fisherman offered to teach his less fortunate friend the method of preparing the bouillabaisse. During the cooking stage, the instructor shouted, "Et quand ça commence a bouillir, baisse." Hence the name "bouillabaisse"; you must stop when it starts to boil. Just at that moment the fish must be snatched from the fire; otherwise, it would spoil if cooked a split second longer. That's how the dish got its name.

The usual Creole custom was to use red snapper and redfish, instead of the sturgeon and perch, as the red snapper abounded in Gulf waters. The sturgeon was not available, so the Creole had to work with the materials at hand. However, they did very well.

The Creole launched their bouillabaisse by first boiling the head of a red snapper in 2 quarts of water in order to get a good fish stock. They put 1 sliced onion in the pot along with a bouquet of herbs consisting of thyme, bay leaf and parsley. When the boiling had reduced the contents to 1 pint, they strained the water and set it aside.

They then took 6 slices of redfish and 6 slices of red snapper of equal size, and rubbed them with salt and pepper. They minced 3 sprigs of thyme, 3 sprigs of parsley, 3 bay leaves and 3 cloves of garlic. Then, 6 berries of allspice were ground very fine and mixed with herbs and garlic. Each slice of fish was rubbed with this exhilarating liniment until it was permeated by the herbs, spice and garlic. The success of the dish depended on this operation. Now, 2 tablespoonfuls of olive oil were poured into a very large pan. The pan was large enough to allow the slices of fish to be laid out in state without one piece overlapping the other. 2 chopped onions were added to the heating oil. The fish was laid in, slice by slice, and allowed to simmer for 10 minutes, being turned over once to enable each side to become partly cooked.

The fish was then taken out of the pan and the slices placed on a dish. ½ can of tomatoes was poured into the pan and allowed to boil well. When the tomatoes were boiling, ½ a lemon, cut in thin slices, was dropped in, and over this was poured the pint of liquid in which the head of the snapper was originally boiled. This was seasoned strongly with salt and a liberal pinch of cayenne pepper. This whole was allowed to boil until reduced to ½. Then, the slices of fish were returned to their former resting place in the pan, great care being taken that the slices did not touch. In the meantime, ¼ of a teaspoon of saffron had been chopped very fine, set in a small deep dish and a little of the sauce in which the fish were boiling was poured over the saffron to dissolve it. When the fish had been boiling about 5 or 6 minutes, the saffron sauce was poured over it in the pan and—boull-ir—baisse. It was done.

It was then taken quickly from the heat, and each slice of fish was laid out separately on a piece of toast which had been fried in butter. The sauce was poured over it and it was served at once.

The finished bouillabaisse was well worth the waiting. It was served in several of the famous restaurants in New York: Delmonico's, Rector's and the old Brevoort, but they found it difficult to compete with the Creole kitchens in the South.

Stuffed Baked Shad

Cleanse and wash the shad for baking. Prepare the stuffing with 2 cups bread crumbs that have been soaked in milk. Mash 6 hard-boiled eggs and break up the shad roe into little bits. Chop some parsley, thyme and other herbs that may appeal to your taste. Season the whole with salt and pepper. Knead the egg, roe and herbs into a paste, then mix with bread crumbs and stuff the fish with this mixture. Sew the shad up as you would a turkey and place in a long fish kettle. Cover the shad with plenty of butter. If the butter is sweet, you can add a little more seasoning. Put it into the oven and baste very often with the drippings.

Shad Roe Omelet

★

The Norman chef does some surprising things with shad roe, and he excels his own imagination when he uses it in an omelet. Two shad roes are sufficient for 6 people:

They are washed carefully and bleached by steeping for 5 minutes in boiling water that has been slightly salted. Sometimes a piece of tuna fish as large as an egg is hashed in with the roes. Season with a little minced shallot. After it is well mixed, the roe mixture is placed in a saucepan with a lump of butter and allowed to fry lightly. This procedure is the important part of the recipe.

Next, beat 12 eggs. Take the hot shad roe and pour it over the eggs, stirring until well mixed. Cook 2 or 3 omelets in the usual manner. In order to make them perfect, follow Madame Poulard's method of pouring in a dash of cream at the right moment. (See Eggs for Omelet Poulard.)

Broiled Shad Roe, Ravigote Butter

Wash shad roe, dry carefully, season with salt and pepper and dip in oil. Broil under moderate heat, allowing about 10 minutes to each side. Remove roes to hot platter and spread with Ravigote Butter. (See Prepared Butters.)

Shad Roe à la Newburg

Drop 1 pair of shad roe in boiling, salted water and simmer 15 to 20 minutes, depending on size of roes. Drain, and when cool enough to handle, remove pieces of membrane and cut roes into pieces about the size of a walnut, season lightly with salt and a few grains of cayenne. Add roe to 1 cup of Newburg Sauce. (See Shellfish for Sauce.)

Shad Roe, Sauce Mornay

Poach shad roe by following directions contained in Fillet of Sole, Mornay.

Shad Roe, Sauté Meunière

Carefully wash shad roe, remove bits of membrane, but be careful not to cut thin skin over roe. Dip in flour and fry in clarified butter over moderate heat until nicely browned. Arrange roes on a hot platter, squeeze a little lemon juice over them and sprinkle finely chopped parsley on top. Add 2 tablespoons of butter to pan and just as it turns brown, remove it from heat and pour it over the roes.

Broiled Salmon Steak, Fines Herbes

Cut salmon steaks ¾ inch thick. Sprinkle lightly with salt and pepper and dip in oil. Broil under moderate heat allowing about 12 minutes for each side. Add a piece of butter to pan and baste frequently with melted butter and oil. Place on hot platter when cooked, and carefully remove the skin. Sprinkle each steak with ¼ teaspoon finely chopped parsley, ¼ teaspoon finely chopped chervil and ¼ teaspoon finely chopped chives. Add the juice of 1 lemon to the pan containing the melted butter and oil. Heat for 1 or 2 minutes until it is hot—then pour it over the salmon. Allow about 2 tablespoons for each steak.

Boiled Salmon, Mousseline Sauce

Cook a 3-pound piece of salmon in Court Bouillon 40 to 45 minutes (See Court Bouillon for boiling fish). Drain, remove skin, arrange fish on hot platter, garnish with parsley and Hollandaise Potatoes (see Potatoes). Serve sauce separately. (See Index for Mousseline Sauce.)

Broiled Salmon Steak, Anchovy Butter

Cut salmon steaks 1 inch thick. Sprinkle lightly with salt and pepper and dip in oil. Broil under moderate heat allowing 12 minutes for each side. Add a piece of butter to pan and baste frequently while broiling. Remove steak to hot platter and spread over 2 tablespoons Anchovy Butter. (See Prepared Butters.) Garnish with sprigs of parsley and lemon.

Cold Salmon, Sauce Vert

Cook a 3-pound piece of salmon in Court Bouillon (see Index) 40 to 45 minutes. Drain, cool, remove skin and chill in the refrigerator until wanted. Arrange whole piece of salmon on a bed of crisp lettuce leaves. Serve sauce separately, as follows:

Sauce Vert

To 1 cup of mayonnaise, add 2 level tablespoons of strained green pulp, which is obtained by macerating in a mortar the following ingredients: 6 sprigs parsley, 6 spinach leaves, 1 small bunch watercress, 6 green tarragon leaves and 6 blades of chives. Work herbs in a mortar until reduced to a pulp. Rub pulp through a fine sieve until desired amount is obtained.

Escalloped Salmon

Canned salmon or cold boiled salmon may be used in this recipe. Remove skin and bone and flake 2 cups of salmon. Make 2 cups of White Sauce (see Index) and add a grating of onion to it. Butter a small baking dish, add a layer of salmon, cover with White Sauce and continue layers of salmon and White Sauce until all is used, having sauce end on top. Sprinkle with bread crumbs and dot with small bits of butter. Bake in a moderate oven until nicely browned—about 35 minutes.

Salmon and Macaroni Timbales

Cook long pieces of macaroni in boiling, salted water for 20 minutes. Drain, hold under cold running water and drain again. Butter timbale molds and line with macaroni which have been cut in pieces to fit interior of mold. Fill center of molds with Salmon Forcemeats made as follows: Cook ½ cup milk and ½ cup bread crumbs together for 8 or 10 minutes, then add ⅔ cup cold cooked salmon which has been picked apart and sieved. Also add 2 tablespoons of butter, 2 tablespoons heavy cream and 1 slightly beaten egg. Season to taste with salt and pepper. Place timbale molds in pan of hot water and bake in moderate oven for 25 to 30 minutes. Serve with Béchamel Sauce. (See Index for Sauce.)

Brook Trout, Sauté Meunière

Clean and wash the brook trout, cut off fins and tail but leave the head on. Dip lightly in flour and fry in clarified butter until browned.

Place trout on hot platter, squeeze lemon juice over them and sprinkle over some finely chopped parsley. Add 2 tablespoons of butter to pan in which the trout were cooked, and when the butter turns brown, remove it from heat and pour it over the fish.

Broiled Whitefish, Maitre d'Hotel

Select a medium-sized whitefish; split and bone for broiling. Season with salt and pepper and dip in oil. Broil under moderate heat until nicely browned. Remove fish to hot platter and spread with Maitre d'Hotel Butter (see Prepared Butters).

Planked Whitefish, Rector

Clean and bone a whitefish weighing about 4 pounds. Season with salt and pepper and rub entire fish with soft butter. Place it on a buttered plank (a plank is a cooking board) and cover empty space of plank with salt (this will keep plank from burning). Bake in moderate oven 30 minutes. Remove plank from oven, brush off all the salt and make a potato border around edge of plank by using a pastry bag and tube. Fill in the space between edge of fish and potato border with baked stuffed tomatoes, small mounds of string beans and small mounds of cauliflower. Place plank in hot oven to brown potato border. Remove from oven, garnish with parsley and lemon and serve from plank. Cover mounds of cauliflower with Hollandaise or Cream Sauce. (See Index for Sauces.)

Baked Finnan Haddie

Since finnan haddie is a dried smoked fish, it is advisable to soak it in cold water for at least 1 hour. This will also remove some of the salt. Lay the finnan haddie, skin side down, in a baking pan. Cover with cold milk, add 1 small bay leaf, a pinch of thyme and about 10 whole black peppercorns. Heat the finnan haddie very slowly over low heat for about 30 minutes without letting the milk boil. Drain off the milk and seasonings, reserve milk, spread fish with butter and place in a moderate oven to bake for 20 minutes. Baste fish occasionally with melted butter during the baking. Mix ½ cup cream with ½ cup reserved milk and pour it over fish just as it leaves the oven. Sprinkle top with paprika.

Finnan Haddie, Rector

This was one of the popular chafing dish specialites of the Rector Restaurant in Chicago and was later introduced in New York. Soak the finnan haddie in a baking pan with just enough milk to cover. Let it stand about 1 hour, then place it over low heat to simmer gently for 20 minutes. Lift the fish carefully out of the pan when cooked, and flake into pieces. Be sure to remove all bone and skin while flaking the fish. To every 3 cups of fish, add 2 cups of Rich Cream Sauce (see Index for Sauce); 2 hard-boiled eggs, finely chopped; 1 tablespoon green pepper, finely chopped; and 1 tablespoon chopped pimiento. Sprinkle liberally with paprika and serve on toast.

Steamed Haddock, Egg Sauce

Select a 3-pound haddock. Cook for 20 minutes by steaming over boiling water. Remove fish to hot platter and carefully peel off the skin. Garnish with Hollandaise Potatoes (see Potatoes) and thin slices of hard-boiled egg. Serve with Egg Sauce. (See Index for Egg Sauce.)

Baked Stuffed Haddock

Prepared in the British Manner, this is about the best fish you will have ever tasted.

Purchase a fresh haddock. The other ingredients are: 2 tablespoonfuls of bread crumbs, 1 dessert-spoonful of chopped parsley, 1 teaspoonful of dried herbs, 1 ounce of suet, 1 egg, 2 ounces of fat, salt, pepper and 12 oysters which have been cut into quarters.

Wash and cleanse the fish thoroughly, then dry with a cloth. Put the bread crumbs into a bowl and mix with the parsley, herbs, shredded suet, salt and pepper. Beat the yolk of the egg and add it to the mixture. Combine the oysters and stuff the fish with the Oyster Forcemeat. Sew the haddock up with cotton thread and truss it into the shape of the letter S. Place it in a baking pan which has been well greased. Beat the white of the egg very little and then brush it over the fish. After the fish is brushed with the white of the egg, sprinkle the haddock with more bread crumbs. Now, bake in a moderate oven for 30 minutes, basting very often with butter. When cooked, remove the cotton thread and serve on a hot dish. A garnishing of parsley is palatable, and Anchovy Sauce is another splendid garniture. (See Index for Sauce.)

Baked Haddock, Savory Stuffing

Purchase a 4-pound Haddock for baking. Wash, dry and sprinkle with salt. Make a stuffing of 2 cups of bread crumbs, ¼ cup chopped onion, ¼ teaspoon of summer savory, ¼ teaspoon whole sage and salt and pepper to taste. Mix ingredients well and moisten with 4 tablespoons melted butter, add just enough water to make the stuffing moist but not wet. Fill fish with stuffing and sew the edges together. Rub fish with melted butter and lay it in a greased baking pan, dredge lightly with flour and lay 3 slices of salt pork on fish. Bake in a moderately hot oven, allowing 15 minutes to the pound. Baste every 10 minutes with the salt pork drippings. Serve with Creole, Poulette or Egg Sauce. (See Index for Sauces.)

Boiled Cod, Anchovy Sauce

Have 3 or 4 pounds of cod fish cut in 1 piece for boiling. Place it on rack and lower it into fish kettle containing enough boiling, salted water to cover. Add 2 tablespoons of vinegar to water as this will keep the cod white. Simmer until fish is cooked—20 to 25 minutes. Remove fish from kettle and carefully peel off the skin. Arrange on a hot platter and garnish with parsley and Hollandaise Potatoes (see Potatoes). Serve Anchovy Sauce separately. (See Index for Sauce.)

Baked Cod, Espagnole

Select a 4-pound cod; split and cut into pieces with all bone and skin removed. Rub the pieces with soft butter and season with salt and pepper. Arrange them in a buttered casserole and sprinkle 1 tablespoon finely chopped onion on top. Moisten with 6 tablespoons white wine or Fish Stock (see Stock) and place in a moderate oven to bake, basting occasionally. When fish is cooked, carefully lift it onto a hot platter, add 1 cup of Creole Sauce and 1/4 cup thick Tomato Sauce to casserole and stir until mixed. Return sauce to hot oven for 5 minutes. Pour sauce over fish and sprinkle a little finely chopped parsley on top. (See Index on Sauces.)

Cod Tongues, Sauté Meunière

Trim and wash the cod tongues and dry them on a towel. Season with salt and pepper and roll them lightly in flour. Fry them in clarified butter until nicely browned. Arrange them on a hot platter, squeeze a little lemon juice over them and sprinkle lightly with finely chopped parsley. Add 2 tablespoons of butter to pan, let it turn brown, remove from heat and pour it over tongues.

Cod Tongues, Sauce Poulette

Trim and wash the cod tongues. Cover them with a Fish Stock (Court Bouillon, see Index) and simmer for 10 or 12 minutes. Drain, arrange tongues in serving dish and pour Sauce Poulette over tongues. (See Index for Sauce Poulette.)

Scrambled Codfish

This recipe calls for salted codfish. Wash codfish in cold water and soak overnight. This will remove enough of the salt to make it edible. Never cut salted codfish with a knife but tear it or shred it with fork. Beat 4 eggs and gradually add 1 pint of milk and 1 cup of shredded codfish. Turn into hot buttered frying pan and cook over moderate heat until the eggs and codfish are set. Stir occasionally and do not cook too long; otherwise the eggs will become hard and dry. Garnish with crisp parsley and triangles of fresh toast.

Creamed Codfish

Shred 2 cups of salted codfish, which has been soaked in water overnight. Cover with fresh cold water and bring to a boil. Reduce heat and SIMMER for 3 or 4 minutes. Drain water off and add 1 cup of fresh cream. Heat slowly until boiling point is reached. Remove from heat and serve on large rounds of toast.

Salt Codfish au Gratin

Shred 2 cups of salted codfish, which has been soaked in water overnight. Cover with fresh cold water and bring to a boil. Reduce heat and SIMMER for 5 minutes. Drain. Fry 1 finely chopped onion in 2 tablespoons of butter 5 minutes, taking care not to brown butter or onion. Add the drained codfish, season with a few grains of cayenne, add 1 clove of crushed garlic and 1 teaspoon finely chopped parsley. Cook over moderate heat 2 minutes, then add 1½ cups of Cream Sauce (see Sauces) and pour into a buttered shallow casserole. Sprinkle top with buttered bread crumbs and grated Parmesan cheese. Place in a moderate oven until browned.

Broiled Scrod

A scrod is a young codfish and is perfectly delicious when broiled. Select one weighing about 2 or 3 pounds. Split it for broiling and remove the entire backbone. Place it on a greased broiler (open side up) and cook under moderate heat until nicely browned—about 20 minutes. Baste it with melted butter while it is broiling; otherwise it is apt to be dry. A small fish of this weight does not have to be turned in the cooking. The heat of the broiler will penetrate to the skin, and when the open part is nicely browned, the fish will be sufficiently cooked. Carefully remove to hot platter and spread with fresh butter and season with salt and pepper. Serve with quartered lemon.

Broiled Smelts, Maitre d'Hotel

Select the large smelts and remove bones if not already boned. Place on broiler and dot with fresh butter and cook until nicely browned. It will only be necessary to broil on one side (the open side). Then arrange them on a hot platter and spread with Maitre d'Hotel Butter, which should be made in advance. (See Prepared Butters.)

Fried Smelts, Tartare Sauce

Clean smelts, trim fins and tail but leave the heads on. Season with salt and pepper and dip lightly in flour, beaten egg and bread crumbs. Deep-fry until nicely browned. Drain on paper, arrange on hot platter and garnish with fried parsley. Serve sauce separately. (See Index for Tartare Sauce.)

Fried Smelts, Figaro Sauce

Clean smelts, trim fins and tail, but leave the heads on. Season with salt and pepper, dip lightly in flour, beaten egg and bread crumbs. Fry in clarified butter until nicely browned. Remove to hot platter and garnish with fried parsley and lemon. Serve sauce separately. (See Index for Figaro Sauce.)

Broiled Fresh Mackerel, Anchovy Butter

Split and bone a 2-pound mackerel for broiling. Season with salt and pepper and dip in oil. Lay it skin side down on broiler and cook under moderate heat until nicely browned. It is only necessary to broil a fish of this size on the open flesh part. Remove to hot platter and spread with Anchovy Butter. (See Prepared Butters.)

Broiled Fresh Mackerel, Maitre d'Hotel

Follow above directions. Spread with Maitre d'Hotel Butter instead of Anchovy Butter. (See Prepared Butters.)

Fish and Cheese Timbales

Make 1 cup of Cream Sauce and season it with 1 teaspoon of A.1. or Worcestershire sauce. Add 1 cup of cold cooked chopped fish (halibut, cod or bass will do very nicely). Place over low heat, and in the meantime, butter the timbales and sprinkle the buttered surface with grated cheese. Fill the timbales with fish mixture and set the timbales in a pan of hot water and bake in a moderate oven 15 minutes. Serve with Cheese Sauce. (See Index for Sauces.)

Broiled Deviled Sardines on Toast

Select large sardines. Carefully remove skin and cover with Deviled Butter made as follows: Cream 2 tablespoons of butter, add 1 level teaspoon English mustard and a few drops of Worcestershire sauce. When thoroughly blended, spread sardines with mixture and dip in crackermeal. Broil under quick heat until brown. Serve on freshly made toast and garnish with parsley and lemon.

PREPARED BUTTERS

5

Terrapin Butter

Mash 3 hard-boiled egg yolks. Thoroughly blend them with ¼ pound of creamed butter. Season with salt, a few grains of cayenne and a few grains of nutmeg. Press through a sieve and keep in refrigerator until needed.

Anchovy Butter

Remove skin and bones from 1 ounce of anchovies. Dry thoroughly and pound them in a mortar. Add 1 teaspoon of Anchovy Paste (see Index) and pound with pestle until thoroughly blended. Then work in ¼ pound of sweet butter and rub through a fine sieve. Keep in refrigerator until needed.

Maitre d'Hotel Butter

Cream 2 tablespoons of butter and add ½ teaspoon salt, a pinch of cayenne pepper, 1 teaspoon of finely chopped parsley and gradually add 1 tablespoon of strained lemon juice. To be spread over hot broiled fish, also, used for basting.

Hazel-Nut Butter

Melt ¼ pound of butter in a saucepan. When hot, it will froth and then settle down to brown. Let it brown but do not burn it. Carefully pour it into a hot dish, leaving the sediment in the saucepan. Season with a little salt, a few grains of cayenne pepper and 1 tablespoon strained lemon juice.

Creamed Butter

Cream ½ pound of fresh butter. When soft, beat it well with a fork or wire whisk. Season with a little salt, a pinch of grated nutmeg. Gradually add ¼ pound of sifted flour and beat until thoroughly blended. To be used for thickening soups or sauces. Keep covered in a cool place until needed.

Deviled Butter

Cream 2 tablespoons of butter, add 1 level teaspoon English mustard and a few drops of Worcestershire sauce. Blend thoroughly. Spread thinly on fish to be broiled.

Horseradish Butter

Cream ¼ pound of butter, add ¼ cup fresh grated horseradish, a little salt and a few grains of cayenne. Blend thoroughly. Spread on hot broiled steaks or chops.

Lobster Coral Butter

Remove the coral or eggs from a female lobster and work it in a mortar with 4 tablespoons of butter. Season with a little salt and rub it through a fine sieve.

Shallot Butter

Chop and blanch 6 shallots. Sieve and mix with 6 tablespoons of butter. Used for frying meats and fish.

Lemon Butter

Cream 4 tablespoons butter, gradually add 1 tablespoon strained lemon juice and a few grains of cayenne. To be spread over hot broiled fish.

Black Butter (Beurre Noir)

Melt 4 tablespoons of butter in frying pan, and when it turns brown (almost black), add 3 tablespoons cider vinegar. Remove from heat immediately. Shake pan several times to mix butter and vinegar.

Tarragon Butter

Cream 2 tablespoons of butter and add ½ teaspoon salt, a pinch of cayenne pepper, 1 teaspoon finely chopped tarragon leaves and gradually add 1 tablespoon of strained lemon juice.

Ravigote Butter

Blanch 10 or 12 spinach leaves, 4 chives and 4 shallots. Drain, put them in a mortar and macerate until the green juice is extracted. Add ¼ pound of sweet butter, season with a little salt, and when thoroughly blended, press through a fine sieve. Keep in a cool place till needed.

Clarified Butter

Place butter in a small saucepan. Melt it over low heat and the salt will settle on the bottom of the pan. Carefully pour melted butter into another saucepan or dish, leaving the salt on the bottom.

BEEF

6

Chateaubriand, Maitre d'Hotel

Chateaubriand is the name given to the center cut of a fillet of beef and should be cut about 3 inches thick. Trim fat and flatten with the flat side of a cleaver. Dip in olive oil, season with salt and pepper and broil under moderate heat, allowing about 10 minutes to each side. (If your fillet is not 3 inches thick, adjust heat accordingly until nicely browned.) Remove to hot platter and spread with Maitre d'Hotel Butter: Cream 2 tablespoons butter, add ½ teaspoon salt, a few grains of cayenne pepper, 1 teaspoon finely chopped parsley and gradually add 1 tablespoon strained lemon juice.

Broiled Sirloin Steak, Bordelaise

Have broiler oven hot before putting in the steak. Place steak on greased broiler and expose both sides of steak to intense heat until entire surface is seared. Lower heat to moderate and broil until cooked. The average steak, which should be cut about 2 inches thick, will take 20 minutes to broil. In turning steak on broiler, never insert fork in the meat but rather in the fat to prevent loss of juice. Remove steak to hot platter, season with salt and pepper and pour sauce over steak and sliced marrow:

Bordelaise Sauce

2 shallots, finely chopped
½ small onion, finely chopped
1 small carrot, sliced
1 sprig parsley
¼ bay leaf
10 peppercorns
½ cup dry red wine (4 oz.)
1 cup Brown Sauce
1 tablespoon butter
1 tablespoon lemon juice
1 tablespoon parsley, finely chopped
10 slices poached beef marrow (cut ¼ inch thick)

Cook shallots, onion, carrot, parsley, bay leaf and peppercorns with red wine until quantity is reduced to ½. Strain, add wine to hot

Brown Sauce (see Index on Sauces). Add butter bit by bit, and when thoroughly blended, stir in the lemon juice and finely chopped parsley. Season to taste with salt and pepper. Arrange sliced poached marrow on top of steak and carefully pour sauce over all. Poached Marrow: Carefully remove marrow from marrow-bones, slice, and poach in boiling, salted water for 5 minutes. Keep water at simmering point while poaching marrow.

Filet Mignon, Sauce Béarnaise

Select thick fillets, which are uniform in size. Dip each fillet in melted butter and broil for 10 to 15 minutes under moderate heat. Season with salt and pepper and arrange them on a bed of Sauce Béarnaise, as follows:

Sauce Béarnaise

2 shallots, finely chopped
Pinch thyme
4 tablespoons vinegar
1 cup of Hollandaise sauce
¼ bay leaf
2 sprigs parsley
10 peppercorns (crushed)
12 green tarragon leaves
½ tablespoon tarragon leaves, finely chopped
½ tablespoon parsley, finely chopped

Cook shallots, thyme, bay leaf, parsley, crushed peppercorns and tarragon leaves with vinegar until quantity is reduced to ¼ . Strain, add to Hollandaise Sauce (see Index on Sauces) and stir in finely chopped tarragon leaves and finely chopped parsley.

Filet Mignon, Marguerite

Start with thick fillets that are uniform in size. Sauté in clarified butter until cooked. Cover bottom of hot platter with Sauce Colbert (see Index for Sauce) and arrange small rounds of toast on top of sauce. Place fillets on top of toast and garnish with Baked Stuffed Tomatoes: Select 6 firm tomatoes of uniform size. Core out the center with a sharp knife and prepare the stuffing as follows: Put into a large mixing bowl the pulp of the tomatoes, which you have just removed. Add ½ small onion, finely chopped, ⅛ teaspoon mixed herbs, 1 cup cold cooked meat (ham, tongue, chicken or veal, finely chopped) and 1 cup bread crumbs. Moisten with melted butter and season with salt and pepper. Stuff tomatoes with mixture, place on greased baking pan and bake in moderate oven 30 minutes.

Braised Beef, Schmorbraten
Potato Dumpling

Start with a thick flank of beef. Lard it with larding pork (see Techniques) to make it tender, and then, stew it slowly in a casserole with a couple of ham bones, a few bay leaves, a few peppercorns, carrots and onions. Throw in a big pinch of salt. When the meat has become almost cooked, add 2 tablespoons of flour, and at the same time, fill the casserole, in which the meat is cooking, with Consommé (see Stock). Allow the Consommé to reduce by slow boiling to a rich essence. A few minutes before the dish is cooked entirely, add several fresh tomatoes, cut in quarters. To prepare this German specialty in the right manner, requires from 2 to 3 hours. Another variation is to substitute sauerkraut for the fresh tomatoes. The sauerkraut can be added very early in the preparation.

A Potato Dumpling is served with the Schmorbraten on the same platter; the dumplings are made separately: Take medium-sized potatoes and boil them. After they are boiled, peel and mash them. Add 4 or 5 eggs, a little flour, a dash of nutmeg, some salt seasoning and a little ground rice to the mashed potatoes. Stir all these ingredients together in a bowl, and then shape it into small balls about the size of plums. Drop the dumplings into boiling water and allow them to remain until cooked. It is not necessary to boil the dumpling in salt water, as you have already seasoned it when mixing the ingredients. When the dumplings are ready for the table, place on a hot platter and pour the following sauce over them:

Take 2 cupfuls of crumbs made from stale bread, put them in a deep sieve and then lower the sieve into a pot of hot, boiling fat. Allow the sieve to remain in the fat until the bread crumbs are a rich golden brown. Sprinkle the bread crumbs over the potato dumplings and pour over the whole platter some browned butter made from 6 pats of butter.

★

This is an example of real German cooking. The recipe was obtained from one of the oldest establishments in Berlin called the Weinstube, operated by Lutter and Weger.

A weinstube is not a restaurant, but a cellar where you go in for the purpose of drinking wine, and the stubes are usually dark tunnels disguised as taverns. The Weinstube Restaurant, as it was named, was actually built over a weinstube. I hope that's not confusing.

Another form of Schmorbraten, called Sauerbraten, was prepared at Luchow's, a restaurant on Fourteenth Street in New York. The basic difference is that this one is marinated:

The beef is placed in a crock containing equal parts of vinegar and water. Put in a few peppercorns and bay leaves and allow it to remain in the vinegar and water for 2 days before cooking. After the 2 days, the Sauerbraten is treated exactly like the Schmorbraten.

Beef Sauté de France

Cut some very thin slices of meat from the hip or sirloin. Place a large piece of butter in a saucepan and then put the slices of beef in the pan. Season with salt and pepper and add some thin slices of onion. Cook the beef for 5 minutes over medium-low heat. Then turn the meat over and allow it to cook for another 5 minutes. Care should be taken not to allow the onions to burn. Add 4 ounces of hot Bouillon (see Stock), which has been already mixed with a little flour. During the cooking, if you would like more flavor, add 1 teaspoonful of vinegar. When the Bouillon is added, the dish is ready to serve.

Larded Fillet of Beef, Mushroom Sauce

The whole fillet or tenderloin weighs about 3 pounds. Trim the lard for roasting, also obtain several pieces of pork to put in the pan while the fillet is roasting. Place the fillet in a roasting pan with the extra pieces of pork around it and start to cook in a hot oven (450°) for 15 minutes. Reduce to moderate heat (325°) and cook 30 minutes longer basting every 10 minutes. This length of time cooks the fillet medium-rare; so judge accordingly, if you want the fillet cooked rare, medium-rare, or well-done. When the fillet is cooked, sprinkle it with salt and pepper and place it on a hot platter while you make the Mushroom Sauce:

Mushroom Sauce

Add 1½ cups of well-seasoned Brown Stock (see Index) to fat in pan (there should be 2 tablespoons of fat) and stir bottom and sides of pan until all essence is dissolved. Thicken with 1 tablespoon of flour which has been mixed with a little cold water. Bring to a boil and strain into a small saucepan while you prepare the mushrooms. Melt 1 tablespoon of butter in a frying pan. When hot, add ½ pound of thinly sliced mushrooms, cook over moderate heat for 5 minutes, remove from heat, add 1 tablespoon of lemon juice, then pour gravy into pan containing mushrooms. Season to taste and add 3 drops of Worcestershire sauce. Garnish fillet with crisp watercress and serve the sauce separately.

Steak and Kidney Pudding

¾ lb. fine steak meat
¼ lb. beef kidney
1 teaspoon flour
½ teaspoon salt
¼ teaspoon pepper

For the pastry you need 6 ounces of flour, 3 ounces of suet, ½ teaspoonful of baking powder, a pinch of salt, and cold water to mix. To make the pastry: Sieve the flour, salt and baking powder, shred the suet finely and mix with the flour, add sufficient water to make a stiff paste. Cut off a small piece for the lid, roll the rest out and line a greased basin or deep pie dish.

Wipe the meat with a damp cloth, remove all fat and gristle, and cut into strips about 3 inches long and 1 inch wide. Mix the flour, salt and pepper on a plate and then flour the strips of meat with this mixture. Put a small piece of kidney and a tiny piece of fat on each strip and roll them up. Fill the lined basin with these rolls, adding any trimmings of kidney or meat, shake over the seasoned flour left on the plate and half-fill the basin with Stock (see Stock). Put on the lid of pastry, seal the edges well together, cover with greased paper and steam from 3 to 4 hours.

For a variation with vegetables—onions, carrots, turnips or potatoes can be washed, peeled, cut into dice and cooked in the pudding along with the meat and kidney.

When cooked, the pudding is served in the same basin, with a napkin pinned around it. Note: The water must be boiling when the pudding is placed in the steamer, and kept boiling the whole time; otherwise the pudding will not be properly cooked and the pastry will be soggy. As the water in the pan vaporizes, fresh boiling water must be added. Never add cold water—so be sure the added liquid is at the boiling point; there must be no change of temperature during the cooking.

Roast Beef, Yorkshire Pudding

Select a cut of beef for roasting—rib, sirloin or round. Choice depending on size of family or individual taste. Place meat in a hot oven (475°) for 30 minutes. Reduce to moderate heat (350°) and continue roasting allowing 20 minutes to the pound. Baste meat every 10 minutes and before removing from the oven, season top and sides with salt and pepper. Make Yorkshire Pudding as follows: Mix 1 cup of flour and ¼ teaspoon of salt together, gradually add 1 cup of milk and stir until perfectly smooth, then add 2 well-beaten eggs. Pour batter into shallow pan, which has been greased with some of the hot roast beef drippings. Bake in moderate oven 30 minutes, and cut in small squares for serving.

Braised Beef en Casserole

Cut 2 pounds of top round into small pieces about the size of a walnut, season with salt and pepper and dredge lightly with flour. Cover bottom of large frying pan with beef suet drippings, and when hot, add meat and brown quickly on all sides. Remove meat to casserole, add ½ cup of uncooked potato balls, cut with French vegetable cutter, ½ cup uncooked carrot balls, about 10 small white onions (uncooked), about 20 string beans (split lengthwise), ½ small bay leaf and 1 clove of garlic (crushed). Pour 1 cup of seasoned Beef Stock (see Stock) over meat and vegetables, cover casserole, and place in moderate oven until meat and vegetables are tender—about 1 hour. When casserole is taken from oven, enrich sauce by adding 1 tablespoon of butter and ½ teaspoon meat extract, stirring until butter and extract are thoroughly blended into sauce. Baste meat and vegtetables with sauce before casserole is placed on the table.

Pot Roast, Family Style

This roast is most delicious when cooked and seasoned properly. Top sirloin, cross-rib or bottom round may be used for this recipe.

Purchase a 4 or 5 pound pot-roast. Wipe with a piece of clean, damp cheesecloth. Season with salt and pepper and roll in sifted flour. Grease skillet and put pot-roast in to sear and brown on all sides. Then lower the heat under the skillet and add 1 cup of hot water, 1 large sliced onion, 1 cup canned tomatoes and 2 outer stalks of celery and leaves, also 10 peppercorns and 1 bay leaf. Simmer slowly until tender and add hot water or tomato liquid to the pan as the original amount reduces. Turn the meat on all sides while cooking. Remove celery, bayleaf and peppercorns before you make a gravy from the juices.

Bitki (Cossack Steak)

Make 1 pound of fresh ground beef into 7 or 8 small round flat cakes and season with a little salt and pepper. Now, make an egg omelette with 1 egg, 1 tablespoon of water and a pinch of salt. In another pan, melt a small piece of butter and fry ½ cup of chopped mushrooms and ½ cup of onions together until cooked. When mushrooms and onions are cooked, sprinkle them with finely chopped parsley. Cut the egg omelette into fine shreds and mix it with the mushrooms, onions and parsley. Fill this mixture into the center of the meat cakes and pinch the edges together. Fry in beef suet drippings until nicely browned. Serve with Tomato Sauce (see Sauces) mixed with an equal portion of sour cream. Very delicious, and it offers a new way to present hamburger.

Hamburger Dumpling

Take 1 pound of beef and 1 pound of pork. Run the meat through the grinder. Put it into an earthen bowl and add 3 eggs, 12 chopped anchovies, and season with salt and pepper. This is stirred thoroughly with a spoon, and then formed into the dumplings. The dumplings are cooked in Consommé (see Stock) and spiced with marjoram.

They are served with a sauce made from the Consommé in which the dumplings have been boiled. To this stock, add a little flour, to make a cream sauce. In the cream sauce, pour in 2 hard-boiled eggs which have been chopped very fine, and add 1 tablespoonful of capers.

★

One of the restaurants, which preserved the old traditions of Berlin, was the Kempinski House. It was founded in 1862 by Granddad Kempinski, who was the biggest wine merchant in the country, but his Restaurant was his pride and joy. The Kempinski Family was totally involved in the restuarant business and opened several other restaurants in Germany and Amsterdam. One of their establishments, called the Ulfa Building, could seat 5000 people at one time, and it was the largest restaurant on the European continent and probably in the world.

One of their finest recipes was for the Königsberger Klopse (Hamburger Dumpling). Königsberger Dumplings taste their best when served with plain, boiled potatoes.

Smoked Beef Tongue, Sauce Piquante

Soak Beef tongue overnight in cold water to cover. Drain, cover with fresh cold water, add 1 small onion, 2 sprigs parsley, 3 cloves, ½ small bay leaf, 10 peppercorns and a large piece of lemon rind. Bring slowly to the boiling point, let boil for 5 minutes, remove scum, lower temperature to simmering point and cook until tongue is tender—4 to 5 hours. Remove tongue to cutting board, when cool enough to handle, trim off skin and throat cords. Place on large hot platter and pour sauce over and around tongue. (See Index on Sauces.)

Corned Beef Hash

To 2 cups of chopped corned beef, add 2 cups of chopped cooked potatoes, 1 small onion, finely minced and 1 tablespoon of finely minced green pepper. Season with salt and pepper. Bank the hash to one side of the pan to shape it and turn onto a hot platter brown side up. Garnish with fresh sprigs of parsley.

Beef Loaf Aspic

Soak 1 level tablespoon of gelatin in ½ cup of cold water 5 minutes. Meanwhile, slice 1 small onion, 1 heart of celery and boil for 3 minutes in 1 cup of highly seasoned stock. Strain, add 1 teaspoon Worcestershire sauce and pour it into soaked gelatin. When mixture begins to stiffen, add 1 cup of chopped cold roast beef, ¼ cup canned pimentos, cut in very thin strips, and 1 heaping teaspoon of finely chopped parsley. Turn into a wet loaf mold and chill. Garnish with crisp lettuc leaves and asparagus tips which have been dipped in French Dressing. Slice with a sharp knife when serving. (See Index for Dressing.)

Roasted Short Ribs, Raisin Sauce

Sear a 5-pound short-rib roast under broiler for 5 minutes. This process is important because it prevents the meat juices from escaping. Place the roast in a roasting pan with 2 cups of boiling water, season roast with salt and pepper. Add 1 teaspoon celery salt, 3 whole cloves, several peppercorns, a small piece of bay leaf and a bit of thyme. Place in moderate oven and cook about 3 hours. The Raisin Sauce is made as follows: Cook ½ cup of raisins in 2 cups of water and 1 tablespoon of strained lemon juice. Simmer slowly for about 30 minutes. In another saucepan, melt 3 tablespoons butter, blend in 2 tablespoons flour, add a pinch of salt and stir until it is a perfectly smooth mixture, add the raisin mixture slowly and stir continuously. Simmer for 10 minutes. Pour around the roasted short ribs and serve.

Rolled Roast, Provençal

3 to 4 pounds of beef roll
1 cup of chopped celery and leaves
1 large onion, chopped fine
1 clove of garlic, chopped fine
2 tablespoons fat
1 tablespoon flour
1 teaspoon salt
⅛ teaspoon pepper
1 cup of tomatoes
1 head cauliflower, separated into flowerettes.

Brown the celery and onion in melted fat, add the garlic and flour and stir until the flour is thoroughly blended. Add the tomatoes and the beef roll. Sear in a hot oven (450°) for 10 minutes. Reduce heat to 350°, season with salt and pepper. Cover roaster and cook for 1½ hours, then add the parboiled flowerettes and continue cooking until tender—about 1 hour.

Meat Loaf

Start with 1 pound of ground beef, ½ pound lean ground pork and ½ pound ground veal. Mix together and add ½ cup of bread crumbs and ½ cup of milk. Season with 1 teaspoon of salt and ⅛ teaspoon of pepper, and add 1 egg slightly beaten. Shape into loaf and lay across top 2 or 3 slices of salt pork. Place in a hot oven to roast and baste every 10 or 15 minutes until cooked—about 1¼ hours. Serve with Tomato Sauce. (See Index for Sauce.)

Beef à la Mode

2 pounds flank steak
½ cup of flour
Salt and pepper
2 tablespoons fat
1 cup potatoes cut in cubes or small balls
1 cup of small onions
2 tablespoons chopped parsley
1 cup of tomato pulp
½ cup bread crumbs
1 cup White Sauce (see Sauces)

Pound the flour into the steak and season with salt and pepper. Cook for 30 minutes in the hot fat and then transfer the steak to a casserole. Cover with vegetables, White Sauce and sprinkle the bread crumbs over the top. Bake in a moderate oven for 40 minutes and serve from the casserole.

Filet Mignon à la Stanley

Purchase, or slice from a tenderloin of beef, fillets weighing 5 or 6 ounces apiece. Also flatten them to 1-inch thickness by wrapping tightly in a towel and pound, using the flat side of a cleaver, into round shapes. Dip each fillet in melted butter and broil from 8 to 12 minutes. Have ready rounds of fresh buttered toast (same size as fillet) arranged on a platter and place each broiled fillet on a round of toast. Brush the fillets with glaze viande (beef extract) and surround with Horseradish Sauce. Sprinkle each fillet with finely chopped parsley taking care not to get any in the sauce. Place a quarter of fried banana on each fillet and serve:

Horseradish Sauce

Fry in butter without browning ¼ cup finely chopped onion. Add 1 cup of cream and reduce by cooking for several minutes. Strain through a sieve and thicken with 2 egg yolks which have been beaten with a little cream. Then add freshly grated horseradish until it is quite thick. Season with salt. Do not allow to boil again, but the sauce can be kept warm by placing pan in hot water.

Fried Bananas

Allow ¼ banana for each Filet Mignon à la Stanley. Peel firm bananas and split in halves, lengthwise, and then cut each half a-cross. Roll the pieces in flour and fry in deep hot fat until a golden brown. Drain on unglazed paper.

Ragoût of Beef, Bourgeoise

Cut 2 pounds of top round into small pieces. Season with salt and pepper and dust lightly with flour. Melt beef drippings in stew-pan, and when hot, put in meat and brown all sides. When meat is well browned, add 1½ cups of Brown Stock (see Stock) and bring to a boil, then add a small bay leaf, salt and pepper to taste, 1 bunch small carrots, about 10 small onions and potatoes cut in uniform size. Simmer until vegetables are cooked. Thicken with brown flour and a dash of Kitchen Bouquet (a liquid seasoning).

Boiled Beef, Horseradish Sauce

Select a nice piece of fresh beef for boiling. A thick flank will do nicely for this purpose. Cover meat with boiling water, add a few sprigs of parsley, a few celery tops, 1 small bay leaf and about 10 peppercorns. Simmer gently and allow 30 minutes for each pound of meat. Boiled beef must be cooked until it is very tender, and the quality of beef has a lot to do with time allowed for cooking. A 5-pound piece of beef should be tender after 2½ hours of gentle simmering. About 45 minutes before meat is cooked add 6 medium-sized carrots, which have been washed and scraped, and also add a few small white turnips. When meat is cooked, place it on a large platter and garnish with carrots at one end of the platter and turnips at the other end. Sprinkle a little finely chopped parlsey on the carrots and a few grains of paprika over the turnips. Serve the sauce separately. Horseradish Sauce: To 1 cup of milk, add 3 tablespoons of cracker crumbs and cook in top part of double boiler for 20 minutes. Remove from heat and add 1 tablespoon of butter, ⅛ teaspoon salt and a few grains of pepper and stir until butter is dissolved, then add 4 tablespoons of freshly grated horseradish and serve.

Beef à la Mode (Cold Roast Beef)

This recipe is to be made from cold roast beef. Cut the roast beef into small cubes and place them in a saucepan with hot gravy or Beef Stock (see Stock) to cover. To every 2 cups of diced beef, add: ½ cup of seedless raisins, which have been picked over and washed, and 1 tablespoon of vinegar. Simmer slowly until beef is very tender. Add 1 teaspoon sugar and a little salt and pepper. Thicken sauce with a little cornstarch or flour that has been dissolved in cold water. Bring to a boil and serve.

Beef Steak Pie

This dish needs little recommendation, and all the goodness and flavor of the round steak is enhanced by this method of preparation. Cut 2 pounds of round steak into small pieces and brown them in hot fat, and at the same time brown 1 cup of sliced onion with it. Season with salt and pepper, 1 tablespoon of Worcestershire sauce and 2 tablespoons of chopped parsley. Cover with boiling water and simmer gently for 30 minutes. Add 2 cups of diced potatoes and cook for 45 minutes longer. Thicken with flour and butter creamed together. Pour into a deep dish, cool slightly, cover with a thin crust of Biscuit Dough (see Index) and bake in a moderately hot oven until crust is browned.

Beef Liver, Creole

Cut 1 pound of beef liver into thin slices. Remove skin and veins and wipe with a damp cloth. Roll in flour and fry in hot fat until brown. When liver is cooked, add 1 cup of sliced onions, 1½ cups of canned tomatoes and 1 sliced green pepper. Cover and cook slowly for 25 minutes, then season to taste with salt and pepper. Thicken with 2 tablespoons flour dissolved in cold water and boil for several minutes longer. Now, make a border of boiled rice on a large platter and pour the Beef Liver Creole in the center of the rice.

Liver Balls

The ingredients are: 2 pounds of ground liver, ¼ pound chopped bacon, 1 heaping cup of dry bread crumbs, 2 medium-sized grated onions, 1 small bunch of finely chopped parsley, 3 eggs, salt, pepper and a pinch of marjoram. Mix all together. Do your mixing with a tablespoon, which will then be used to measure the meat for the balls. You take a heaping tablespoonful for each ball and shape the ball with your hands. Drop these balls into boiling Consommé or Stock (see Stock), which should be freshly prepared. The Consommé is made easiest from cubes of meat extract. When the meat balls are dropped into the boiling stock, they will sink immediately to the bottom. As soon as they are cooked, they will rise to the surface. Spoon the meat balls out and place them on a hot platter. These liver balls are served covered with a sauce made as follows:

Chop finely, 2 medium onions and sauté very lightly in butter and lard. Pour this over the Liver Balls and serve with sauerkraut and mashed potatoes.

★

This was a favorite dish of Frankfort, which is not in the Rhine Valley, but it is close enough to enjoy all the aromas of the many fine dishes of the Rhineland. It was prepared by the chef of the Frankfurter Hof-on-the-Main.

Leberknodël, as it is called, is popular all over Germany and is a true example of that country's cuisine. When serving this dish, don't forget the onion sauce, sauerkraut and mashed potatoes, for each one has its special flavor and all are essential to the success of the recipe.

Casserole of Liver

2 lbs. liver (in one piece)
¼ cup drippings
¼ cup flour
1 small onion
2 carrots
1 small bay leaf
1 cup celery
2 cups potatoes
1 teaspoon salt
½ teaspoon pepper
¼ lb. salt pork, finely diced
1 can tomatoes (2½ cups)

Place drippings in hot frying pan. Dredge liver with flour and place in frying pan and sear on all sides until nicely browned; then transfer it to a casserole. Add thinly sliced onion, sliced carrots, bay leaf, chopped celery, diced potatoes and seasoning. Pour tomatoes over all and sprinkle with diced salt pork. Cover casserole and bake in a moderate oven (350°) for 2½ hours.

Marinated Beef, Alfredo

Begin with 5 to 6 pounds of shoulder of beef; it should be cut about 2 inches thick rather than a chunky piece. Make a Marinade as follows: 1 cup vinegar, 1 cup water, 1 bay leaf, 10 peppercorns, 1 sliced onion, 1 blade of mace and 2 or 3 cloves. Bring water, vinegar and spices to boiling point and remove from heat and cool. When cool, pour over meat and let stand in the refrigerator for 48 hours. Then remove the meat from the marinade, wipe it dry and dip in flour. Sear it on all sides in a hot frying pan, and then transfer it to a roasting pan with 3 or 4 slices of fat salt pork and roast in a moderate oven for 2½ hours. Garnish with parsley and serve with Noodles Alfredo:

Noodles Alfredo

Cook noodles in boiling, salted water for 20 minutes. Drain in colander and hold under cold water to separate, then hold under hot water to heat. Drain, place noodles on a large hot platter, sprinkle top with grated Parmesan cheese and add 3 lumps of butter. Now take a large spoon and fork and lift noodles from platter until butter and cheese are thoroughly blended with the noodles.

New England Boiled Dinner

Select a nice piece of corned beef; the cut depending on individual choice. If lean beef is desired, purchase the rump, and if a little fat is desired, then, I would suggest the brisket. Personally, I like the brisket corned beef. Put the corned beef in a large saucepan and cover with cold water. Bring slowly to the boiling point and remove scum that rises to the top. Continue to cook over very low heat until the meat is tender. A 5-pound piece of corned beef should cook for 5 hours to be perfectly tender. When cooked, remove the meat to a warm dish and skim the water of all fat and cook the various vegetables, (cabbage, turnips, carrots, potatoes) in the water in which the meat was cooked. If the turnips, carrots and potatoes are small, they may be cooked whole; otherwise, cut them into pieces. The head of cabbage is to be cut into ¼ or ⅛-inch pieces. Boiled beets also are included in this dinner, but they are to be cooked alone in another saucepan. Start them well in advance of the other vegetables as they take longer to cook. When vegetables are cooked, lift the corned beef onto a large hot platter and place the carrots, turnips and potatoes around it. Beets and cabbage served in separate dishes. To 3 parts melted butter, add 1 part vinegar and pour over cabbage and beets.

Hungarian Goulash

3 pounds of chuck of beef
Beef suet drippings
3 pints of Beef Stock (see Stock)
2 cloves garlic
1 bay leaf
1 tablespoon paprika
1 teaspoon salt
Few grains cayenne
6 medium-sized potatoes, cut same size as the beef

Cut meat into 1½-inch pieces. Brown quickly in beef suet drippings. Add the stock, garlic, bay leaf, salt and cayenne and simmer very slowly for 2½ hours. Add the potatoes and simmer for 35 to 40 minutes longer. Add the paprika and thicken the sauce (there should be 3 to 4 cups) with roux made by creaming 3 tablespoons of butter and adding 3 tablespoons of flour. Add the roux gradually and stir until well-blended and smooth. Serve with a green vegetable.

★

I believe there is not another dish that was so widely advertised as goulash. In America veal, pork, mutton, beef or anything that would goul was goulash. But the right name is Gulyas of Beef, and only beef will do. A Hungarian does not know what you mean by the word "goulash."

Goulash contains everything necessary to sustain life—meat, butter-fats and vegetables. In preparing goulash, many times, lard is used instead of butter because tests have shown that butter will not improve the dish as much as lard.

The following recipe is the way it was prepared in the best eating places in Hungary—Gundle's, The Hungaria, Diofa, Spolarich, the Erbely-Borozo and at the Gerbeaud:

In a large saucepan, cook partially in lard, 2 medium onions. Now add about 2 pounds of beef, preferably cut from the round steak. This meat must be cut into medium-sized cubes about 1 to 2 inches square. Cook very slowly in the oven. Shortly after the meat has started to cook, season with a liberal amount of paprika (Since the paprika is from the sweet red pepper, you can add as much as you desire without making it any hotter.), a pinch of caraway seed, a few leaves of bay, ¼ cupful of vinegar and a little finely chopped garlic. A little water should be placed in the pan at the start of the cooking, and more water added when required. When the meat is well cooked and tender, add a small quantity of Beef Broth (see Stock). If the sauce of gravy is too thin, thicken with flour. Add some freshly boiled potatoes that are similar to the size of the meat. Stir the potatoes in with the goulash, and it is ready to serve.

Because of the liberal amounts of sauce in this dish, rice is usually served on the plate with the goulash. And, for variety, there is the popular Szekely Goulash which has, as an extra ingredient, 1 medium cabbage, cut into cubes the size of the meat, and added with the seasonings.

Ox Tail en Casserole

Wash and dry on clean towel 2 ox tails that have been cut into joints. Brown in large frying pan with half butter and beef drippings. When nicely browned, season with salt and pepper and add 1 pint of strong Beef Stock (see Stock), a bouquet of celery leaves and parsley, a little mace and about 6 peppercorns. Boil for 1 minute and transfer to covered casserole dish to finish cooking in moderate oven. Ox tail requires long slow cooking so allow 3 to 4 hours in the oven. Add small white onions and carrots to casserole about 1 hour before serving. It will also be necessary to add stock as it reduces during the oven cooking. Skim off surface fat and thicken with very little brown flour. Serve from casserole dish.

Honeycomb Tripe and Onions

Purchase 2 pounds of honeycomb tripe. Wash it well in cold water and cut into 1½-inch squares. Cover with boiling water, add 1 sprig of parsley, 1 sliced carrot, a tiny piece of bay leaf, a few celery leaves, 6 peppercorns and 1 clove. Simmer very slowly until tender —about 3 hours. In the meantime, peel about 20 small white onions—cover with boiling, salted water and cook until tender— 20 to 25 minutes. Also prepare 2 cups of Rich Cream Sauce (see Sauces) and flavor with ⅓ cup of tripe stock. Put the tripe and onions in the sauce and bring to the boiling point and serve while hot.

Tripe à la Mode de Caen

Purchase 3 pounds of honeycomb tripe, wash it well in cold water and cut into pieces about 2 inches square. Cover the bottom of a large earthen crock with sliced carrots, 2 thin slices of onion, a pinch of thyme, a tiny bit of bay leaf, 1 clove and 3 peppercorns. Sprinkle a little salt on top. On the vegetable and herb foundation, arrange a layer of tripe, 2 small pieces of calves foot, 1 teaspoon of butter and 1 teaspoon of beef marrow. (Ask the butcher to give you marrow bones when purchasing tripe and calves feet.) Continue building layers until crock is half full and end with carrots and herbs on top. Cover with cider (almost to the top of the crock), place cover on crock and set in a moderate oven to cook for 7 hours. The longer tripe cooks the better it is, and I have found from experience that 8 or 9 hours in the oven makes the tripe more mellow and gives a rich quality to the liquid or sauce, which is the secret of this particular recipe.

★

This recipe came from the Pepin-Chandivert restaurant in Caen, of France. The Norman area is famous for its cider used in the preparation. The original recipe called for apple cider to be added with water and that is how it was mixed at the well-known Kinsley Restaurant, on Adams Street in Chicago. The secret of the tenderness of Kinsley's Tripe was that he boiled it overnight to break down its natural toughness.

When Kinsley opened the Holland House in New York, he made honeycomb tripe his specialty, and the Holland House was considered the greatest hotel/restaurant in the United States by the epicureans.

The preparation of Tripe in the Kinsley Manner should include washing the tripe until it is perfectly white. The quantity of beef marrow should be added to the tripe to make it rich and mellow, and when cooking for 6 persons, you should use about 1½ pounds of butter and 1 pound of beef fat, layered with the mixture.

Chevreuil à la Chasseur

★

This is an old Creole recipe for "Venison, Hunter's Style," which can also be used for rabbit. The Creole's finest trait is their ability to soften up tough sinewy meat by braising. Braising is one of the secrets of Creole cookery. It is a cooking process halfway between baking and frying. The meat is in a covered saucepan, which prevents the moisture and flavor of the meat from going up in steam.

Chop the venison into pieces about 2 inches square. Salt and pepper liberally. Drop 2 tablespoonfuls of butter in a saucepan with venison and allow it to brown slowly. When it is almost brown, add 1 onion chopped very fine and let this also brown slightly. Then add an egg-size bit of ham which has been minced well; 1 clove of garlic, 2 sprigs of thyme and 2 bay leaves which have been chopped fine. Stir in with the venison and allow to brown about 2 minutes. Add 1 tablespoon of flour and brown several minutes longer. Pour in 1 pint of warm water and let it all simmer for another 5 minutes. Add about 1 quart of Consommé (see Stock) and cook for 1 hour. Season again according to taste and add ½ can of chopped mushrooms and the grated rind of a lemon. Again season to taste and cook all for another 30 minutes. Serve on a hot dish with croutons which have been fried in butter.

LAMB

7

Lamb en Casserole, Caramello

Cut 2 pounds of lean lamb in pieces for serving. Sprinkle with salt and pepper, dredge lightly with flour and brown lamb in large frying pan with 2 tablespoons of olive oil. Remove lamb to casserole, add 2 cloves of crushed garlic, 2 whole leeks, 1 green pepper that has been cut into eighths and all seeds removed, and ¼ bay leaf. Sprinkle ½ teaspoon of salt over meat and vegetables and pack the casserole with eggplant that has been peeled and cut into pieces about the size of a walnut. Add 2 tomatoes, that have been cut in halves, with centers scooped out and seeds removed. Pour over 1 cup of well seasoned lamb stock, cover casserole and place in a moderate oven (350°) to cook for 3 hours. Uncover casserole, baste over the top with some of the essence in bottom of casserole, return casserole to oven, uncovered, and baste 3 times at 5 minute intervals. Serve from casserole.

Lamb Steak, Sauté

Allow 1 lamb steak for each portion. Each steak should be about ½ inch thick. Season with salt and pepper and sauté in butter until cooked—about 15 minutes. Arrange each steak on a large plate, garnish with 6 whole mushroom caps which have been fried in butter, and with a small portion of O'Brien Potatoes (see Index). Add 1 tablespoon of butter to frying pan after chops are removed, and just as it is turning brown, remove it from heat and pour over chops and mushrooms.

Roast Forequarter of Lamb, Rector

Purchase a forequarter of lamb, trim fat and remove bone for stuffing. The stuffing to be made as follows: 6 cups of soft bread crumbs, ⅓ cup melted shortening, 1 teaspoon salt, ½ teaspoon pepper, ½ teaspoon sage, ½ teaspoon thyme, 1 tablespoon chopped parsley and 1 cup of chopped mushrooms. Mix thoroughly by tossing lightly with a wooden spoon. Stuff the lamb and place in a very hot oven for 20 minutes. Reduce heat to moderate (325° to 350°) and continue roasting, allowing 20 minutes for each pound. Baste occasionally and season with salt and pepper just before removing from the oven. Place lamb on a hot platter, pour off all but 2 tablespoons of the lamb drippings from the pan in which the lamb was roasted. Mix 2 tablespoons of flour in the pan with the drippings. When flour and drippings are thoroughly mixed, add gradually 1 cup of water and ½ cup strained tomato juice. Stir over low heat until the boiling point is reached, scraping and stirring all particles of meat essence well into the sauce. Remove from heat and season with salt and pepper, 1 tablespoon of lemon juice and a dash of Worcestershire sauce. Strain and serve with the lamb.

Lamb Chops, Soubise

Broil thick lamb chops under moderate heat allowing about 5 to 10 minutes to each side. Cover bottom of hot platter with Sauce Soubise (see Index for Sauce) and arrange broiled chops on bed of sauce. Garnish platter with small mounds of boiled string beans which have been seasoned with salt and pepper and moistened with butter.

Lamb Stew, with Dumplings

Cut 2½ pounds shoulder of lamb in uniform-size pieces. Dredge lightly with flour, season with salt and pepper and brown in 4 tablespoons of hot oil. Add 2 quarts of water and bring to boiling point and simmer for 1 hour. Add 7 or 8 small white onions and 6 small carrots and simmer 10 minutes longer. Add 2 cups of diced potatoes and 1 cup of diced celery and cook until potatoes and celery are soft—about 30 minutes. If fresh green peas are available, add 1 cup to the stew along with the potatoes and celery. The dumplings can be dropped into the stew 20 minutes before it is ready, or the batter can be dropped into boiling water. Still another way is to steam the dumplings for 20 minutes. Make Dumpling Batter as follows: Sift together 1 cup of flour, 4 teaspoons baking powder and ½ teaspoon salt. Add 1 cup of dry bread crumbs and mix well. Now, add 2 tablespoons of melted shortening to 1 cup of milk, stirring until mixed; add it to flour and bread crumb mixture, working it with a spatula until it is a soft dough. Drop from tablespoon into stew or boiling water and cook for 20 minutes. Keep pan uncovered during the first

10 minutes of cooking, and then cover tightly for the last 10 minutes.

Roast Leg of Lamb, Mint Sauce

With a sharp skewer puncture the leg of the lamb in 6 different places (top and underside) and insert strips of garlic as the skewer is withdrawn. Place meat in hot oven (475°) for 30 minutes. Reduce heat to moderate (350°) and continue roasting allowing 20 minutes to the pound. Baste meat occasionally, and just before taking from the oven, season with salt and pepper. Remove leg of lamb to hot platter, pour off all but 2 tablespoons of fat in baking pan, add 1½ cups of hot water and stir. Scrape bottom and sides of pan to dissolve meat essence. Thicken with 1 tablespoon flour that has been mixed with a little cold water. Bring to boiling point, season with salt and pepper and strain gravy into sauce boat. Mint Sauce as follows:

Mint Sauce

To ½ cup of mild vinegar (if vinegar is strong, dilute it with water), add 1 tablespoon of powdered sugar. When dissolved, pour it over 2 tablespoons of finely chopped mint. Let stand on warm part of stove for 30 minutes before using.

Lamb Hash

Dice cold leg of lamb—taking care to remove skin and gristle. Moisten with Brown Sauce (see Index for Sauce). To every 3 cups of diced lamb, add 1 cup of cooked potatoes which have been cut into small cubes. To this, add 1 small green pepper, which has been cut into small dice and cooked in boiling, salted water for 5 minutes. Season to taste with salt, pepper and paprika. Stir in 2 tablespoons tomato catsup. Serve with freshly made toast.

Roast Leg of Lamb, Mint Sauce

Curry of Lamb

A curry recipe must be made from lean meat. Cut 2 pounds of lean lamb from the forequarter or leg and cut into pieces about the size of a walnut. Put meat in a large saucepan, add 1 small onion, 2 sprigs parsley, a few celery leaves and 1 teaspoon salt. Cover with cold water and bring to boiling point. Simmer gently until meat is tender. Remove meat to another saucepan, strain stock and skim top of all fat. (There should be 3 cups of stock.) Melt 3 tablespoons butter, blend in 3 tablespoons of flour and 1 tablespoon of curry powder. Gradually add 3 cups of hot stock, stirring constantly until sauce comes to a boil. Let boil 2 minutes, add lamb to curry sauce. Serve with boiled rice.

Boiled Shoulder of Mutton, Caper Sauce

Purchase a shoulder of mutton weighing about 4 or 5 pounds. Wash the meat and place it in a saucepan with 2 quarts of boiling water, a small piece of bay leaf, 1 onion, 2 slices of lemon and 1 teaspoon of salt. Boil hard for 8 or 10 minutes. Reduce heat and simmer allowing 30 minutes for each pound of meat. Caper Sauce as follows:

Caper Sauce

Melt 3 tablespoons of butter and blend 3 tablespoons of flour, ½ teaspoon of salt and ⅛ teaspoon pepper. Gradually add 1½ cups of hot mutton stock that has been skimmed and strained. Boil 5 minutes, remove from heat and add 2 tablespoons of butter, broken into small pieces, and ½ cup of capers, drained from their liquor, and moistened with 1 teaspoon of strained lemon juice.

Baby Lamb en Casserole, Ulpia

You need 2½ pounds of rib, breast or shoulder of lamb. Cut up into small pieces about the size of stew lamb. Salt, pepper and sauté the lamb in pure olive oil. While the lamb is cooking in the olive oil, chop 1 button of garlic and a little rosemary very fine; put it in ½ cup of vinegar. Set it aside. Now, see that the lamb is cooked a nice, golden brown and give it a high heat prior to adding the vinegar, rosemary and garlic. Put the cover on very tight. Allow it to simmer over a low heat about 5 minutes. Then serve.

★

This characteristic recipe came from the Ulpia Restaurant, which was located in the center of the busiest section of the old Roman ruins. The Ulpia was unique because it was built underground and was a museum of sorts—being filled with ancient artifacts.

Kidney Stew à la Kessler

Cover 6 lamb kidneys with cold water and let stand 1 hour. Drain, dry on towel and cut in slices about ¼ inch thick. Season with salt and pepper and dredge lightly with flour. Sauté in butter until all sides are browned. In another saucepan, melt 3 tablespoons of butter, add 1 tablespoon of finely chopped shallots and cook 5 minutes at low heat without letting butter or shallots turn brown. (If heat is properly regulated, shallots will be soft and yellow.) Add 2 tablespoons of flour and stir until thoroughly blended. Gradually add 1 cup of Brown Stock (see Index) and stir until boiling point is reached. Pour sauce into pan with kidneys, add ½ cup sliced fresh mushrooms that have been cooked in butter 5 minutes, and 1 small green pepper which has been thinly sliced and cooked in boiling water for 8 minutes. Season with salt, paprika and a few grains of cayenne. Just before serving add 1 tablespoon of butter and 2 tablespoons of sherry.

English Grill

A large blue plate should be used to serve the English grill, which consists of a broiled English mutton chop, 1 lamb kidney split and broiled, 1 slice of broiled bacon, 1 sausage and 1 thick slice of tomato sprinkled with bread crumbs and broiled. This combination is to be served on each blue plate as a portion. Start the English mutton chops to broil first—as it will take 20 to 25 minutes to cook them. When they are half cooked, start the kidney, sausage and the breaded tomato. Baste the tomato occasionally with the drippings from the meat. As the bacon will only take a few minutes to broil, start it to cook toward the last. Serve with baked potato, which can be cooked in the oven while using the broiler.

Lamb, Richelieu

The average lamb roll will weigh about 5 pounds. The method of this recipe is pot-roasting. Take a large saucepan and melt sufficient lamb drippings to cover bottom of the pan. Add 2 chopped onions, 2 sliced turnips, 2 sliced carrots, 1 clove of garlic, a small bay leaf and a sprig of thyme. Let the vegetables cook in the fat for 8 or 10 minutes over low heat, so the vegetables will cook without burning. Add the lamb roll and sear on all sides. Add 2 cups of boiling water and 2 cups of tomato pulp. Season with salt and pepper, cover the saucepan and cook slowly until the meat is tender (about 2 hours).

VEAL

8

Veal, Parapluie

Purchase veal cutlets, 1 inch in thickness. Lay one flat on the cutting board and with the dull side of a large knife begin pounding it. At the same time add grated Parmesan cheese—do this to both sides of the cutlet. When the pounding is finished, the veal will be about ½ an inch thick. The pounding spreads the veal to almost double its size. Season with salt and pepper and dip in beaten egg, and then in bread crumbs. Fry in clarified butter until both sides are nicely browned. You will enjoy the flavor of the veal with the Parmesan cheese, and notice also the tenderness because of the pounding process.

Blanquette of Veal

Purchase 2 pounds of breast of veal and cut into small pieces. Place in a saucepan and cover with water (or White Stock, if you have it). Bring to a boil and skin. Add 3 small onions with 1 clove stuck in each one, also 2 carrots cut up in small pieces, a few sprigs of parsley and 2 outer stalks of celery. Season to taste and cover saucepan. Simmer gently for 1 hour. Take out the meat and strain the gravy. Thicken the gravy with flour mixed with cold water. Bring to a boil and let simmer for 5 minutes. Remove from the heat and add well-beaten yolk to the gravy. The best way to introduce beaten egg yolk into hot gravy is to take a tablespoonful of gravy and stir it into the egg—do this until you have used up about ½ cupful of gravy, then pour the egg into the pan with the rest of the gravy. This method prevents the egg from curdling when it mixes with the hot gravy. Now place the veal on a platter and pour the gravy over it. Sprinkle the top with finely chopped parsley and garnish with bread cut in diamond shape. Serve with green peas.

Veal Loaf

Purchase 4 pounds of shank of veal and crack the bone in several places. Wipe the meat with a damp cloth and place it in a saucepan with ½ cup diced carrots, ¼ cup sliced onion and ¼ cup diced celery. Cover over with 1 quart of boiling water and simmer gently until meat is tender. Drain, reserving broth. Remove meat from the bones and return undesirable particles and bones to the broth. Simmer the broth until it is reduced to 1 cup. Strain and skim the top of any fat. When the veal is cold, dice it into small pieces and add it to the strained broth with ½ teaspoon salt and ¼ teaspoon pepper. Now, decorate bottom of mold with slices of hard-boiled egg and slices of cooked carrot cut in fancy shapes. Bits of parsley and pimiento may also be introduced. (The artistry of decoration I shall leave entirely up to you.) Put veal mixture in the decorated mold and let stand until cold and firm. (No gelatin need be used in this recipe.)

Veal and Kidney Pie

Purchase 2 pounds of veal and 2 veal kidneys—cut into small pieces for stewing. Take a large frying pan and render some of the fat from the kidneys and brown the veal and kidneys in it. Add 1 sliced onion to brown at the same time. When the meat is browned, add 1 cup of canned tomatoes, 1 cup of water, (or White Stock, if you have it) and a Soup Bunch consisting of 2 branches of celery, 2 sprigs of parsley, 1 bay leaf and 1 clove of garlic. Simmer over a low heat until the meat is tender. About 30 minutes before meat is cooked, add 1 cup of diced potato. If necessary, add more liquid while cooking. When potatoes are cooked, remove the soup bunch and flavor the liquid with 1 tablespoon of Worcestershire sauce, and salt to taste. Thicken with flour mixed with cold water and pour the stew into a casserole dish, cool and cover with pie crust dough. Make a few perforations in the dough so the steam can escape. Bake in a moderate oven until the crust is browned. (See Index on Pie Crust.)

Calves Liver à la Bourgeoise

★

Bergue's Place in New York in the old French Market is where this particular recipe originated. Bergue was a butcher who opened a restaurant in conjunction with his shop. Here, he experimented and developed a number of recipes for his restaurant. His specialties were Kidney Stew and Calves Liver. In this recipe for Calves Liver, Bergue uses a unique process called Larding. It was started in

France when an Italian chef came north to compete with the French cooks, who were preparing the dinner to celebrate the marriage of one of the Medici to the son of Francis I. The French cooks gave this chef fish to prepare. Being dissatisfied with the dryness of the fish, the Italian was struck with the idea of larding, or stuffing the fish with bacon. This was a revolutionary thought in cuisine. Now, when you stuff a turkey with oysters or a roast with mushrooms, you are actually larding them. Larding permeates the meat and supplies the necessary moisture. This prevents the meat from becoming parched and falling flat. (See Techniques.)

Here is the recipe as given by chef Bergue:

"Prepare the liver first by washing it in cold water. Then lard it with bacon. The larding is done with a long, hollow larding needle. The bacon or soft pork is sliced in thin strips and drawn through the liver by the larding needle. This leaves the liver laced with long thin threads of bacon. Place a large piece of butter in the frying pan. When the butter is hot, add an onion, a carrot and a turnip, all sliced very fine. Then drop a powdered bay leaf in and allow the mixture to brown. Add the liver to the pan, along with a pint of Consommé (see Stock). Season highly with cayenne pepper, cover the pan very tightly, set on low heat and allow it to simmer for about 30 minutes."

Calves Liver Patties

Put 1 pound of calves liver through the meat grinder, add 2 cups of soft bread crumbs, ½ cup grated onion, 1 teaspoon salt, ½ teaspoon pepper, 4 tablespoons bacon drippings and a pinch of marjoram. Mix thoroughly and shape into round patties about ½ inch thick—roll in sifted flour and fry in bacon drippings. Serve with crisp grilled bacon.

Veal Cutlet, Sauce Figaro

Start with a veal cutlet, ½ inch thick and pound it with the dull edge of a knife until it is thin and made somewhat tender by the pounding. Season with salt and pepper and cut into uniform-size pieces for serving. Dip in Light Batter and fry in deep hot oil (350° to 375°) until browned. Test temperature of oil by dropping in a piece of bread; if it browns in 1 minute, it is the right temperature to receive the uncooked mixture. Drain on paper and serve sauce separately. (See

Index on Sauces.) Light Batter: ½ cup flour, ¼ teaspoon salt, 1 teaspoon baking powder, ¼ cup milk and 1 egg. Mix and sift dry ingredients, add milk gradually and egg which has been well-beaten.

Calves Brains in Muffin Tins

Cover calves brains with cold water and let stand 1 hour. Free from all skin and membrane. Plunge them into boiling Acidulated Water which has been slightly salted. Add 2 sprigs parsley, a few celery leaves, 1 small onion and ¼ bay leaf. Boil gently for 20 minutes. Drain, cool and cut into small pieces. Make a Rich Cream Sauce (see Index on Sauces), add calves brains and some slices of fresh mushrooms that have been cooked in butter for 5 minutes. Season with salt and a few grains of cayenne and pour into muffin tins. Sprinkle top with paprika. For Acidulated Water add 1 tablespoon of lemon juice to 1 quart of water.

Calves Brains au Beurre Noir

Cover calves brains with cold water and let stand 1 hour. Free from all skin and membrane and plunge them into boiling Acidulated Water that has been slightly salted. Boil very gently for 20 minutes. Drain, and put brains in cold water. When cool, drain and dry carefully with a towel. Dip in flour, and fry in hot melted butter until nicely browned. Remove to hot platter and add 2 tablespoons of butter to the hot frying pan. When butter has turned brown, add 2 tablespoons of vinegar. Remove immediately from heat and shake the pan a few times, so butter and vinegar will mix. Pour over calves brains, which have been sprinkled with finely chopped parsley. The Acidulated Water is made by adding 1 tablespoon of vinegar or lemon juice to 1 quart or water.

Sweetbread Croquettes

Cut the membranes into small dice and add the same quantity of coarsely chopped mushrooms. Then hash a large onion and brown it in a saucepan with a ¼ pound of fresh butter. Add 1 spoonful of flour, without allowing the flour to brown, and pour into the pan about 3 cupfuls of milk. Now, add the sweetbreads and the chopped mushrooms and allow them to simmer in the sauce for 10 minutes. Remove from the heat, and before it cools, stir 4 whole eggs into this preparation, using a wooden spoon for the stirring. Pour into a flat dish, which is large enough to allow the mixture to spread to an even depth of about 1 inch. Smooth off the surface and add butter to the top to prevent a crust from forming, and allow it to cool in the refrigerator.

After it has cooled off, then cut it in oblongs about 2 inches by 1 inch and cover the rectangles with a batter made of white bread crumbs and beaten eggs. Deep fry in hot lard for several minutes, until they are brown. Serve hot with Tomato Sauce. (See Index for Sauce.)

★

This recipe calls for not only the sweetbreads but also the membranes. It is a well-known fact that very few cooks, and that includes good chefs, can make use of the membranes. If you follow this recipe, you will find that you can use the membranes and convert them into a delightful, edible entrée.

Sweetbread Croquettes, Croquettes de Ris de Veau, was served at Foyot's in a calm and dignified manner. Foyot's was the dining place of senators, deputies and ministers of departments. It was located in the shadows of Luxembourg. Its dishes were many and varied, including of course, the classic "caneton" and "poularde or chicken sauté."

Sweetbreads, Braised

Sweetbreads are a great delicacy and when other foods lose their appeal, try sweetbreads with tiny green peas. Sweetbreads come in pairs—separate them and soak in cold water for 1 hour. Plunge into boiling, salted Acidulated Water (see Glossary) and cook slowly for 15 or 20 minutes. Drain and plunge into cold water to harden. Remove any pieces of wind pipe and membrane. Place the sweetbreads under a light weight to restore to original shape. Lay them in a shallow casserole and dot each piece with small bits of butter. (Do not split the sweetbreads.) Place in a moderate oven and in 5 minutes, baste with some of the melted butter and spread each sweetbread lightly with glaze viande (beef extract). Return sweetbreads to oven and bake for 5 minutes longer. Baste again and season very lightly with salt and pepper. Place on hot platter and pour the sauce (melted butter and glaze viande) over them. Garnish with parsley and serve with fresh green peas.

Veal Cutlets Sauté

Select 6 medium-sized cutlets and arrange them around the frying pan. Season them with salt, paprika and 1 spoonful of dry white wine mixed with "fines herbes" (parsley, chervil, tarragon and chives). Sauté the cutlets in butter. Make a border of rice mixed with truffles. Place on each cutlet, a slice of ham already browned in butter. On top of the ham, put 1 small spoonful of chopped pimientos. The cooking of the veal cutlets results in an essence being left in the pan to which a large piece of butter is added and stirred until amost brown. When the cutlets are on the serving platter, this combined essence and butter is poured over each individual cutlet.

★

Stewed Chicken

This recipe for Veal Cutlets, or Escalopes de Veau, is from chef M. Montagné, who was the owner of a café on the Rue de l'Echelle in Paris, France. The best restaurant is the one in which the proprietor is the chef, and M. Montagné was a leader in this class. He would restrict his Bill-of-Fare to a few specialties each day and work enthusiastically in the kitchen preparing them. This is not to say that he knew only a few recipes; M. Montagné was an expert chef and a great writing authority on culinary matters. Another one of his specialties was Étuvée de Poulet la Padou, Stewed Chicken:

Prepare a chicken as you would for a fricassee. Season the pieces of chicken with salt and pepper, and place them as flat as possible in a frying pan. Cover them with finely minced onions which have been cooked in butter until not quite browned. Cover the pan and cook the pieces. When the chicken is done, remove it from the pan and set the chicken on a platter on one side of the stove to keep hot, while you prepare the following sauce from the essence, which has been left in the pan: Add 1 small glass of madeira to the essence and allow it to reduce a little on slow heat. Add 2 cupfuls of Chicken Stock (see Stock) and let it reduce until only 1 cupful remains in the pan. Put in ½ cupful cream and a piece of fresh butter. Stir this around with a wooden spoon, but stir very gently, until the cream, stock and butter are well blended together. Do not allow it to come to a boil. Set this aside to remain hot. Now, for the garniture: In another saucepan, cook some sweetbreads chopped in small pieces, some very little pork sausages and fresh mushrooms cut in small pieces. When this garniture is ready, lay the pieces of chicken on a bed of boiled white rice, which has been cooked with truffles and minced ham. Lay the sweetbreads, pork sausages, and mushrooms over the chicken. Then over all, pour the prepared sauce, which has been kept hot.

One distinct feature of French cuisine, as exemplified in the recipes given here by M. Montagné, is that the Paris chef never overlooks a chance to build up a sauce from the essence in the pan. He considers it willful waste to lose anything from the pan, which includes the essence, fragrance and any stock remaining after cooking.

Wiener Schnitzel

★

Paprika Huhn

Apfelstrudel

These recipes are from the Heumuble Restaurant in Vienna, which was run by Miss Hess. The Heumuble was originally opened as a cooking school attended by the daughters of prominent Austrian families, who went there to study domestic science. It was at this school where they learned to make the illustrious Wiener Schnitzel, Paprika Huhn and Apfelstrudl:

The Wiener Schnitzel is a slice from the shoulder of veal, and is a breaded veal cutlet much lighter in bulk than a normal veal cutlet. Its secret is in its crispness and lightness. It's prepared as follows:

From the shoulder of the veal, slice, not too thick, a piece of meat. Flatten this a little with a cleaver and season with salt and pepper. Make a light batter consisting of 1 egg and very fine bread crumbs.

Dip the veal in this batter and fry in lard. No sauce is ever used in Vienna for Wiener Schnitzel, except mayonnaise on the side in a small sauceboat.

Paprika Huhn:

Cut a chicken into 4 pieces. The skin is removed. Some bacon fat is sliced into small pieces and placed in a pan, along with a little lard, which is allowed to simmer. Then, the chicken is put in to cook in the bacon fat and lard. After 5 minutes the chicken is seasoned with plenty of paprika, which blends all through the ingredients in the pan. When the chicken is thoroughly cooked, 1 cupful of sour cream is poured over it and stirred slowly around to enable the cream to mix with the sauce. The sour cream makes the dish, which is taken quickly from the heat and poured out on a plate.

I suspect that most everybody has tasted Apfelstrudl, or Apple Strudel. The following recipe is a good one, except the weights are confusing. Keep in mind your metric system—a dkg. is a dekagram and a kg. is a kilogram. A kilo is a fraction over 2 pounds and a gram is 1/1000th of a kilo. A dekagram is 10 grams. Here is an exact translation of an original recipe for Apfelstrudl. It's rather like a crossgram puzzle, but do your best:

"Put ½ kilogram of flour on your board, take 1 whole egg, 10 dekagrams melted butter, a pinch of salt, about ½ of a litre of lukewarm water and work it until it is smooth and comes off your hands. If it should turn out to be too hard, then add a little more water. Sprinkle flour on the board and turn your paste into a round loaf and leave it to rest for 1 hour, covered, in a dish.

Spread a tablecloth on your table, sprinkle it with flour and place the paste in the center. Begin to pull the paste until you get it nearly as thin as paper, then put 6 chopped apples, 6 tablespoons bread crumbs (which have been fried in butter), 1 cup raisins, 1 cup powdered sugar and a liberal sprinkling of cinnamon over the top of the spread-out paste. Take two corners of the tablecloth and use them to roll up the strudel. Grease your pan with lard or butter and bake slowly." Baste several times with butter during the baking. Remove from the oven when slightly browned.

After the strudel is baked in a long loaf, it is sliced up to be served. There are many kinds of strudels—flat, long or dumpling—but the secret of the rolled strudel is that it holds in the juices and the flavor of the fruits and spices. It is not a light pastry, rather heavy for dessert, but delicious. The Austrian likes it smothered with whipped cream.

Veal Chops à la Zingara

Purchase 4 veal chops cut rather thick. Lard one side of the chops with alternate pieces of salt pork and lean ham (see Techniques). Brown the chops in frying pan with sufficient butter to keep from burning or becoming too brown. Add 1 tablespoon of finely chopped shallots, ¼ cup thinly sliced carrots, 2 ripe tomatoes that have been peeled and centers scooped out to remove seeds and water, and also add ⅓ cup of white wine. Simmer gently for 20 minutes. In the meantime, sauté ½ cup sliced mushrooms in butter until cooked—about 5 minutes. Add mushrooms to chops and season to taste with salt and pepper. Remove chops to hot platter, add 1 tablespoon of butter to sauce and reduce sauce by cooking over high heat for 3 minutes. Remove from heat, pour sauce over and around chops.

PORK

9

Roast Pork, Savory Apples

Select an inexpensive but lean cut of meat for this recipe. Preferably a pork shoulder roast, weighing 4 to 4½ pounds. Dredge the roast with flour and sear in a hot oven (450°) for 10 minutes. Reduce oven heat to moderate (350°) and season with pepper and salt. Add enough water to keep roast from burning. Cover roasting pan and bake for 45 minutes. Remove from oven. Place around the roast 4 or more apples that have been cored and stuffed with chopped dates and brown sugar. Place 1 clove on top of each stuffed apple. Return to oven and bake until apples are cooked—about 1 hour.

Fresh Spare Ribs, Jardinière

Purchase a strip of spare ribs weighing about 3½ to 4 pounds. Wash, season with salt and pepper and dredge with flour. Cut raw potatoes in French ball shape or small dice, cut several carrots in fancy shapes or slices, 1 cup of diced celery, a few shelled peas and a small head of cauliflower, cut into separate flowerettes, also peel and slice a medium-sized onion. Place all the raw vegetables in a roasting pan and lay the spare ribs over them. Add 2 cups of boiling water and place in a moderate oven (350°) to cook, allowing about 1¼ to 1½ hours.

Roasted Spare Ribs

Select a nice strip of fresh spareribs (about 2 pounds) and wipe them with a piece of damp cheesecloth. Season with salt and pepper and a pinch of sage and lay them in a baking pan. And start them to cook in a moderate oven. After they have been in the oven 15 minutes, baste them with the melted drippings and baste every 15 minutes thereafter until they are roasted. It will only take 1 hour to roast spareribs, so gage the rest of your dinner accordingly.

Ham Mousse, Cumberland Sauce

For a Mousse of Ham, you will need ½ pound cooked ham, 8 ounces of well-flavored stock (see Stock), 1 tablespoon gelatin, white pepper, a small pinch of cayenne and very little salt, if any, and ½ pint of cream plus a small quantity of aspic jelly.

The ham must be free of skin and fat. Run it through the meat grinder that is set on fine grind or run it through a regular grinder several times. Then pound it in a mortar with the stock and season with the white pepper and the cayenne. Melt the gelatin in some additional stock (set a little of the gelatin aspic aside to cool to pour on the mousse) and strain it into the ham mixture. When it is smooth, add the cream, which has already been whipped, and then whip the whole mixture until it is light and frothy. Place the purée in a soufflé dish and smooth the top as evenly as possible without pressing down the mixture too heavily. Just as it is settling, pour some cold liquid aspic gently on the mousse and decorate to taste. (See Index for Cumberland Sauce.)

Ham Risotto

1 cup diced cooked ham
2 cups boiled rice
2 cups canned tomato
1 cup broth (any kind)
½ cup green pepper, finely minced
1 teaspoon grated onion

Cook the green pepper in the broth for 5 minutes. Add the tomato, onion and cooked rice. Bring to a boil and add the diced ham. Risotto is to be served moist but not watery; so, if there is too much liquid, reduce it with a few minutes of cooking. Season with a dash of Worcestershire sauce, salt, pepper and paprika. Place a piece of butter on each serving. Very delicious, and I am sure that you will agree.

Baked Ham, Cider Sauce

Select a ham weighing from 10 to 12 pounds. Take a small brush and scrub it well in cold water. Place in large saucepan with cold water to cover. Add 1 small bayleaf, 1 sliced onion, 2 or 3 branches of celery, 2 sprigs of parsley and 2 sliced carrots. Bring to the boiling point and carefully peel off top skin. Leave a little skin around the shank end of ham. Place ham in baking pan (fat side up) with 1 cup of hot water and 1 cup cider. Place in moderate oven for 1 hour and baste every 10 or 15 minutes during this time. Remove pan from oven to table and score fat surface evenly and spread with brown sugar and bread crumbs. Stick a few cloves into fat at regular intervals. Return to oven to brown. Do not baste after sugar, crumbs and cloves have been added.

Cider Sauce

In a saucepan, make a sauce by adding 1 cup of the ham liquor to the pan that the ham was baked in. Thicken with 1 tablespoon butter and 1 tablespoon flour creamed together and bring to a boil while adding ⅓ cup of cider. Season with a few grains of paprika and strain sauce before serving.

Creamed Ham, Rice Border

Wash ¾ cup rice in cold water, drain, cook in top part of double boiler with 2½ cups of milk until rice is cooked... about 1¼ hours. Season with salt and pepper and stir in 1 tablespoon of butter. Pack rice into buttered ring mold, place mold in pan containing hot water and set it in moderate oven 20 minutes. In the meantime, prepare the creamed ham. Melt 2 tablespoons of butter, blend in 2 tablespoons of flour and gradually add 1½ cups of scalded milk. Stir constantly until sauce is smooth and reaches boiling point. Season with a few grains of nutmeg and add 1½ cups of diced cooked ham. Bring to boiling point, remove from heat, add 2 egg yolks (slightly beaten) and stir until thoroughly blended with the sauce. Taste sauce and season with salt. If ham is salty, omit adding salt. Place a large platter on top of rice mold, invert and carefully unmold rice. Pour creamed ham in center of rice and decorate rice border with a sprinkling of finely chopped parsley.

Ham Mousse, Epicurean Sauce

2 cups cold boiled ham
1 tablespoon gelatin

½ cup of hot water
½ cup heavy cream
1 teaspoon prepared mustard
⅛ teaspoon paprika
Few grains cayenne

Chop the ham very fine and pound in a mortar. Dissolve the gelatin in a very little cold water, and then in hot water and add to the prepared ham. Season with mustard, paprika and cayenne and add the cream which has been stiffly beaten. Turn into a mold dipped in cold water. Set in the refrigerator to chill. Unmold and garnish with parsley. Serve Epicurean Sauce separately:

Epicurean Sauce

½ cup heavy cream
4 tablespoons mayonnaise
1 teaspoon English mustard
2 tablespoons fresh grated horseradish
1 tablespoon tarragon vinegar
¼ teaspoon salt
Few grains cayenne

Beat cream until stiff, stir in the mayonnaise, grated horsradish and the balance of the ingredients which have been mixed together.

Deviled Virginia Ham à la Rector

Cut thin slices from a cold cooked ham about ¼ inch thick. Prepare a paste of English mustard and bread crumbs. Spread paste lightly on both sides of sliced ham and arrange the slices on a platter which will stand oven heat. Allow slices of ham to overlap each other about 1 inch and arrange a risotto border around the ham—Risotto: 2 cups cooked rice, 1 tablespoon finely chopped pimiento, 1 tablespoon finely chopped green pepper, 1 tablespoon chopped onion that has been cooked in a little butter for 5 minutes, and 1 large canned tomato that has been cut up or chopped. Add enough stock to moisten. Season with salt and few grains of cayenne. Risotto must not be too moist as it must hold its shape as a border. Dot ham with small bits of butter and place under moderate broiler to brown.

Breaded Pork Chops, Sauce Piquante

Have rib pork chops cut of uniform thickness . . . season with salt and pepper. Dip the chops in melted butter, then in white bread crumbs and broil under moderate heat for 15 or 20 minutes. When nicely browned, remove to a hot platter and trim the rib bones with white paper frills. Sauce Piquante as follows: (Brown Sauce must first be made for Sauce Piquante.):

Brown Sauce (Espagnole)

Brown Stock or Broth (see Index) is the base for Brown Sauce. Melt 2 oz. butter (¼ cup) and add 1 tablespoon chopped onion, 1 tablespoon chopped carrot, a sprig of parsley, a sprig of thyme, 1 small bay leaf and 10 whole peppercorns. Cook until well-browned, but do not allow the butter to burn. Add 4 tablespoons flour and stir, mixing thoroughly. Gradually add 2 cups of Brown Stock or Broth and bring to the boiling point. Allow to simmer for 2 or 3 minutes. Strain and season with salt and pepper to taste.

Sauce Piquante

To 1 cup of thick Brown Sauce (Espagnole), add 2 tablespoons of tarragon vinegar, 1 teaspoon shallots, finely chopped, 1 tablespoon chopped capers and 1 tablespoon chopped vinegar pickle. Season with a few grains of cayenne and place on very low heat for 15 or 20 minutes before serving.

Pork Chops, Florentine

Purchase 6 shoulder pork chops. Dredge them with flour and season with salt and pepper. Sear both sides in a skillet; reduce the heat and cook 30 minutes. Put a layer of hot, cooked spinach in an oven casserole and arrange the chops on top. Prepare 1½ cups of White

Sauce (see Index); just as you remove it from the heat, add 2 beaten egg yolks to it. Pour sauce over chops and spinach and sprinkle with grated Swiss or American cheese. Place in a hot oven or under broiler to melt cheese and slightly brown it.

Pork Chops, Creamed Gravy

Select fresh pork chops. Trim fat and set aside for frying. To ½ cup cracker meal, add 1 teaspoon of poultry seasoning, ¼ teaspoon salt and ⅛ teaspoon pepper. Mix thoroughly and dip the chops in the seasoned crackermeal. Fry chops in melted pork fat drippings, and when nicely browned, remove them to a platter. Arrange the chops to overlap each other, either in a straight line or circle. To the fat remaining in pan (there should be about 1 tablespoon), add 1 level tablespoon of flour, stir until thoroughly mixed and gradually add 1 cup of scalded milk. Keep stirring until gravy reaches boiling point. Pour around chops.

Crown of Pork à la Rector

Trim the fat off a loin of pork, form the chops into a crown, and cover each chop bone with bacon. Stuff cavity of crown with a Savory Rice Stuffing made as follows: to 2 cups of plain boiled rice add ½ cup of finely minced green pepper, 1 finely minced pimiento, a slight grating of onion and ½ teaspoon of sage. Mix thoroughly and moisten with 3 tablespoons of melted butter. Place crown in roasting pan, fill with prepared rice, cover with a piece of buttered paper and sear in a hot oven (450°) for 20 minutes. Reduce heat to moderate (350°) and continue roasting until crown is cooked... about 2½ to 3 hours, basting occasionally during that time. Remove bacon from bones and dress each bone with a small paper frill.

Suckling Pig, Piedmontese

Have a young pig dressed for roasting. Wash, stuff with Ham Risotto (see Index for Risotto) and sew cavity together. Place in dripping pan and cook in moderate oven until skin is crisp and browned. Baste every 15 minutes and cook about 3 hours. Remove pig to large platter, garnish with watercress and serve with a tart apple sauce.

Broiled Pork Tenderloin

Select thick tenderloins and split them for broiling. Rub them with melted butter and season with salt, pepper and a tiny pinch of sage or poultry seasoning. Broil under a moderate heat until nicely browned. Serve with tart apple sauce.

Chow Mein

Cut 1 pound of pork tenderloin into strips 2 inches long. Heat frying pan and add ¼ cup pork drippings. When hot, add the sliced pork tenderloin and reduce the heat and simmer slowly for 15 or 20 minutes without browning the meat. Then add 1 cup bamboo shoots, cut en Julienne (which simply means strips about 2 or 3 inches long and ⅛ wide), ½ pound of water chestnuts, cut into shreds, and 1 cup of celery, cut en Julienne. Moisten with ½ cup White Stock (see Index) and simmer gently until vegetables are cooked. Season with 1 tablespoon of Soy sauce and thicken with a little cornstarch mixed with cold water. Serve on a bed of crisp fried noodles and garnish top with egg threads. For Egg Threads: Beat 1 egg and fry in large oiled frying pan without browning. Cut into threads about 2 inches long.

POULTRY

10

Poulet Maison

Select a tender chicken and cut in 4 to 6 pieces. Put a large lump of butter into a saucepan and cook over high heat. Season the chicken with salt and pepper and place the slices in the pan before the butter changes color. When the slices start to brown, turn them over. Then put the lid on the saucepan and place it in a moderate oven. Take 12 raw mushrooms and chop them into small dice. Add them to the chicken when the chicken is almost cooked. Before you take the bird out of the oven, sprinkle with a small quantity of truffles, which has been sliced en Julienne and soaked in madeira wine. Let it boil down, and then blaze the chicken with a glass of good cognac. Pour in 4 ounces of heavy cream and let it simmer just a moment.

Arrange the chicken carefully on a silver platter. The sauce still remains in the pan, so add a couple of tablespoons of butter into the sauce and move the pan around on top of the heat, taking care that it does not come to a boil; otherwise, the sauce will break, and the cream will curdle. Pour the sauce over the chicken on the platter. Make a garniture of sliced smoked ham around the edge of the platter, and on each slice of ham, lay a bouquet of hot asparagus tips.

★

This was the specialty in the restaurant of the Hôtel de la Couronne in the French province of Normandy. This is a classic Norman process of Poulet Maison due to the use of cognac. During the blazing process, the cognac is deprived of its alcoholic qualities, and only the flavour of the liqueur remains. This is quite different from sherry or madeira in Lobster Newburg, because that dish is not ignited in the preparation and the liqueur retains its high-powered kick.

Boiled Chicken, St. Simeon

Wash chicken in cold water, drain and truss. Place it in a saucepan with some celery tops, 2 sprigs of parsley, 1 small onion and a tiny bit of bay leaf. Cover with boiling water and simmer gently until chicken is cooked. Add 1 tablespoon of salt to pan 30 minutes before chicken is cooked. A 5-pound fowl will have to simmer 3 to 4 hours before it is tender. A smaller chicken will cook in 1 to 1½ hours. Remove chicken from pan, drain and place it on a hot platter. To 1 cup of scalded cream, add 2 tablespoons of Tarragon Butter (see Prepared Butters) and stir until butter is thoroughly blended with cream. Thicken with 2 egg yolks, slightly beaten with 1 tablespoon cream. Pour sauce over boiled chicken and serve.

Roast Chicken, Sausage Stuffing

Follow directions contained in Roast Turkey. Sear in hot oven (450°) for 10 minutes. Reduce heat to moderate (375°) baste every 15 minutes and allow 20 minutes for each pound:

Sausage Stuffing

½ pound sausage meat
3 cups stale bread crumbs
1 tablespoon sausage drippings
1 tablespoon melted butter
1 tablespoon finely chopped parsley
1 teaspoon salt
1 teaspoon poultry seasoning
⅛ teaspoon pepper

Cook sausage meat over moderate heat and drain off and set aside fat. Remove from heat, add bread crumbs, parsley and seasoning. Toss lightly until all ingredients are mixed, then add sausage drippings and melted butter to moisten:

Giblet Gravy

After fowl has been removed to hot platter, pour off all but 3 tablespoons of drippings remaining in baking pan, add 2 tablespoons of flour and stir until flour and drippings are blended, gradually add 1½ cups of stock in which gizzard, heart and liver have been cooked. Stir until perfectly smooth and bring to a boil, strain into small sauce pan and add finely chopped giblets. To cook giblets cover with boiling water... about 2 cups, add 1 slice of salt pork and simmer until tender. Pour gravy over Sausage Stuffing.

Breast of Chicken, Rector

Select 2 or 3 medium-sized chickens. Remove the breast skin and cut out entire breast. Sprinkle lightly with salt and pepper and dip in heavy cream, and then in flour. Fry the chicken breasts in butter until lightly browned. You need 1 slice of broiled ham for each chicken breast. Cut ham thin and have it the same size as the breast. Arrange broiled ham on piece of buttered toast and place chicken on top. Pour over with Supreme Sauce made as follows: Melt 2 tablespoons of butter in pan in which breasts were cooked, add 2 tablespoons of flour and stir until well-blended. Then pour on gradually 1 cup hot Chicken Stock (see Stock) and ½ cup heavy cream. Stir constantly and bring to the boiling point and season with salt and a few grains of nutmeg. Remove from heat and add 1 egg yolk slightly beaten. Stir for 1 minute, strain and pour over chicken breasts. Garnish with cooked mushroom caps.

Chicken Wings and Legs, Deviled

The wings and legs may be kept in the refrigerator for several days and utilized when the occasion demands. Wash in cold water. Dry thoroughly and sprinkle with salt and pepper. Make the following mixture and rub it on the wings and legs: Cream ¼ cup butter and add 1 teaspoon of hot mustard, either English or French, ½ teaspoon paprika, ½ teaspoon salt, a few grains of cayenne and 1 teaspoon vinegar. After wings and legs are thoroughly covered with deviled mixture, place them in a baking pan and sprinkle over with buttered bread crumbs and bake in a moderate oven until tender and crumbs are browned.

Chicken Sauté, Boivin

Quarter a chicken weighing about 2 pounds. Season with salt and pepper and dredge lightly with flour. Melt a piece of butter in a

saucepan and brown chicken on all sides. Cover saucepan and cook over low heat until chicken is cooked... about 20 to 25 minutes. Then add 1 cup of cooked potatoes cut in 1 inch dice or small ball shape, 1 cup of cooked small white onions and 2 artichokes which have been cooked and quartered, lengthwise. Be sure to remove needles from center of artichokes. Allow vegetables to cook with chicken until they are thoroughly heated. Remove chicken and vegetables to hot platter while making the sauce by adding 1 cup of Stock (see Stock) to saucepan along with ½ teaspoon beef extract. Stir and reduce a little by cooking over high heat for several minutes. Pour sauce over chicken and vegetables.

Chicken à la King

Remove the entire breast from a cold boiled fowl and slice it into pieces about ¼ inch thick and 1½ inches in diameter. Melt 1 tablespoon of butter, blend in 1 tablespoon flour and gradually add ½ cup of hot Chicken Stock (see Stock) and stir until thoroughly blended. Then add 1 cup of scalded cream and bring to the boiling point. Add ½ cup sliced mushrooms, which have been cooked in butter for 5 minutes, 1 tablespoon of diced pimiento and 1 tablespoon diced truffles (if available). Add 2 egg yolks to thicken sauce and do not allow to boil after egg yolks have been added. Add fowl to sauce and heat over hot water 5 minutes until fowl is thoroughly heated.

Chicken Sauté à la Rector

Cut chicken into 8 pieces. Wash in cold water and dry thoroughly. Season with salt and pepper and sauté in clarified butter until lightly browned. Cover chicken with 1 cup of raw mushrooms, which have been chopped into dice, cover pan and place in a moderate oven to finish cooking... about 25 minutes. Keep pan tightly covered while in the oven. Remove pan from oven and skim off fat. Place it over low heat, add 2 tablespoons sherry and stir in ¾ cup scalded cream. Thicken sauce with 1 egg yolk just before removing from heat. Remove chicken from pan and arrange in crown shape on a hot platter. In the middle of the crown, arrange several thin slices of Virginia Ham (see Pork) rolled horn-shape to hold small bunches of hot asparagus. Pour the sauce over chicken and sprinkle over sauce 2 tablespoons of finely chopped truffles or mushrooms.

Chicken Fricassee

Disjoint chicken for stewing. Wash in cold water and place into stewpan. Add 1 clove garlic, 2 sprigs of parsley, 1 small onion, a few celery tops and boiling water to cover. Simmer gently until chicken is tender. Season with salt when chicken is half cooked. Lift pieces of chicken onto a hot platter while making the gravy. Strain Chicken Stock (there should be about 3 cups), skim off fat. In another saucepan, melt 3 tablespoons of butter, blend in 3 tablespoons of flour and gradually pour on the hot Chicken Stock, when perfectly smooth, add ½ cup of cream and season with salt and pepper. Pour hot gravy over the chicken and serve with boiled rice and little Baking Powder Biscuits:

Baking Powder Biscuits

1 cup flour
2 teaspoons baking powder
¼ teaspoon salt
1 tablespoon shortening
⅓ cup milk

Sift dry ingredients together. Cut in shortening and gradually add milk. Roll out on a lightly floured board to ½ -inch thickness. Cut into biscuits 2½ inches in diameter and bake on an ungreased cookie sheet at 450° for 10 minutes.

Chicken Pie à la Rector

Disjoint a fowl or chicken for stewing. Place in stew pan, add 6 pieces of diced salt pork, 1 clove of garlic, 1 small onion, 2 sprigs of parsley, a few celery tops and boiling water to cover. Simmer gently until chicken is tender. Season with salt when chicken is half cooked. When fowl is cooked, carefully lift it into a hot dish while making the gravy. Strain chicken stock, (there should be about 4 cups) and skim off fat. In another saucepan, melt 3 tablespoons butter, blend in 3 tablespoons flour and gradually pour on the hot chicken stock. Stir constantly until perfectly smooth. Bring to a boil and season to taste with salt and pepper. Arrange chicken in a baking dish, remove as many of the small frame bones as possible, add cooked diced salt pork, 1 cup of boiled potatoes, that have been cut ball shape with a French cutter, ½ cup boiled, sliced carrots and about ½ cup of boiled white onions. Pour gravy over the chicken and vegetables and cool before covering with a pie crust. Meat pies only have a top crust; so therefore, a rim must be put around edge of baking dish. Wet edge of rim with cold water and make a slight impression to hold edges together. Make a few incisions in top crust to allow escape of steam. Bake in moderate oven (350°) until crust is nicely browned. Pie Crust as follows:

Basic Pie Crust

1½ cups flour
½ teaspoon salt
½ cup shortening
Cold water (about 4 tablespoons)

Sift flour and salt and cut in shortening until it is well distributed. Add gradually sufficient water to make stiff paste. Toss on floured board, pat and roll out.

Chicken Pot Pie

★

Chicken Pot Pie, or Volaille sous la Cendre, prepared in the following manner was given by Julien, a graduate of the Café de Paris in Paris, France. He was then acting director of Ciro's in Monte Carlo and Paris, and Chicken Pie was his specialty. This is a very complicated dish, but very delectable:

Purchase a chicken weighing about 3½ pounds. Heat 3 tablespoons of fresh butter, ½ an onion, minced, and 3½ ounces of rice. Stir over the heat until the rice is well-done, moisten with 1 pint of Chicken Broth (see Stock), cover and place in a moderate oven for 20 minutes. Remove rice from oven, strain from broth and set broth aside. Put the rice in another pan, add 3 tablespoons of butter, a little at a time—stirring with a wooden spoon to keep the grains of rice separate. To the rice, add the chicken liver, chopped into cubes, and 2 fresh truffles, quartered. Salt and pepper the whole, add a dash of spices and 2 tablespoons of the Chicken Broth. Mix the whole very carefully and taste the seasoning; if necessary, add a dash of cayenne pepper.

Stuff the chicken with the rice mixture. Cook the chicken with butter in a deep saucepan for about 20 minutes to brown it thoroughly on all sides. When the chicken is completely cooked, remove the chicken from the saucepan and place it on a cutting board. Scoop the rice into a pie dish. With a sharp knife, remove the meat from the carcass and mix in with the rice.

The saucepan in which the chicken was browned still contains some sauce. Keep that sauce and to it add a chopped shallot and 7 ounces of minced mushrooms. Cook over slow heat for 10 minutes and finish off with 4 ounces of port. Allow this to cool and add the pint of chicken stock, boil down for 5 minutes and add 3 tablespoons of butter and chopped tarragon, chervil and parsley. Pour this sauce over the chicken in the pie pan. Then cover the chicken with Pie Crust. (See Index for Pie Crust.) Make certain that the crust is well sealed over the edges of the dish. Bake in a slow oven for 1 hour and serve.

Fried Chicken, Creamed Gravy

Cut a young chicken into 8 pieces. Wash in cold water, drain and sprinkle with salt and pepper. Dip in flour and fry in sausage drippings until all sides are nicely browned. When chicken is cooked, remove it to hot platter, drain off all the fat in frying pan, add 2 tablespoons of butter, blend in 1 tablespoon flour and gradually add 1 cup of thin cream. Bring to boiling point, stirring constantly until perfectly smooth. Season with salt and pepper. Pour sauce in platter with chicken.

Breast of Chicken, Melba

Individual cassolettes (earthen dishes with glass or metal bell-shaped covers) are necessary for this recipe. With a sharp knife remove the 2 breasts from a broiler; season with salt and a few grains of cayenne pepper. Butter cassolette dishes and lay a round piece of

toast in each one, cover each piece of toast with a thin slice of cooked Virginia Ham (see Pork) and place the raw chicken breast on top of ham. Pour ¼ cup cream over each chicken breast, add 3 or 4 peeled mushrooms and a few slices of truffle (if available). Cover with glass bell and place in a moderate oven to cook 35 to 40 minutes. Add a little more cream to cassolette while cooking, as toast will absorb quite a quantity, and there should be about 2 tablespoons of cream in dish when it is served. When adding cream, do not remove cover from cassolette, but pour it in from the side of the dish. Covers are removed at table when dish is served.

Poscharski (Chicken Croquettes)

Remove enough meat from a cold cooked fowl to make 2 cups. Chop it fine. Season with salt, a few grains of cayenne, ⅛ teaspoon celery salt, 1 teaspoon minced onion and 1 teaspoon finely chopped parsley. Bind together with 1 cup of thick White Sauce (see Sauces) and shape into croquettes. Dip in crumbs, then in egg and again in crumbs. Deep-fry at 350° and drain on paper. Place a tiny sprig of parsley in the top of each croquette and serve with a Rich Cream Sauce:

Rich Cream Sauce

Melt 2 tablespoons of butter and blend in 2 tablespoons of flour and ½ teaspoon of salt. Pour on slowly 1½ cups of thin cream (scalded) stirring constantly until the boiling point is reached. Boil 2 minutes and serve.

Chicken Sous Cloche

Cut the breast from a chicken. Season with cayenne pepper and salt. Place it in a small glass casserole (originally the chicken was cooked under a glass bell, called a cassolette). The breast of chicken rests on a piece of toast. A piece of butter is placed under the toast to prevent it from scorching, and also to supply the necessary juices for the cooking. Now, place a slice of cooked ham between the chicken and the toast. Pour over the chicken a small quantity of cream. Place a couple of mushrooms or a few slices of truffles on top of the chicken. Last, put your glass top on the casserole dish and place in the oven, which has been set on low heat. It will require about 50 minutes to cook thoroughly. Add a little cream, now and then, while the chicken is cooking to keep it moist.

★

This recipe was originated in Maryland by the chefs of The Baltimore. Sous Cloche by the nature of its name means under the bell. The bell is glass, except in Virginia—where they used paper bags. The bags were greased with butter or lard. When cooking vegetables or a dish in which water was added, the bag was not greased. The reason for this is that the moisture of the vegetable or water kept the bag from drying out.

Broiled Chicken, Maitre d'Hotel

Purchase a young chicken (broiler) and split for broiling. Wash in cold water and dry thoroughly. Season with salt and pepper, rub with soft butter and fasten tip of wing under shoulder blade. Broil under moderate heat until nicely browned and baste several times during the broiling. Remove to hot platter, breast side up. Spread with Maitre d'Hotel Butter, and garnish with parsley. (See Prepared Butters.)

Chinese Chop Suey

Purchase a frying chicken with a plump breast as it is only the breast of chicken that will suffice for this recipe. Remove the entire breast and cut the meat in strips about 2 inches long. Melt 1 tablespoon of butter in a saucepan, and when it is hot, add the sliced chicken meat. Cook for several minutes but do not allow the meat to brown. Then add 2 cups celery cut in thin slices, crosswise, 1 cup of thinly sliced onion and ½ pound of Chinese water chestnuts that have been peeled and sliced. Stir these ingredients well and add 1 cup of bean sprouts—that have been well rinsed in cold water—over the top. Cover the saucepan and let steam, or cook slowly, for 15 minutes. (If there isn't enough moisture in the meat and vegetables to create steam, then add very little Chicken Broth (see Stock). When chicken and vegetables are tender, add sufficient Chicken Broth to moisten but do not make the suey too liquid. Thicken with 2 tablespoons of cornstarch, mixed with 2 tablespoons of water and 1 tablespoon of Soy sauce. Bring to the boiling point and simmer for several minutes. Serve with plain boiled rice.

Chicken Livers en Brochette

Cut chicken livers in halves. Cut sliced bacon in 1 inch pieces. Fill skewers with alternate pieces of chicken liver and bacon. Place a medium-sized mushroom on the end of each skewer, dip in melted butter and roll in bread crumbs. Broil under moderate heat, basting occasionally and turn skewers until all sides are browned. Season with salt and pepper and garnish with sprigs of parsley.

Rissoles

Roll Puff Paste to ⅛ inch thickness and cut in rounds, 3 inches in diameter. (See Index for Puff Paste.):

Chicken Filling

1 cup finely chopped cooked chicken
3 tablespoons butter
1 cup scalded milk
½ cup finely chopped cooked ham
3 tablespoons flour
Salt and pepper

Make a thick white sauce by melting butter, blending in flour and gradually adding hot milk. Bring to boiling point and let boil 2 minutes. Add finely chopped cooked chicken and cooked ham to white sauce and season to taste with salt and pepper. Place 1 tablespoon of the creamed mixture on a round of Puff Paste, moisten edge with cold water and lay another round of Puff Paste on top. Press edges together, place on a baking sheet which has been covered with 2 thicknesses of brown paper and bake in a hot oven. Serve with a well-seasoned Tomato Sauce. (See Index on Sauces.) Smaller Rissoles may be made by using only 1 round of Puff Paste and folding like a turnover.

Chicken en Casserole

Select young chickens weighing from 2½ to 3 pounds. Disjoint and brown the pieces in hot butter, then transfer the chicken to a hot casserole dish to finish cooking in the oven for 45 to 60 minutes at 350°. Keep the bottom of the casserole dish covered with Chicken Broth (see Stock) as this creates steam and helps to cook the chicken. Also keep casserole dish covered tightly while in the oven. Now parboil some small white onions, a few young carrots and white potatoes that have been scooped into ball shapes. Drain off the water from vegetables and add them to casserole dish about 30 minutes before chicken is cooked as this will finish cooking the parboiled vegetables. When casserole is ready to remove from oven, have ready about 12 medium-sized mushrooms that have been dipped in flour and fried in butter, to add to it. Serve at table in casserole dish.

Mexican Tamale

★

A gourmet cookbook would not be complete without this classical delight. This recipe for tamales was served in the Casa Del Rio, in San Francisco and cooked by Felipe and Maria. Here is the established Mexican recipe:

"Boil a chicken until the meat separates from the bones. Then, the meat should be chopped fine and moistened with the juice in which it was cooked. Boil 6 good-sized chili peppers in a little water and cook them until they can be sieved through a very fine strainer. Add the chopped chicken to this, with a little chopped parsley, and salt to taste. Now work some corn meal into a lump of butter about the size of an egg (6 tablespoons). Add boiling water (1 quart) and continue working in the corn meal (which should total about 3 cups) until the corn meal is a paste about the consistency of biscuit dough. Before this operation you should parboil the soft inner husks of green corn for 5 minutes. Spread a lump of dough about the size of a walnut on each husk and work it into a flat cake covering the husk. Put a teaspoon of the chopped chicken meat in the center of the dough, add some minced olives and roll together. Put several tablespoonfuls of chopped meat on a larger husk and add more minced olives. Roll this together and lay other husks on them until the tamales are the desired quantity. Tie the ends together with fine husks stripped into strings and cook in boiling water for at least 20 minutes."

Some Mexican chefs substitute veal and pork for the chicken while others seem to use all three.

Chicken in the Shell

Place a young chicken in a large saucepan containing a quart of water. Drop in one sliced onion, 1 blade of mace, 2 cloves, 6 peppercorns and 1 bay leaf. Cover the pan and allow it to simmer for 1 hour, and then set aside to cool. After it is cool, remove the skin and throw it away. Then pick the meat from the bones and cut it into small dice. Mix 1 tablespoonful of butter and the same amount of flour in another saucepan, but do not allow it to brown. Add ½ pint of cream and stir well until it boils. Add 2 dozen finely chopped mushrooms, season with white pepper, and then add 1 truffle and the diced chicken. Allow the whole to stand in a chafing dish until hot. Add the yolks of 2 eggs and allow to cook for 2 minutes. Stir in a glass of sherry and serve. When this recipe was developed, it was served in cockleshells; thus, Chicken in the Shell.

★

The original recipe for Chicken in the Snell was from the Iron Horse in San Francisco, which created some of the first distinct Western specialties. The Iron Horse was quite a step upward for San Francisco and the West Coast, because it wasn't until the Iron Horse that the West could compete with the cuisine of Chicago, not to mention New York. There just weren't any cooks between Chicago and the Pacific Coast. The Iron Horse and then the El Dorado, among others, finally began to respond to the miners' demands for better food by importing cooks.

Emincé of Chicken or Turkey, Sauce Mornay

Cold roast chicken or turkey may be utilized in this recipe. Cut chicken into small thin slices and heat slightly by covering with hot Chicken Stock (see Stock). Drain, arrange slices on a platter which will stand oven heat, cover with Sauce Mornay (see Index on Sauces) and place it under the broiler until the sauce is slightly browned.

Boiled Turkey

Rub a turkey all over with lemon juice. Have ready a large saucepan of boiling water on the stove and place the turkey in it with a few slices of carrots, onions and a small bunch of herbs, 3 stalks of celery, ¼ pound of butter, a little mace and cloves, and salt and pepper to taste. Boil the turkey slowly, skimming off the grease and waste as it rises to the top.

In the meantime, prepare the following Oyster Sauce: Parboil 2 dozen oysters in their own liquor, drain them and remove beards. The liquor should be strained and set aside. Put 1 tablespoon of butter in a stewpan, and when it is melted, add 1 tablespoonful of flour and mix over the heat. Then stir in the oyster liquor with sufficient milk to make the required quantity of sauce. Add ½ blade of mace, 1 bay leaf, salt and pepper to taste and a very small quantity of cayenne pepper. When the sauce is done, remove the mace and bay leaf from the sauce, squeeze in a small quantity of lemon juice, strain the sauce, and then add the oysters.

When the turkey is cooked, drain it, place on a hot dish and serve with the sauce. The turkey is our national dish. It is a native American bird, but I must admit that the British have made some improvements on the original chassis.

If you prefer another sauce, rather than the Oyster Sauce, try it with Celery Sauce:

Cut the stalks off some hearts of celery, peel the hearts, wash them and stew. When tender, drain the hearts of celery, cut them into pieces about 1 inch long and put them into some hot Béchamel Sauce (see Sauces). When the turkey is cooked, drain it, put it on a hot dish, pour the sauce over and serve.

★

Alfred Willes, then head Chef of Simpson's on the Strand, London, England, gave us these recipes for Boiled Turkey and Sauces. The Simpson's was once a wayside tavern, which was the last remaining link in the chain of pure Anglo-Saxon cuisine. Now, big corporations control all the historic taverns, which were bought and sold very quickly, but it wasn't unusual to find waiters who had worked forty or fifty years in the same restaurant. The chefs began as scullions or dishwashers, and worked their way through the ranks, they remained with the same tavern until they retired.

Roast Turkey, Chestnut Stuffing

Wash turkey and fill with stuffing—sew opening together and truss. Sprinkle turkey with salt and rub over with soft butter. Place it in baking pan, dust with flour, lay 2 pieces of salt pork on breast and place it in hot oven (450°) for 10 minutes. Reduce heat to moderate (350°) and baste every 15 minutes until turkey is cooked allowing about 3 hours to cook a medium-sized turkey of 8 or 9 pounds. Start basting turkey with ½ cup of butter melted in ½ cup of hot water. When this has been used up, then baste from baking pan.

Chestnut Stuffing

1 quart of chestnuts
2 cups bread or cracker crumbs
¼ pound butter (melted)
¼ cup cream
1 teaspoon salt
Few grains of pepper

Cover chestnuts with boiling water and simmer gently until cooked... about 35 minutes. Drain, cover with cold water and drain again. Remove shells, mash, season with salt and pepper and stir in the cream and half of the melted butter. Add bread or cracker crumbs and the balance of the melted butter and stir until thoroughly mixed.

Roast Stuffed Duck

Wash duck thoroughly. Dry on clean towel and fill it with stuffing. Prepare stuffing as follows: Mix 2 cups of cracker crumbs with 1 cup of finely chopped peanuts... moisten with 1 cup of cream and about 3 tablespoons melted butter. Season with a few drops of onion juice scraped from an onion, salt, pepper and a dash of cayenne. The stuffing should be light and moist but never wet. Tie tail securely with a piece of white string and fasten to crossed drumsticks. Dredge with flour and pepper and salt. Place in a hot oven (475°) for 30 minutes, then reduce heat to moderate and finish roasting, allowing 20 minutes for each pound. Baste every 10 minutes during last ½ hour of baking.

Roast Duck, Danish Stuffing

Wash duck thoroughly. Danish Stuffing to be made as follows: Soak 1 cup of prunes overnight, remove pits and chop prunes. Combine chopped prunes with 1 cup of chopped apples and 1½ cups of bread crumbs. Season with ½ teaspoon salt and moisten with cold water... about ½ cup of water should be used to moisten the stuffing. The stuffing should be light and moist but never wet. Stuff duck... sew up cavity, tie legs together. Dredge lightly with flour, pepper and salt and place in a hot oven (475°) for 30 minutes. Then reduce heat to moderate and finish roasting, allowing 20 minutes for each pound. Baste every 10 minutes during last ½ hour of baking. Serve with Sauce Bigarade:

Sauce Bigarade

3 tablespoons drippings
1 tablespoon flour
1 cup Brown Stock (see Stock)
½ teaspoon salt
½ teaspoon paprika
½ teaspoon sugar

Few grains cayenne
Finely shredded rind of ½ orange
¼ cup strained orange juice

Make the sauce in baking pan after duck is removed to hot platter. Pour off all but 3 tablespoons of drippings, blend in the flour, add hot stock and stir constantly until perfectly smooth. Add salt, paprika, sugar and cayenne and simmer 10 minutes. Remove from heat and add shredded orange rind and orange juice. The orange rind must be peeled off the orange, so there is no white pulp on it, then shred it into pieces to resemble threads. If you happen to have any port wine, add 1 tablespoonful to sauce just before serving.

Rouen Duck

Purchase a large, plump duck. Allow the bird to roast in a medium oven from 15 to 25 minutes per pound, depending on the size. Place the roast duck on a silver platter and blaze for quite some time with ½ cup cognac. The carcass and the rest of the bird, which has been cut up in advance, are put in a pressoir, or press, and all the essence that is extracted by the pressing is mixed with boiling cognac. This mixture is then stirred with a spoon to blend the 2 liquids. The liquid is poured into a chafing dish and a generous lump of butter added. When it is all thoroughly melted and blended in the chafing dish, it is seasoned well with pepper. The duck is cut into thin slices, and the slices are dropped into the sauce in the chafing dish. With a spoon, keep working the sauce over the slices until they are saturated. It is then ready to serve.

★

Rouen Duck is from Rouen, Normandy, inland from Harve on the Seine in France. It has been disputed that Norman cuisine is lacking in the masterful touch of the chefs of Burgundy and Provence, but you might find this disagreement unsound when you taste the nectar of the Rouen Duck.

The cognac, or fine champage, used in this recipe is essential—there is no substitute that I can suggest. The use of cognac and champagne plays an important role in most of the cooking in Normandy.

Caneton à la Presse

Purchase a duck for roasting. Place the duck in a hot oven, 450° for 20 minutes; the idea is to have it very much underdone. The liver is mashed and mixed in a dish with a mixture of 2 ounces of cognac and 4 ounces madeira. The practically raw duck is then sliced and the legs are removed to be broiled. The remaining bones are squeezed in a special machine press, and the juices extracted are poured in a chafing skillet with the slices of the breast of the caneton, the mashed liver mixture and the juice of a lemon. These ingredients are then heated by the chafing fire, and the caneton is cooked until the sauce takes the thickness and color of clear melted chocolate. This requires about 25 minutes, and during that time, the sauce is constantly spooned up and poured back over the duck.

The bird is served from a silver platter. The broiled legs are served separately as a second course. One caneton is enough for 4 people.

★

Soufflé of Fish
Onion Soup
Frogs à la Provençal

This was a specialty from one of the quaint old places of Paris, the Tour-d'Argent founded in 1582. The cooking of the Caneton à la Presse in the chafing dish was performed right on a service table in front of the patrons, who were at liberty to criticize the operation and to advise the chef at all times. Which was one of the charms of the Tour-d'Argent, because if the dish was not exactly right, it was your own fault, as you were the superintendent of the job.

Some of the diners of Tour-d'Argent were Cardinal Richelieu, Henry III and the Court favorites of Henry IV. They dined on soup made from the milk of almonds, swans roasted on the spit and white goose garnished with stewed plums. The Farmers-General of the time of the Fifteenth Louis ate there to be followed in turn by the Directoire and the expert gourmets of the Restoration. It was at the Tour-d'Argent that George Sand met Alfred de Musset for the first time; Dumas smacked his appreciative chops here, and so did Sarah

Bernhardt and Edward VII.

It was during the Third Republic that the Tour-d'Argent reached its climax of renown under the guidance of a chef known as the Great Frédéric.

Other specialities of his include:

Croustade de Filet de Barbue Lagrene, which is Soufflé of Fish and it followed the Caneton à la Presse, as a third course. The secret of the dish is the mixture of egg, as anything with egg, it always comes out fluffy and light.

For 2 persons put 1 tablespoonful of Sauce Béchamel (see Sauces) in a saucepan. Add 2 ounces of grated Parmesan cheese and let it heat until the cheese and the sauce are blended. Then add 1 egg yolk, some salt and cayenne pepper and stir this mixture well together. Now whip 2 egg whites into the preparation. Meanwhile, two pieces of fillet of any fresh white fish should be cooking in a Fish Stock (see Stock) which has been seasoned with a glass of white Bordeaux wine.

Fix a bed of very dry mashed potatoes on a silver platter. Place the fillet of fish on these mashed potatoes and over it pour the sauce, which you have first prepared. Scatter some mixed bread crumbs and grated Parmesan cheese over the whole thing, and on top of all, put some small pieces of butter. Then put the platter in the oven to brown.

The stock in which the fillets were cooked should be made thicker with an egg yolk; butter should be added while cooking; and this extra sauce is served on the side when the platter is removed from the oven to the table.

The proprietors of the Tour d'Argent boasted of Frogs' Legs and Onion Soup:

The Onion Soup is delicious:

For six persons mince a plateful of onions. Brown them in butter in a frying pan and add 8 cupfuls Beef Broth (see Stock) to the minced onions. Cook over slow heat for 1 hour and pour off into an earthen crock. Cut some rolls in fine slices and brown them. Then place the slices of bread in the soup until they cover the whole top, and over them, place a thick coating of grated Parmesan and Gruyère cheese. A spoonful of cream is added to each plate of soup when it is served.

If you are not in the mood for Onion Soup, try the Frogs à la Provençal:

Ten frogs are enough for 4 people (consider the size of the legs).

Wash the frog legs in milk, drain off on a napkin, and then powder with flour. Melt a large piece of butter in a very large frying pan, and add 3 spoonfuls of olive oil while the butter is melting. Place the frog legs in the pan and fry over high heat. Just before they are cooked, add a clove of garlic, 2 shallots and a sprig of parsley, all chopped fine. Lastly, add a large fresh tomato, which has been peeled and pressed in order to remove the seeds. The tomato is crushed into the pan with the hand. The tomato gives the preparation a distinct flavor.

Wild Duck

Wild ducks are plucked, singed, the head cut off, drawn and trussed like fowls. They are never stuffed or seasoned as the flavor of the duck is delicious in itself. Canvasbacks, mallards and black ducks are always cooked rare, so have the oven very hot when you put the duck in. Cook in the hot oven 20 to 25 minutes. No gravy is served with wild duck—but use the natural juice coming from the duck as it is carved. Serve with currant jelly, grilled sweet potatoes and fried hominy. Also a green vegetable and celery salad.

Roast Goose, Savory Rice Stuffing

Select a young plump goose. Wash in cold water. Place 1 cored apple and unpeeled, gashed orange in cavity. Tie legs securely to body with piece of white cord. Place in hot oven (500°) for 30 minutes. Remove from oven, untie cord, take out fruit and pour off excess fat. When cool enough to handle, fill with Savory Rice Stuffing made as follows:

Savory Rice Stuffing

Moisten 2 cups of cooked rice with 2 tablespoons of goose drippings. Add a small green pepper, finely chopped, 1 pimiento, finely chopped and ½ teaspoon sage. Mix all together and stuff goose. Sew skin together, salt and dredge lightly with flour. Return to oven and reduce heat to 300° and finish baking allowing 25 minutes to each pound. Baste every 10 minutes with hot water during last 30 minutes of roasting.

Squabs en Casserole, Printanière

Wash 2 jumbo squabs in cold water and drain. Rub entire surface with soft butter, truss, and put them in a casserole. Set uncovered casserole in hot oven 10 minutes, then add ½ cup raw potato balls, about 10 small white onions (uncooked) and ½ cup fresh green peas. Pour 1 cup of seasoned Chicken Broth (see Index) over vegetables and squabs, cover casserole, and place in moderate oven to cook until tender... about 1 hour. Remove casserole from oven, enrich sauce in bottom of casserole with 1 tablespoon of butter and ½ teaspoon beef extract, and stir gently until butter and extract are thoroughly blended into sauce. Serve from casserole.

Broiled Squab, Maitre d'Hotel

Follow directions contained in Broiled Chicken, Maitre d'Hotel.

Quail

Small birds are usually served on toast, with gravy and browned bread crumbs, which are placed on the plate with the quail. A Panada or Bread Sauce is also a delicious accompaniment with quail. Quail may be roasted whole or split and broiled. Rub them well with butter and baste frequently with the melted butter. If they are to be roasted, they can be treated exactly as a roast chicken and stuffed with a chestnut stuffing. Cover the breast with a piece of fat (salt pork or bacon) for the first 10 minutes of cooking. Have the oven hot, baste the quail frequently; otherwise, the meat may be dry. 20 to 25 minutes is ample time to roast a quail. Serve with a Brown Sauce (see Sauces), fried bread crumbs and Panada which is made as follows: Stick 1 small onion with 2 whole cloves and put it in a saucepan with 1 pint of milk... bring it to a boil and pour it over 3 oz. of bread crumbs. Return it to the saucepan and let it stand in a warm place on the stove until the bread has absorbed the liquid. Remove the onion and cloves, beat well with a fork and season to taste with salt and pepper. If Panada is too thick, dilute it with a little milk, if not thick enough, add more bread crumbs. Just before serving, add 2 tablespoons butter cut into small bits. Stir until butter has melted into the Panada.

Rabbit à la Normandy

First remove all the bones. Keep the legs, liver and hind-quarters, which are to be retained for the fillets. Chop the other pieces of meat. The fillets are to be cut, lengthwise. Add 1 pound of ground pork. Mix the rabbit meat and the pork well together, adding salt, pepper, a dash of nutmeg and a spoonful of cognac. Trim an earthenware dish, which should be deep, with strips of bacon and spread a layer of the mixed rabbit meat and pork over this. Then put a layer of bacon over the meat and a layer of fillet over that. Repeat these layers until the dish is full. Cover the dish with strips of bacon and add 1 leaf of laurel and 1 of thyme. Then put the dish into the oven and permit it to cook for 2 hours.

This is a Rabbit Pâté. And like all other pâtés it is served cold; so after cooking, place it in the refrigerator and keep it there until it is ready to serve.

Rabbit à la Andermahr

Select a rabbit for frying. Season with salt and pepper and dredge lightly with flour. Sauté pieces in a hot mixture of 2 tablespoons of butter and 3 tablespoons olive oil. When the pieces of rabbit are lightly browned, remove them from the pan and set aside. In the pan, melt 4 tablespoons of butter and sauté 1 medium onion, chopped, and ½ pound of mushrooms for 5 minutes. Add 1 clove of garlic, minced, 1 tablespoon parsley, chopped, and stir. Add the rabbit to this mixture with ¾ cup white wine and 1 tablespoon of Beef Broth (see Stock). Cover pan and simmer over low heat for 45 minutes. Serve over rice and garnish with parsley.

Rabbit Stew

Cut a rabbit into neat jointed pieces for stewing. Wash the pieces and season with salt, pepper and a tiny bit of mace. Cut 4 slices of bacon into 1-inch pieces and fry them in a saucepan. When the fat of the bacon melts, put in the pieces of seasoned rabbit and 1 small onion that has been finely minced and fry over moderate heat until the meat is lightly browned. Then add 1 quart of warm Stock (see Stock) and the following herbs which are to be tied in a muslin bag: 2 sprigs of parsley, a piece of lemon peel, 3 whole cloves and about 8 or 10 peppercorns. Cover the saucepan and cook slowly over low heat for 2 or 3 hours, the time depending on the size of the rabbit. Remove the bag of herbs and enrich the liquid with 1 teaspoon of glaze viande (meat extract). Just before serving, add 2 tablespoons of sherry.

SAUCES

11

Volumes could be written about sauces, especially when one is interested in the French cuisine. The French chefs have made a serious study of sauces. They are careful to save the essence of the fish, poultry, and other meats that have been sautéed, which results in the finest base for their sauces. The French chefs believe in thrift in the kitchen, which means saving everything—to be utilized in one form or another. This thrift is the basic ingredient of fine sauces.

White Sauce

1 tablespoon butter
1 tablespoon flour
¼ teaspoon salt
Few grains pepper
1 cup scalded milk

Melt butter, blend in flour, salt and pepper, gradually add milk and stir until perfectly smooth. Bring to boiling point and let boil 2 minutes.

Cream Sauce

1 tablespoon butter
1 tablespoon flour
¼ teaspoon salt
Few grains pepper
1 cup scalded cream

Melt butter, blend in flour, salt and pepper, gradually add cream and stir until perfectly smooth. Bring to boiling point and let boil 2 minutes.

Brown Sauce

4 tablespoons butter
1 tablespoon chopped onion
1 tablespoon chopped carrot
1 sprig parsley
1 sprig thyme
1 small bay leaf
10 peppercorns

4 tablespoons flour
2 cups Brown Stock

Melt butter, add onion, carrot, parsley, thyme, bay leaf and peppercorns and cook until well-browned but do not allow the butter to burn. Stir in the flour, and when well-browned, add the Brown Stock. Bring to the boiling point and let boil 2 minutes. Remove from heat, strain and season to taste with salt and pepper. (See Index for Stock.)

Piquante Sauce

1 cup Brown Sauce
2 tablespoons tarragon vinegar
1 teaspoon shallot, finely chopped
Few grains cayenne
1 tablespoon vinegar pickle, finely chopped
1 tablespoon capers, finely chopped

Add vinegar, shallots, capers, vinegar pickle and cayenne to Brown Sauce. (See above Sauce.) Place on low heat 15 minutes before serving.

Béchamel Sauce

1½ cups White Stock
1 sprig parsley
6 celery leaves
½ small onion
¼ bay leaf
6 peppercorns
3 tablespoons butter
3 tablespoons flour
1 cup scalded milk
¼ teaspoon salt
Few grains cayenne
Few grains nutmeg

Cook White Stock with parsley, celery leaves, onion, bay leaf and peppercorns until quantity is reduced to 1 cupful. Strain. Melt butter, blend in flour and seasonings and gradually add the strained White Stock and scalded milk. Bring to boiling point and let boil 2 minutes. Strain sauce through a fine strainer before using. (See Index for

Stock).

Creole Sauce

1½ cups canned tomatoes
1 green pepper, thinly sliced
1 medium onion, thinly sliced
½ cup Brown Sauce
½ cup mushrooms, thinly sliced
1 tablespoon butter
1 tablespoon flour

Cook tomatoes, green pepper, onion and mushrooms together 10 minutes. Add Brown Sauce and cook 2 minutes longer. Thicken with butter and flour that has been creamed together. (See Index for Brown Sauce.)

Curry Sauce, American

2 tablespoons butter
1½ tablespoons flour
1 tablespoon curry powder
¼ teaspoon salt
1 cup hot White Stock
1 egg yolk
2 tablespoons heavy cream

Melt butter, blend in flour, curry powder and salt. Gradually add hot White Stock and bring to the boiling point. Let boil 2 minutes, remove from heat and add egg yolk slightly beaten with cream. (See Index for Stock.)

Mornay Sauce

3 cups Cream Sauce
¼ cup grated Parmesan cheese
¼ pound sweet butter
¼ cup grated Gruyère cheese
Few grains cayenne pepper
Salt

Place saucepan containing Cream Sauce in a very hot oven until a brown crust has formed on top. Remove from oven, discard brown crust, beat sauce with wire whisk while adding small bits of butter, alternating with both kinds of grated cheese. It is important that the butter and cheese are immediately whipped into the Cream Sauce as the intense heat of the sauce must melt not only the butter but also the two kinds of grated cheese. Season with cayenne and add salt to taste. Strain through a fine sieve. A delicious sauce to serve with poached fish fillets, poached eggs, various vegetables or sliced cooked chicken. After food is covered with Mornay Sauce place it in a moderate oven until lightly browned. (See Index for Cream Sauce.)

Tomato Sauce

2 cups canned tomatoes
½ small onion
1 sprig parsley
½ bay leaf
½ clove garlic
10 peppercorns
¼ teaspoon salt
1 teaspoon sugar
3 tablespoons butter
3 tablespoons flour

Cook tomatoes, onion, parsley, bay leaf, garlic, peppercorns, salt and sugar together—20 minutes. Rub through a sieve and thicken sauce by adding it to butter and flour, which have been blended together. Bring to boiling point and let boil 2 minutes.

Sauce Italienne

1 cup thinly sliced mushrooms
5 shallots, finely chopped
2 tablespoons butter
4 tablespoons white wine
1 cup Brown Sauce (see Index)
1 cup Tomato Sauce (above)
1 tablespoon butter
1 tablespoon parsley, finely chopped

Cook mushrooms and shallots with 2 tablespoons butter for 5 minutes. Add wine and cook 5 minutes longer, then add Brown Sauce and Tomato Sauce and bring to the boiling point. Let boil 2 minutes, remove from heat and stir in 1 tablespoon butter and finely chopped parsley.

Velouté Sauce

2 tablespoons butter
2 tablespoons flour
¼ teaspoon salt
Few grains cayenne pepper
1 cup White Stock

Melt butter, blend in flour, salt and cayenne, gradually add hot White Stock (see Stock) and stir until perfectly smooth. Bring to boiling point and let boil 2 minutes. Strain sauce through a fine strainer before using.

Sauce Soubise

1 cup Velouté Sauce (see above)
3 medium-sized onions, sliced
½ cup cream
1 tablespoon butter
Salt

Cover onions with boiling water and cook until soft. Drain, rub onion pulp through a sieve into the Velouté Sauce, add cream and stir until the boiling point is reached. Remove from heat and stir in butter. Season to taste with salt.

Celery Sauce

1 cup Velouté Sauce
2 cups celery, thinly sliced
3 tablespoons cream
1 tablespoon butter

Cover celery with boiling water and cook until soft. Drain, force pulp through sieve into Velouté Sauce. Bring to boiling point, stir in cream, remove from heat and add butter in small bits. Season to taste with salt. (See Index for Velouté Sauce.)

Cheese Sauce

3 tablespoons butter
3 tablespoons flour
¼ teaspoon salt
1½ cups scalded milk
1 cup grated American cheese
Few grains pepper

Melt butter, blend in flour, salt and pepper, gradually add milk and stir until perfectly smooth. Bring to boiling point and let boil 2 minutes. Remove from heat and gradually beat in the grated cheese.

Villeroi Sauce

Follow recipe for Velouté Sauce (see Index), bring to boiling point and thicken with 2 slightly beaten egg yolks. Remove from heat and add 1 tablespoon finely chopped chives and 4 tablespoons minced cooked mushrooms.

Sauce à la Normande

Follow recipe for Velouté Sauce (see Index), add 4 tablespoons strong Fish Stock (see Court Bouillon), 4 tablespoons white wine and bring to boiling point. Thicken sauce with 2 slightly beaten egg yolks, remove from heat, stir in 1 tablespoon butter and the juice of half a lemon. Strain sauce through fine sieve and serve.

Sauce Allemande

2 tablespoons flour
2 tablespoons butter
¼ teaspoon salt
Few grains cayenne
Few grains nutmeg
1 cup Chicken Stock
¼ cup cream
1 egg yolk
1 teaspoon lemon juice

Melt butter, blend in flour and seasonings, gradually add hot Chicken Stock and cream. Bring to boiling point and let boil 2 minutes. Add slightly beaten egg yolk, remove from heat and stir in the lemon juice. Strain sauce through a fine strainer before using. (See Index for Stock.)

Parsley Sauce

Follow recipe for Sauce Allemande (see above). Add 2 tablespoons finely chopped parsley to sauce as it is removed from the heat.

Sauce Poulette

Follow recipe for Sauce Allemande (see Index). Add ½ cup sliced cooked mushrooms.

Egg Sauce

2 tablespoons butter
2 tablespoons flour
¼ teaspoon salt
1 cup hot Fish Stock
2 hard-boiled eggs, chopped
1 teaspoon finely chopped parsley
Few grains pepper

Melt butter, blend in flour, salt and pepper, gradually add hot Fish Stock and stir until perfectly smooth. Bring to boiling point and let boil 2 minutes. Add chopped eggs and parsley. (See Index for Stock.)

Curry Sauce, Indienne

¼ pound butter
3 medium-sized onions, chopped
¼ pound raw ham, chopped
½ teaspoon celery salt
20 peppercorns
3 cloves
Pinch of thyme

¼ teaspoon salt
2 tablespoons curry powder
1 quart White Stock
3 egg yolks
½ pint cream

Cook chopped onions in butter until lightly browned. Add chopped ham, celery salt, peppercorns, cloves and thyme. Let cook over low heat 15 minutes, then add salt and curry powder. Stir ingredients, gradually add hot White Stock, and cook 20 minutes longer. Strain through a double thickness of cheese cloth, add cream, bring to a boil and thicken with slightly beaten egg yolks. Do not allow sauce to boil after yolks are added. (See Index for Stock.)

Anchovy Sauce

2 tablespoons butter
2 tablespoons flour
⅛ teaspoon salt
Few grains pepper
1 cup hot Fish Stock (see below)
2 tablespoons Anchovy Butter

Melt butter, blend in flour, salt and pepper, gradually add hot Fish Stock and stir until perfectly smooth. Bring to boiling point and let boil 2 minutes. Add Anchovy Butter bit by bit, stirring until it is thoroughly blended with the sauce. (See Prepared Butters.)

Fish Stock

1½ pounds fish (flounder, blackfish or red snapper)
1 cup oyster liquor
1 cup cold water
½ cup onion, sliced
1 small carrot, sliced
1 sprig parsley
10 peppercorns
¼ teaspoon salt
¼ bay leaf

Cut your fish into small pieces but do not remove head or bones. Cover with cold water and oyster liquor and add the rest of the ingredients. Bring to boiling point and simmer 30 minutes. Strain stock before using.

Fish Velouté

3 tablespoons butter
2 tablespoons flour
¼ teaspoon salt
Few grains cayenne
1 cup hot Fish Stock (see above)
1 teaspoon lemon juice

Melt butter, blend in flour, salt and cayenne, gradually add hot Fish Stock and stir until perfectly smooth. Bring to boiling point and let boil 2 minutes. Add lemon juice and strain through a fine strainer before using.

Oyster Sauce

1 pint oysters and liquor
2 tablespoons butter
2 tablespoons flour
¼ teaspoon salt
Few grains pepper
1 cup milk

Wash oysters, strain liquor over them and cook 5 minutes. In another saucepan, melt butter, blend in flour, salt and pepper. Gradually add hot milk, oyster liquor and oysters. Bring to the boiling point and let boil 2 minutes.

Hollandaise Sauce

4 egg yolks
½ cup sweet butter (melted)
¼ teaspoon salt
¾ cup boiling water
2 tablespoons strained lemon juice
Few grains cayenne

Beat egg yolks, gradually add melted butter, seasonings and boiling water. Put into top part of double boiler and cook over water until sauce thickens. When sauce thickens, remove immediately from heat as too much heat will cause Hollandaise to separate. Stir in lemon juice and serve. If Hollandaise separates, the sauce may be brought together by working it into ¼ cup thin Cream Sauce (hot), and remove from heat immediately. (See Index for Cream Sauce.)

Mousseline Sauce

1 cup Hollandaise Sauce (see above)
½ cup whipped cream

Gradually beat whipped cream into Hollandaise Sauce.

Figaro Sauce

1 cup Hollandaise Sauce (see above)
¼ cup thick Tomato Sauce (see Index)
1 tablespoon finely chopped parsley

Gradually beat Tomato Sauce and chopped parsley into Hollandaise Sauce.

Sauce Béarnaise (Hollandaise)

2 shallots, finely chopped
Sprig thyme
¼ bay leaf
2 sprigs parsley
10 peppercorns, crushed
12 green tarragon leaves
4 tablespoons vinegar
1 cup Hollandaise Sauce
½ tablespoon tarragon leaves, finely chopped
½ tablespoon parsley, finely chopped

Cook shallots, thyme, bay leaf, parsley, crushed peppercorns and tarragon leaves with vinegar until quantity is reduced to ½. Strain, add to Hollandaise Sauce and stir in finely chopped tarragon leaves and finely chopped parsley. (See Index for Hollandaise Sauce.)

Sauce Béarnaise

6 shallots, finely chopped
Few branches green tarragon
12 peppercorns, crushed
1 cup vinegar
4 egg yolks
½ cup melted butter
½ teaspoon tarragon leaves, finely chopped
½ teaspoon parsley, finely chopped

Add shallots, tarragon branches and crushed peppercorns to vinegar and boil in uncovered saucepan until vinegar is reduced to ¼ of original amount. Strain, gradually add to slightly beaten egg yolks and cook over hot water until mixture thickens. Stir constantly with wire whisk and gradually add melted butter. When thoroughly blended and thick, remove from heat and add finely chopped tarragon leaves and finely chopped parsley.

Babcock Sauce

3 tablespoons butter
1 tablespoon flour
½ teaspoon English mustard
1 cup clam liquor, strained
¼ teaspoon salt
½ teaspoon black pepper, coarsely ground

Melt butter, blend in flour and English mustard, gradually add clam liquor and bring to boiling point. Let boil 2 minutes, add salt and freshly ground black pepper. Freshly ground black pepper is the secret of Babcock Sauce. Grind whole black peppercorns in a small pepper mill until you have the desired quantity. Sauce should be heavily flecked with black pepper.

Mignonette (Spiced Sauce for Oysters)

½ cup tarragon vinegar
1 tablespoon shallots, finely chopped
1 teaspoon parsley, finely chopped
1 teaspoon mustard seed

20 peppercorns, crushed

Mix ingredients together. Serve with oysters on the half shell.

Cumberland Sauce

3 tablespoons red currant jelly
2 tablespoons port wine
2 tablespoons orange juice
1 tablespoon lemon juice
1 teaspoon prepared mustard
1 teaspoon paprika
½ teaspoon ground ginger
3 tablespoons orange rind, finely shredded

Melt jelly over low heat until liquid. Cool, add port wine, orange juice, lemon juice, mustard, paprika, ground ginger and orange rind that has been covered with cold water, brought to a boil and drained. This is a delicious sauce to serve with cold cuts.

★

This recipe for Cumberland Sauce was obtained from the chef, via Sir Francis Towle, of the famous Simpson's on the Strand, London, England. He recommended that the sauce be served with hot or cold tongue and hams.

Bordelaise Sauce

2 shallots, finely chopped
½ small onion, finely chopped
1 small carrot, sliced
¼ bay leaf
1 sprig parsley
10 peppercorns
1 cup Brown Sauce
½ cup dry red wine (4 oz.)
1 tablespoon butter
1 tablespoon lemon juice
1 tablespoon parsley, finely chopped
10 slices poached beef marrow (cut ¼ inch thick)

Cook shallots, onion, carrot, parsley, bay leaf and peppercorns with red wine until quantity is reduced to ½. Strain, add wine to hot Brown Sauce. Add butter bit by bit, and when thoroughly blended, stir in the lemon juice, finely chopped parsley and poached marrow. Poached Marrow: Carefully remove marrow from marrow-bones, slice, and poach in salted water for 5 minutes. Bring water to a boil and reduce heat to simmer and keep water at simmering point while poaching marrow. (See Index for Brown Sauce.)

Mint Sauce

½ cup mild vinegar
1 tablespoon powdered sugar
2 tablespoons finely chopped mint

Dissolve powdered sugar in vinegar. When dissolved, pour it over finely chopped mint. Let stand in warm place 30 minutes before using.

Sauce Colbert

1 tablespoon beef extract
Few grains Nutmeg
1 cup water (hot)
⅛ pound butter
Juice of 1 lemon
2 tablespoons sherry
1 teaspoon finely chopped parsley

Dissolve beef extract in boiling water and let boil 2 minutes. Remove from heat, add butter bit by bit, beating constantly with wire whip until butter is thoroughly blended with sauce... Add lemon juice, nutmeg and sherry. Strain sauce through a fine sieve, then add finely chopped parsley and serve. This may be varied by using 1 teaspoon finely chopped green tarragon leaves instead of parsley.

Sauce Bercy

1 cup Tomato Sauce
2 tablespoons boiling water

1 teaspoon beef extract
1 tablespoon butter

Cook Tomato Sauce until quantity is reduced to ¾ of a cup. Dissolve beef extract in boiling water and add to reduced sauce. Remove from heat and stir in butter. (See Index for Tomato Sauce.)

Caper Sauce

3 tablespoons butter
3 tablespoons flour
½ teaspoon salt
⅛ teaspoon pepper
1½ cups hot Mutton Stock
2 tablespoons butter
½ cup capers
1 teaspoon lemon juice

Melt butter, blend in flour, salt and pepper, gradually add hot stock, which has been skimmed and strained. Boil 5 minutes, remove from heat and add 2 tablespoons butter broken into small pieces, and capers, drained from their liquor and moistened with lemon juice. Use Mutton Stock from Boiled Shoulder of Mutton (see Index on Lamb).

VEGETABLES

12

Canned food comes in handy during an emergency, but I would not recommend it seven days a week. We have a variety of fresh vegetables and fruits in great abundance, and we should avail ourselves of this opportunity to use fresh produce more often.

Many vegetables in this section retain their freshness and nutritional value when steamed, and I would recommend that process wherever possible in preparing these recipes.

Special Baked Potato, Rector

Just a little extra work is going to make this baked potato a real treat. Bake large potatoes in moderate oven until cooked—about 1 hour. Cut a large oval piece of skin from the top of the potato and scrape all the potato from the shell into a warm bowl. Be careful in handling the shells as they are to be used again. Season with salt, pepper, paprika and mash with fresh cream. Sprinkle some finely chopped chives into potatoes while mashing them. Refill potato shells with the mixture and put them in a hot oven to brown. In filling the shells, do not pack the potato in tight but allow some of it to come up over where the potato was cut. Serve immediately.

Scalloped Potatoes

Wash and peel the required number of potatoes and slice in ⅛-inch thickness. Butter a baking dish and cover bottom with a layer of sliced potatoes. Sprinkle lightly with salt, pepper, parsley, grated Gruyère cheese and flour. Dot with several small pieces of butter and sprinkle with nutmeg. Continue layers of potatoes and seasonings until required quantity is used up. Then pour milk over all and bake in a moderate oven 50 minutes. Serve from baking dish in which potatoes have been cooked.

Potatoes au Gratin

This recipe is to be made from hot boiled potatoes. This may sound odd, but try it; the result will be softer, fluffier potatoes than the usual cold potatoes warmed in a hot sauce. For every 2 cups of hot chopped potatoes, allow 1½ cups of Velouté Sauce made as follows:

Melt 2 tablespoons butter, blend in 1½ tablespoons flour and gradually add 1½ cups of strained Chicken Broth (see Stock) stirring constantly until smooth and boiling point is reached. Add potatoes to sauce, season with salt and pepper and pour into a shallow casserole. Sprinkle top with grated cheese and bake in moderate oven until browned.

Boiled Parisian Potatoes

Wash and pare large potatoes. Cut in small balls using a French vegetable cutter. Cook them in boiling, salted water, drain, add a piece of fresh butter and carefully shake pan until potatoes have absorbed butter. Sprinkle with finely chopped parsley.

Browned Parisian Potatoes

Wash and pare large potatoes. Cut in small balls using a French vegetable cutter and parboil 10 minutes in boiling, salted water. Drain, sauté in butter until lightly browned.

Potatoes Bayonne

Wash and pare 6 medium-sized potatoes and drop them into cold water to freshen for 30 minutes. Cook in boiling, salted water until soft. Drain, keep the saucepan uncovered for 2 or 3 minutes to allow escape of steam. Force the hot potatoes through a potato ricer or a coarse strainer into another saucepan. Moisten with 3 tablespoons of strong clear White Stock (see Stock) and 3 tablespoons of cream. Season with salt, pepper and a pinch of nutmeg and beat with a fork until light and creamy. In the meantime, fry 2 chopped shallots in 1 tablespoon of butter until soft but do not let them turn brown. Add this to the potatoes along with 1 teaspoon of finely chopped parsley, ¼ pound of cooked ham cut into tiny squares of about ¼ inch and 2 slightly beaten egg yolks. Beat all together until thoroughly mixed. Now set aside ⅛ of this preparation and form the remainder in a dome-shape on a shallow baking dish. To the ⅛ reserved part add 2 egg yolks that have been beaten with 1 tablespoon of cream. Mix well and then fold in 2 egg whites that have been stiffly beaten.

Cover the potato dome with this lighter potato mixture and sprinkle finely buttered bread crumbs over top. Set in a moderate oven until nicely browned.

Rissolée Potatoes

Wash and pare potatoes of uniform size into oval shape. Cover with cold water and let stand 15 minutes, drain and dry on a towel. Put potatoes in baking pan with a roast about 45 minutes before meat is cooked. Baste and turn during the cooking. Drain on brown paper and sprinkle liberally with salt.

Hollandaise Potatoes

Wash and pare potatoes of uniform size into oval shape about 2 inches long and 1 inch in diameter. Cook them in boiling salt water, drain, cover saucepan with cloth until time of service.

O'Brien Potatoes

Cut cold boiled potatoes into small cubes of uniform size and sprinkle lightly with flour. To every cup of cubed potatoes, add ¼ cup finely chopped pimientos. Fry in hot butter until potatoes are nicely browned. Remove to hot dish and sprinkle top with finely chopped parsley.

Potatoes Anna

Wash and pare potatoes. Cut them in slices ⅛ of an inch thick and 1½ inches in diameter. Cover with cold water and let stand 15 minutes, drain and dry on a towel. Butter a shallow casserole and sprinkle lightly with fine bread crumbs, arrange a layer of sliced potatoes on the bottom, having the slices overlap each other. The bottom layer becomes the top when the potatoes are turned out of the casserole, so arrange them nicely. Cover the layer with soft butter and continue to build layers of potatoes and butter until 2 inches high. Cover casserole and place in a moderate oven to cook for 1 hour. Uncover casserole, place a large dish over top, invert carefully, and now you have Potatoes Anna cooked to a golden brown.

French Fried Potatoes

Wash and pare potatoes of uniform size. Cut lengthwise into strips, about 16 to a potato. Soak in cold water 1 hour, drain, dry on a towel, put potatoes in frying basket and fry in deep hot fat or oil until browned. Temperature of fat or oil should be about 370° or hot enough to brown a cube of bread in 1 minute. Drain potatoes on brown paper and sprinkle liberally with salt.

Green Corn, Rector

Cover corn on the cob with boiling, salted water and cook 10 to 15 minutes. Cut corn off cob by taking a sharp knife and cutting down through the center of the kernels. Scrape corn off cob, leaving as many of the kernel shells on the cob as possible. To every 2 cups of corn, add 1 cup of Cream Sauce (see Index), 4 tablespoons finely chopped pimientos and 4 tablespoons finely chopped green pepper which has been blanched by covering with boiling water. Pour into a buttered gratin dish, sprinkle top with fine bread crumbs and grated Parmesan cheese—dot with small bits of butter and place in moderate oven to brown.

Corn Fritters

4 ears of corn (2 cups)
2 tablespoons flour
⅛ teaspoon salt
1 egg (separated)

Cover the corn with boiling, salted water and boil for 15 minutes. Remove the corn from the cob. This is done by splitting each row of kernels down the center and scraping the split kernels with the dull side of your knife. Leave as many kernel shells on the cob as possible.

To every 2 cups of corn add 1 beaten egg yolk, the flour and salt and mix thoroughly. Then beat the egg white until stiff and fold it into the corn mixture. For each fritter, drop a heaping tablespoon of this mixture into a hot, buttered frying pan and fry until the fritters are golden brown.

Canned Corn, Soufflé

Make a cream sauce by melting 2 tablespoons of butter, blending in 2 tablespoons of flour and gradually add 1 cup of milk. Bring to the boiling point stirring constantly for a smooth mixture. Remove from the heat and stir 1 can of corn into it. Season with salt and pepper and add ¼ cup minced pimiento. Stir in 2 slightly beaten egg yolks and lastly fold in 2 stiffly beaten egg whites. Pour into a buttered oven dish and bake in a moderate oven for 30 minutes. Serve immediately as a soufflé dish soon falls.

French Fried Mushrooms

Select mushrooms of large uniform size. Peel caps, and leave a ½-inch stem on each mushroom. Dip in Light Batter and fry in deep hot fat or oil until lightly browned. Drain on brown paper and sprinkle with salt. Light Batter: ½ cup flour, 1 teaspoon baking powder, ¼ teaspoon salt, ¼ cup milk and 1 egg. Mix and sift dry ingredients, add milk gradually, and egg well-beaten.

Creamed Mushrooms on Toast

Trim the stems from 1 pound of mushrooms leaving a ½-inch stem on each one. Cook them in a frying pan with fresh butter and stir them around until they are all an even brown. Season with salt and pepper and dredge with 1 tablespoon of sifted flour. Pour 1 cup of thin cream over them and cook 5 minutes longer. Serve on fresh toast.

Mushrooms Bouchées

Select the extra large mushrooms for this recipe. Peel the caps and remove the entire stem from 6 large mushrooms. Chop the stems up fine and cook them in 2 tablespoons of butter, add 1 tablespoon of finely chopped shallot, 2 tablespoons of bread crumbs, 2 tablespoons of finely chopped cooked chicken, and 1 teaspoon of finely chopped parsley. Moisten with meat stock (see Stock) and fill the mushroom caps with the mixture. Cover top with fine bread crumbs mixed with an equal quantity of grated cheese. Dot mushrooms with a small piece of butter and place on a greased baking pan to cook in the oven for 15 to 20 minutes.

Mushrooms Sous Cloche (Under Glass Bell)

Individual baking dishes with glass bell-shaped covers are necessary for this recipe. Cover bottom of individual baking dishes with Lemon Butter (see Prepared Butters). Put a small circular piece of toast in baking dish, cover with peeled mushroom caps and build the mushrooms up high toward the center. Pour enough cream around toast to cover bottom of baking dish, cover with glass bell and place in a moderate oven to cook for 30 minutes. Add a little more cream to dish while cooking as toast will absorb quite a quantity, and there should be about 2 tablespoons of cream when dish is served. Bell dishes are sent from oven to table and covers removed at the table.

Cauliflower, Sauce Mornay

Cover a whole cauliflower with boiling, salted water and cook until tender. Drain, place cauliflower in baking dish and cover with 1 cup of Mornay Sauce (see Index on Sauces). Place in moderate oven until lightly browned.

Potato Salad

★

Hiller ran one of the more prestigious restaurants in Berlin. He maintained the highest standards, and his clientele was a reflection of those standards.

You could have seen Crown Prince Wilhelm in there almost any day, along with King Frederick Augustus of Saxony, Foreign Minister

Stresemann and the industrial barons of Germany.

Its popularity was due to the fact that when the rest of Berlin was on quarter rations, you could always get fine food and drink in Hiller's. Hiller was known for his Kartoffel Salat or Potato Salad:

Take some small potatoes and boil until tender. One of the secrets of good Kartoffel Salat is the smallness of the potatoes used. Drain off the water and let them cool. Peel them and slice them ⅕ inch thick. Season with salt and pepper and add some very thick-sliced onions. Pour 1 cup of Consommé (see Stock) over them and allow it to stand until the potatoes have absorbed the Consommé—which should be Chicken, as Beef Consommé will discolor the salad. Add 3 tablespoonfuls of olive oil and 1 tablespoonful of vinegar. Sprinkle a pinch of chopped parsley over all. To improve this dish, add 1 tablespoonful of mayonnaise and mix it thoroughly with the other ingredients. Many Berliners like their Kartoffel Salat served warm. It was used as a side dish for just about everything on the menu.

Cauliflower au Gratin

This is a particularly nice vegetable to serve with roasts or plain broiled meats.

Trim all the outer green leaves off a medium-sized cauliflower and wash well in cold water. Drop into boiling, salted water (stem end downward) and cook until tender. Drain carefully in a colander taking care not to break off any of the flowerettes. Place the cauliflower in an oven dish or casserole and pour 1 cup of Cream Sauce (see Sauces) over it. To another cup of Cream Sauce, add 4 tablespoons of grated Parmesan cheese and the same amount of dried bread crumbs. Pour this over the cauliflower and brown in moderate oven. Serve in the dish in which it was baked.

Artichokes, Ulpia

Select large artichokes of uniform size. Cut off stems and remove some of the bottom leaves. Soak in cold water 1 hour, drain, and cover with boiling, salted water, add 1 clove of crushed garlic, the juice of 1 lemon and 4 tablespoons of olive oil. Cook until artichokes are soft, about 45 minutes. Carefully remove from water, and turn upside down to drain. Gently open artichoke by spreading center leaves and remove choke which is located in center. Serve Hollandaise Sauce separately. (See Index on Sauces.)

Artichokes

★

Pizza alla Pasesana

Peas

Following is a typical Tuscan menu of Italy, which was prepared and served by Giovanni Pisani, capo cuoco, or top chef, of one of Florence's leading hotels:

Prepare a large, flat brioche, unsweetened, about 10 inches in diameter and an inch thick. Place the brioche in a shallow baking pan. On top of the brioche place a layer of sliced tomatoes. Scatter on top of the tomatoes about 10 or 15 fillets of anchovy. Over all place thin slices of Mozzarella cheese. Spray with a little olive oil, season with salt and pepper and cook in oven for about 20 minutes.

The next dish on the menu was Tortino di carciofi Ossibuchi con Piselli alla Fiorentina:

Take 6 artichokes—carciofi—and remove the hard leaves, trimming very close to the heart of the artichokes. Cut each plant into 6 parts from the top down. Sauté in a frying pan, with olive oil. Aside from this, beat about 12 eggs and season with salt. Then add the eggs to the artichokes in a low casserole and cook slowly on top of stove for about 10 minutes. At the last minute, put the casserole in a hot oven and allow to cook until it hardens. You must remove before the eggs get too tough and stringy.

This accounts for the Tortino di carciofi Ossibuchi. Now, for the Con Piselli alla Fiorentina, which means ordinary peas in the Florentine manner:

Place in a saucepan 1 tablespoonful of oil and the same amount of butter. Chop finely a small onion and fry in pan. When onion is brown, add several ounces of small pieces of raw ham. Now add ½ a pound of shelled peas. Fill a saucepan with water to cover all the peas and let it cook until the water has evaporated and the peas are all dry. Serve.

The menu was not complete without Cassata alla Toscana, the Tuscan idea of Neapolitan ice cream, Pasticcini Assortiti (assorted pastries) and Cestini di Frutta or bananas marinated in liqueur.

Giovanni Pisani was very proud of this menu and regarded it as his masterpiece.

Spinach en Casserole

Wash the spinach several times using a large receptacle, so the spinach will rise to the top and the dirt or sand will sink to the bottom. Cut off the roots but leave the stem on the leaves. Pick over carefully, and when perfectly clean, pack into a covered casserole dish and place in a moderate oven to cook for 20 or 30 minutes. Do not hesitate to pack it tight—it will cook down considerably. Add no water to the casserole, since there will be sufficient water on the leaves and stems to create steam enough to cook it. Chop slightly and season with salt, pepper and butter. This recipe or method is especially good as it is rich in lime of calcium and iron, because the spinach has cooked in its own juices.

Spinach à la Crème

Wash and pack the spinach into a saucepan and add just enough water to cover the bottom of the pan so the spinach will not burn. Add a little salt to the water and cook about 15 minutes. Chop finely, and if there is any juice remaining, reduce it by cooking over a high heat. Add enough thick cream to moisten and season with salt and pepper. Pour over spinach.

Spinach à la Noailles

Wash and cook the spinach in just enough water to cover bottom of pan. Chop it finely and force it through a coarse sieve into another saucepan. Add a piece of fresh butter and stir constantly over moderate heat until all moisture is evaporated. Then sprinkle lightly with flour and moisten with Chicken or Veal Stock (see Stock), adding a little glaze viande (meat extract) at the same time. Season with salt and a very little nutmeg, and just before serving, stir in a piece of fresh butter.

Summer Squash au Gratin

5 lbs. squash
¼ cup butter
½ teaspoon salt
⅛ teaspoon pepper
¼ cup grated onion
¾ cup buttered bread crumbs

Break squash into small pieces. Remove seeds and fibers and wash in cold water. Place in a steamer, cover tightly and steam until tender. Scrape squash from shell, mash and season with butter, salt and pepper. Arrange layers of squash, grated onion and bread crumbs in a buttered casserole. Finish with bread crumbs on top. Bake in a moderate oven (350°) 30 to 35 minutes.

Steamed Winter Squash

In selecting winter squash, be sure that it is heavy for its size. Cut a winter squash into small pieces. Remove all seeds and pulpy part. Steam over boiling water until soft. Scrape from shell and mash with butter and season with a little salt and pepper.

Baked Stuffed Tomatoes

Select 6 firm tomatoes of uniform size. Core out the center with a sharp knife and prepare the stuffing as follows: Put into a large mixing bowl the pulp of the tomatoes which you have just removed, add ½ medium-sized onion, finely chopped, ⅛ teaspoon mixed herbs, 1 cup cold cooked meat, finely chopped, (ham, tongue, chicken or veal) and 1 cup of bread crumbs. Moisten with melted butter and season with salt, pepper and paprika. Mix well and stuff the tomatoes with the mixture, place on a greased baking pan to cook in a moderate oven 20 to 30 minutes.

Asparagus, Buca Lapi

Wash asparagus in cold water, trim lower part of stalks and tie together with piece of string. Cover with boiling, salted water and cook until soft, about 20 minutes. Drain, arrange asparagus on hot plates, pour some hot melted butter over tips and sprinkle with grated Parmesan cheese and serve.

Asparagus Hollandaise

Follow directions for boiling asparagus in above recipe. Drain, arrange asparagus on hot plates and pour sauce on the side. (See Index for Sauce.)

Brussels Sprouts au Beurre Noir

Wash 1 quart brussels sprouts in cold water and remove wilted leaves and stems. Cover with boiling, salted water and cook 10 to 15 minutes. Drain, melt 4 tablespoons butter and let it become brown, remove from heat and add 2 tablespoons vinegar. Pour over brussels sprouts and serve.

Braised Lettuce

Select small solid hearts of lettuce. Scald with boiling White Stock (see Stock), drain and cool. Press sides of lettuce gently and lay them in a baking pan (pressed sides down), dot with butter and moisten with ½ cup of White Stock which has been enriched with ½ teaspoon beef extract. Place pan in moderate oven, baste occasionally and cook until lettuce has absorbed most of the liquid.

Braised Celery

Trim off outer stalks and leaves of celery. Split each heart in halves. Cook 1 tablespoon of chopped onion in 2 tablespoons of butter until onion is soft, about 5 minutes, arrange the split hearts of celery on top, moisten with Beef Stock (see Stock), cover pan and cook over very low heat 20 minutes or until celery is soft. Add ½ teaspoon beef extract to pan and blend it in with the Beef Stock and baste top of celery. Place pan in moderate oven, uncovered, add a few small bits of butter and cook until celery has absorbed most of the liquid. Baste celery once or twice while it is in the oven.

Braised Endive

Follow directions in above recipe, using endive instead of celery.

Carrots Vichy

Wash and scrape fresh carrots of uniform size. Cover with boiling water and cook until tender, add a little salt to the boiling water and 1 small bay leaf. Drain, and when cool enough to handle, slice them in thin slices, almost wafer-like. Melt a piece of butter in a frying pan, and when hot, add the sliced carrots to brown. Turn them carefully to brown on all sides. Remove to hot dish and sprinkle with finely chopped parsley.

Glazed Carrots

Wash, scrape and cut the carrots ball shape using a French vegetable cutter. (If a French vegetable cutter is not available, simply slice carrots in uniform size.) Cook them in boiling, salted water until soft... about 20 minutes. Drain, melt 4 tablespoons butter in frying pan and add 4 tablespoons of granulated sugar. When well-blended, add the drained carrots and cook until browned and glazed. Carefully turn while cooking to obtain an even glaze.

Creamed Carrots and Parsnips

Wash, scrape, and cut the carrots in uniform size. Drop them into boiling, salted water and cook until tender—15 to 20 minutes should be ample time. Also wash and scrape the parsnips and cut them into small pieces and start them to cook in boiling, salted water. Do not cook both vegetables in the same water, but use 2 different saucepans for this purpose. You want the individual flavor of the carrots and parsnips, and if they were both cooked in the same water, the parsnip flavor would predominate. When carrots and parsnips have cooked until tender, drain off the water and put the vegetables into a Cream Sauce. (See Sauces.)

String Beans

Wash beans in cold water and remove strings. Cut each bean in halves, lengthwise, oppsite the string side. Cover with boiling, salted water or steam until beans are soft, 30 to 45 minutes. Drain, add a piece of fresh butter and season with salt and pepper.

New Lima Beans

Shell limas and cover with cold water 20 minutes. Drain, cover with boiling, salted water and cook until soft, 20 to 30 minutes. Drain, add a piece of fresh butter and season with salt and pepper.

New Peas

Shell peas and cover with cold water for 20 minutes. Drain, cover with boiling, salted water and cook until soft, 20 to 30 minutes. Drain, add a piece of fresh butter and season with salt and pepper.

Pea Loaf

Soak dried peas overnight. Drain and start to cook in cold water with a small sprig of mint. Drain and rub the peas through a sieve. To every 2 cups of sieved peas, add 1 cup of bread crumbs, 1 egg slightly beaten, 1 teaspoon of chopped onion, salt and pepper to taste and 1½ cups of milk. Turn into a buttered mold and bake in a moderate oven (325°) for 45 or 50 minutes. Turn from mold and serve with Cream Sauce. (See Index on Sauces.)

Haricots Panaché

This is a combination of 3 fresh green vegetables.

Combine equal portions of new string beans, new lima beans and new green peas, which have been cooked separately in boiling, salted water. When vegetables are drained, season with salt and pepper, add cream to cover, heat and serve.

Beets, Home Style

Cover the beets with boiling water and cook until soft. The time required for cooking depends entirely on the size and age of the beets. Skin the beets while hot by holding them under cold water. Slice the beets and keep them hot while you make the following sauce to pour over them: Mix ¾ cup sugar with ½ tablespoon corn starch. Add ½ cup of vinegar, 6 whole cloves and let the mixture boil for 5 minutes. Pour over beets and let stand on a warm part of the range for 30 minutes. Add 1 tablespoon of fresh butter just before serving. Stir and serve.

Baked Beans

Wash and cover 2 cups of pea beans with 4 cups of cold water and place in a cool place to soak overnight. In the morning, if the beans have not absorbed all the water, drain it off and save it; although this proportion is just about right for complete absorption of the water. Start the beans to cook with fresh cold water to cover, about 3½ cups, and cook over low heat in a tightly covered saucepan. Beans must not boil, so remember to keep the heat low and the saucepan tightly covered while they are simmering. By doing this, the process becomes one of steaming, and the beans will swell and gradually absorb some of the water. 1 hour of simmering (from the time the simmering point is reached) is ample time to prepare the beans for the bean pot and oven cooking. Carefully drain the beans, saving the water. Place a slice of salt pork on the bottom of the earthen pot and put in the beans. Now, bury a piece of scored salt pork, weighing about ½ pound, in the center of the beans and prepare the seasoning as follows: ½ cup molasses mixed with ½ cup bean water or ½ cup plain boiling water, ½ teaspoon salt, ½ teaspoon mustard ¼ teaspoon paprika and 1 scant teaspoon of finely chopped onion. Mix thoroughly and pour over beans lifting the beans carefully with a spoon, so the seasoning will go to the bottom of the bean-pot. Cover bean-pot and place in a slow oven to bake for

6 or 7 hours. Uncover the bean-pot the last hour of cooking, so the salt pork can become crisp and browned. It may be necessary to add a little boiling water to the bean-pot during the oven cooking; so exercise your own judgement by looking at the beans every hour or so. Baked beans must not become dry, neither must they be watery. Serve with Boston Brown Bread. (In the following recipes:)

★

Beans à la Bostonnaise
Boston Brown Bread

There must be a thousand recipes for the preparation of beans in the Boston manner, and no two taste alike. Here is one of the best, which was prepared at the old Parker House in Boston, noted for its rolls, coffee and Brown Bread.

Carefully select 1 pound of pea or navy beans. Soak in cold water overnight in a big earthen crock. Drain them off in the morning. Add fresh water and heat them, taking great care not to allow the water to come to a boil. This is to prevent the skin of the beans from bursting. You can determine when the preliminary cooking of the beans is sufficient by examining them to see if the skins will burst easily. A slight touch of the fingers or even a vigorous breath blown on them will break the skins. Drain off the warm water and allow cold water to run over the beans. Cover the bottom of an earthen pot or casserole with a layer of beans, then place a small piece of a rind of fat salt pork over them. Do not pour all the beans into the pot at the same time, as the idea is to season each layer of beans and rind until the crock is full. The seasoning consists of 1 teaspoon of mustard, a little pepper, a teaspoon of salt, ½ cup of brown sugar and 1 cup of pork chopped into small bits. Add a little of this seasoning to each layer and build up until the crock is full. Then pour ½ cup of molasses over the top and add enough water to almost fill the crock. Spread a few slices of salt pork over the beans. Place a lid on the crock and cook slowly for about 7 hours. Shortly before the beans are cooked, remove the cover and allow them to brown.

A night and a day are essential for the correct preparation of beans. The Bostonian starts very early on Saturday morning to cook them, for they are the New England Sunday breakfast. And Sunday breakfast wouldn't be complete without Boston Brown Bread:

The ingredients are 1 cup of rye meal or barley flour, 1 cup of granulated corn meal, 1 cup of Graham flour or oat flour, 2 cups sour milk or buttermilk, 1 teaspoon salt, a short tablespoon of soda and 1 short cup of molasses. By short spoon or cup, I mean about three-quarters full. Some Down East chefs substitute 2 cups of sweet milk for the sour milk, while still others discard both sweet and sour milk and use plain water.

Sift and mix the dry ingredients, add the molasses and milk, stir until the whole is well-mixed, then turn into a buttered mold and steam 3 or 4 hours. The cover of the mold is always buttered before it is placed on the mold. Then it is tied down tight with heavy string. The mold should never be more than two-thirds full.

Any empty tin receptacle will do for a mold. After you are sure that the lid is securely tied down, place the mold on a trivet in a larger pan of boiling water, which should never rise more than half-way up the mold. Add water as needed and steam for at least 4 hours. If the lid has not been tight, it is possible that the bread will need drying out in a warm oven for a few minutes. The oven should not be too hot.

Kidney Beans en Casserole

This is a good emergency recipe to use when you haven't time to soak and cook the dried beans. Purchase the canned kidney beans. Season highly with salt, a few grains of cayenne and a dash of Worcestershire sauce. Place a piece of fat salt pork in bottom of a casserole and pour the beans over it. Insert another piece of salt pork on top of the beans and bake in a moderate oven (dish uncovered) until the pork is cooked and browned.

Sauerkraut, German Style

Sauerkraut requires long slow cooking—6 or 7 hours, so start it well in advance of the rest of the dinner. To 1 quart of sauerkraut, add 2 cups diced apple and 2 tablespoons of drippings or half butter and half drippings. Add enough water to the sauerkraut to keep it covered while cooking. Add a little water every hour or so of cooking and keep the saucepan covered. Toward the last hour of cooking, uncover the saucepan and let some of the water evaporate. Season to taste with salt.

Purée of Parsnips

Wash and scrape 6 medium-sized parsnips. Cut into thin slices and cover with boiling water and cook until soft... 15 to 20 minutes. Drain and force the parsnips through a purée sieve and add a slice of butter and ½ teaspoon of salt. Stir, mix thoroughly and serve. Green peas, beans, chestnuts, spinach and artichokes may be prepared in the same manner.

Glazed Onions

Cook small white onions in boiling water until tender... about 25 to 30 minutes. Drain and dry on a towel. Melt 4 tablespoons of butter in frying pan and add 4 tablespoons of granulated sugar. When well blended, add the onions and cook until browned and glazed. Turn the onions frequently to obtain an even glaze.

Table Celery

Trim off outer stalks and leaves and wash celery in plenty of cold water. Split the celery hearts lengthwise in 4 parts, wrap in wet cheesecloth and keep on ice until needed.

Broccoli, Hollandaise Sauce

Wash broccoli in cold water and let stand 30 minutes. Drain, cover with boiling, salted water and cook 30 minutes or until broccoli is soft. Drain, arrange on hot plates and serve Hollandaise Sauce separately. (See Index on Sauces.)

Escalloped Eggplant

Peel and cut an eggplant in small cubes. Cook in boiling water for 15 minutes. Drain and add ¼ cup of finely chopped parsley, a slight grating of onion, 2 tablespoons of finely chopped green pepper and 1½ cups of White Sauce (see Sauces). Turn into a baking dish, cover top with buttered bread crumbs and bake in a moderate oven for 35 minutes.

Fried Eggplant

Wash eggplant but do not peel. Cut in crosswise slices ½ inch thick. Sprinkle with salt and pepper and roll in flour. Dip in slightly beaten egg, and then in cracker crumbs. Fry in deep hot fat or oil (370°) until nicely browned. Fat should be hot enough to brown a piece of bread in 1 minute.

Zucchini (Italian Marrow)

Zucchini is a member of the summer squash family, and the fact that they are picked from the vine before they attain full growth makes them a delicacy. Zucchini is cooked with the skin on by covering them with boiling, salted water and are served in the same manner as asparagus. Small zucchini are sliced and cooked like eggplant.

PASTA

13

Spaghetti al Tonno —with Tuna Fish

Cook ½ pound of spaghetti in plenty of boiling, salted water until tender. This will require about 15 minutes. While it is cooking, prepare sauce as follows: Chop very fine 1 button of garlic and several sprigs of parsley. Now put 4 tablespoons of pure olive oil in a small saucepan and start to cook over low heat. When oil is hot, put in finely chopped garlic and parsley, a very little salt and pepper, and flaked tuna fish. Let this cook for about 5 minutes, then add 3 tablespoons of thick Tomato Sauce (see Sauces) and a little water. Let cook 5 minutes longer and remove from heat. Strain water off spaghetti and put it on large platters. Pour sauce over top. Mix thoroughly and serve.

★

This recipe, as suggested by Biaglo Moretti, a Roman chef, is prepared in the tradition of true Italian spaghetti. The unusual feature of Spaghetti al Tonno is that there is no Parmesan cheese grated into it like most spaghetti recipes. This is because Parmesan is rarely mixed in with recipes calling for liberal use of olive oil.

Tortellini al Lugo

Prepare a pasta made with 4 cups flour, 4 eggs, a little salt and olive oil—then roll flat. Let it stand like this about 30 minutes and then roll it as thin as possible. From this paste cut out small half ovals and in each put 1 teaspoonful of stuffing made of cooked chicken, liver of chicken and fat of bacon, the whole well-minced and forced through a sieve, and season it with salt, pepper, cinnamon, nutmeg and grated cheese. Then roll up these half ovals from the straight end, seeing that the stuffing is kept well in the pasta. Afterward put together the two ends, forming a ring. Cook these rings—Tortellini—for about 20 minutes in plenty of water.

On the side, prepare a sauce made of the extract of beef, a little butter, just a little onion, carrots, celery and garlic. When this is cooked, add a little red wine; later add a little flour to thicken it, and add some Tomato Sauce. (See index for Sauce.) Serve.

★

Marchese Bufalini, a nobleman of Italy, has given this recipe, which was prepared in his famous restaurant, the Buca Lapi of Florence. Bufalini was the first restaurateur to have the dynamo-equipment to keep his food in a refrigerated capacity. This contributed to maintaining the quality of the menu served in the Buca Lapi.

Tortellini al Lugo was the specialty at his restaurant and was strictly Florentine. The entrée for the pasta was simply a T-bone steak that was broiled over a charcoal grill. The dinner started with the pasta, Tortellini, the steak was then served with white asparagus (from the Tuscan Valley) that was placed in hot clarified butter and garnished with grated Parmesan cheese.

Fettuccine, Alfredo

★

In my opinion, the best form of pasta is fettuccine, and the finest fettuccine was produced by Alfredo, Cavaliere della Corona d'Italia. Fettuccine made Alfredo a cavaliere of Italy, and he was honored by the king for his fine preparation and gourmet quality, which was envied by all the rival chefs of Italy.

His restaurant was located on the Via della Scrofa in Rome. It was here that he achieved Fettuccine:

He put a kilo of flour (which is 2⅕ pounds) into a porcelain mixing bowl. Then, he dropped in 5 egg yolks, a glass of water and a little salt. He kneaded the mixture long and vigorously, and then rolled it out very thin. It was cut into long strips and hung over a line to dry. When it was thoroughly dried out and ready for use, he boiled it for 15 minutes in salted water. Butter and Parmesan cheese were added in the kitchen while the fettuccine was piping hot, and the whole dish retained its heat while Alfredo added his master strokes. (For additional spicing, add chopped parsley, salt and pepper.)

For the second course Alfredo served Golden Escalops with Peas:

From a veal cutlet, cut the veal escalops thin—about the size of the base of a very small cup. Immerse them generously in mixed egg yolks, and flour them with finely grated Parmesan cheese. Fry slowly in butter—don't forget the peas.

BREAD

14

Spoon Bread

Milk
2 cups cornmeal
1 cup boiled rice
2 tablespoons melted butter
2 heaping teaspoons baking powder
2 eggs

Mix the meal, rice, baking powder and butter together with several cupfuls of milk. Break the eggs into it and mix again. The process is the same as making batter bread. Place in baking pan and bake for 30 minutes.

★

Spoon bread, which was called a Poor Man's Pudding, is from Virginia, the state of waffles and presidents. This delicious recipe was acquired from a very old lady in Charlottesville. It derives its name from the fact that it is served so soft that it must be dipped out and eaten with a spoon.

Whole Wheat Cup Cakes

2 cups whole wheat flour
4 teaspoons baking powder
¼ teaspoon soda
½ teaspoon salt
2 eggs
1½ cups sour milk
4 tablespoons vegetable oil
2 tablespoons honey

Mix together flour, baking powder, soda and salt. Stir and add unbeaten eggs, vegetable oil, sour milk and honey. When thoroughly mixed, pour into greased cup cake tins and bake in a hot oven (400°) for 25 minutes.

SALADS

15

Do not forget your vitamins in the daily selection of food. Uncooked fruit and vegetables supply necessary nutrients for the system, and it is just knowing how to select and combine them to get pleasant changes in the diet. Salads dressed with olive oil or a pure mayonnaise are excellent and should be considered an important part of the meal.

One of the tricks of making a real French salad, the kind that is mixed and served from a large salad bowl, is to have a chapon in the bowl while tossing the salad with the French Dressing. A chapon is a dry piece of bread rubbed with garlic and placed in the bowl to impart a slight flavor to the salad. Try combining three or four types of lettuce; such as iceburg, romaine, watercress and escarole with the chapon, and you will be agreeably surprised.

Waldorf Salad

To 1 cup of diced apple, add ½ cup diced celery, ½ cup chopped walnut meats, and ¼ cup of mayonnaise. Mix ingredients together, arrange a bed of crisp escarole or chickory and place the salad in the center. Sprinkle the top with a few grains of paprika.

Salad, Chiffonade Dressing

Select any type of lettuce the market offers; iceberg, romaine, escarole, chickory or endive. Wash the leaves in cold water and place in the refrigerator to chill. Make a French Dressing... 3 parts oil to 1 part vinegar, season with salt, pepper, paprika, a pinch of dry mustard and a tiny bit of sugar. I might suggest that you dissolve the seasonings in the vinegar, and then add the olive oil. To ½ cup French Dressing, add 1 hard-boiled egg chopped fine, 1 tablespoon finely chopped pimiento and 1 tablespoon finely chopped green pepper. Mix all ingredients together and serve on the crisp lettuce.

Avocado Salad

The Avocado is commonly known as the Alligator pear and it is usually split in halves, lengthwise, and a half is a portion. Split the avocado and carefully remove the seed and serve with a highly seasoned French Dressing made as follows: Dissolve 1 level teaspoon of dry mustard, ¼ teaspoon salt and ¼ teaspoon paprika in 3 tablespoons of strained lemon juice. Mix well and stir in 3 tablespoons of olive oil, and when lemon juice and oil are thoroughly blended, pour into a bowl or pitcher to be used at the table.

Asparagus Salad, Vinaigrette

Arrange steamed asparagus tips on lettuce leaves and dress with Vinaigrette Sauce made as follows: To ½ cup of well-seasoned French Dressing (see Index), add 2 tablespoons of finely chopped dill pickle, 1 teaspoon finely chopped chives and 1 teaspoon finely chopped parsley. Mix well and serve.

Endive and Beet Salad, Sour Cream Dressing

Wash endive and cut into quarters, lengthwise. Arrange 3 or 4 quarters of endive on salad plates with some thinly sliced cooked beets and serve with dressing made as follows: Whip ½ cup thick sour cream and add it to 1 cup of mayonnaise. Mix it well and serve.

String Bean Salad, French Dressing

I wonder why so many cooks cut string beans into small pieces instead of splitting them lengthwise. It may be that it saves a fraction of time, but certainly a lot is lost in the appearance of the vegetable.

String small, tender string beans and cut lengthwise, opposite the string side. Drop into boiling, salted water and cook until tender. Drain in a colander, and when cool, marinate in French Dressing (see Salad Dressings). Arrange on lettuce leaves and serve.

Tomato Surprise Salad

Select large firm tomatoes of uniform size. Scald them with boiling water and immediately plunge them into cold water. With a small sharp knife, remove the entire skin. Place them on a cutting board...stem end downward. Carefully cut a ¼-inch slice from the rounded part of the tomato. Lay the slice to one side and carefully scoop out the tomato and refill with finely diced celery and chopped stuffed olives, which have been seasoned with salt, pepper and mayonnaise. Build the filling of the tomato up rather high and cover with the slice of tomato which becomes a cap. Arrange on lettuce leaves and serve cold.

Tomato Aspic Salad

Soak 2 level tablespoons of gelatin in ½ cup cold water for 5 minutes. Cook 4 cups canned tomatoes 15 minutes with 2 tablespoons finely chopped onion, 6 celery leaves, ½ small bay leaf, ½ teaspoon salt and a few grains of cayenne pepper. Remove from heat, add 2 tablespoons vinegar and gelatin and stir until gelatin is dissolved. Strain into wet molds (tomato shape), and when thoroughly chilled, serve on lettuce and garnish with mayonnaise.

Vegetable Salad in Aspic

Soak 1 level tablespoon of gelatin in ¼ cup of cold water for 5 minutes. Add gelatin to 1 cup boiling water and stir until dissolved. Season with ¼ cup vinegar, 2 tablespoons lemon juice, ¼ cup sugar and ½ teaspoon salt. Strain through double thickness of cheesecloth, and just when it begins to stiffen, add 1 cup celery cut in small pieces, ½ cup finely shredded cabbage and 1 finely chopped pimiento. Pour into wet mold, and when thoroughly chilled, serve on a bed of watercress with Boiled Salad Dressing. (See Salad Dressings.)

Salmagundi Salad

To 2 cups of cold diced meat (lamb, beef, veal or pork), add ½ cup cooked diced potatoes, ½ cup cooked diced carrots and ½ cup fresh green peas or ½ cup string beans. Put ingredients in a mixing bowl and pour over ½ cup French Dressing made with equal parts of vinegar and oil... seasoned with pepper, salt, paprika, a pinch of mustard and 1 medium-sized onion chopped very fine. Let the meat and vegetables marinate in the French Dressing for 15 or 20 minutes. Then add ½ cup chopped sweet pickle and 2 hard-boiled eggs which have been chopped fine. Mix all together carefully with a cup of mayonnaise, taking care not to mash the vegetables in the mixing. Arrange on crisp lettuce leaves and decorate the salad with cold sliced beets, cut in diamond shape.

Fish Salad

This recipe can be made from any cold, boiled or steamed fish. Remove the skin and bones and flake it into small pieces. Place in a salad bowl a layer of cold, cooked, sliced potato, some cold, cooked butter beans and make a border of sliced beets. Pile up the flaked fish in the center, cover with Mayonnaise Dressing (see Index) and scatter the sieved yolk of a hard-boiled egg over the mayonnaise. If shrimps are available, they make a delicious addition to the salad. Garnish with parsley... either in sprigs or finely minced.

Chicken and Tongue Salad

To 1 cup of cooked diced chicken, add ½ cup cooked tongue (sliced thin and cut into strips). Make a French Dressing of equal parts olive oil and vinegar—seasoned with pepper, salt and paprika and marinate the chicken and tongue for 1 hour. Now, drain the meat from the marinade and place it in a mixing bowl with ½ cup diced celery. Mix thoroughly and place it on a bed of crisp lettuce leaves. Cover with mayonnaise and decorate the top with pimiento cut into small diamond shape pieces, and 6 rolled anchovies with a caper in the center. Quartered hard-boiled egg may also be added as a garniture.

Chicken and Fruit Salad

Slice the white meat from a boiled fowl and cut into suitable-sized pieces for a salad. Place in a cold salad bowl, and to 2 cups of white chicken, add 1 orange, cut into sections; about 1 dozen large grapes, cut in halves, lengthwise, and seeds removed; 1 dozen Salted Almonds (see Almonds), split in halves; and 1 small banana, thinly sliced. Add ¾ cup mayonnaise and mix well. Serve salad without lettuce. To cut out the entire section of orange, peel the orange first, and with a small sharp knife, remove white pulp with skin. Cut each section out, starting from the outside of the orange—working toward the center. Remove all seeds and membrane.

Fruit Salad

1 orange
1 pear
20 white grapes
1 small banana
½ apple
Lettuce

Cut orange in half and with a small sharp knife remove sections; cut pear in small pieces and cut grapes in halves and remove seeds. Slice banana; cut apple into small dice and squeeze the juice of half a lemon over banana and apple. Moisten salad with Mayonnaise or Fruit Salad Dressing (see section on Salad Dressings) and serve on lettuce leaves.

Hawaiian Salad

Cut up or shredded pineapple is used in this recipe. To 1 cup of pineapple, add ⅓ cup grated coconut, and moisten and mix with mayonnaise. Arrange the individual portions on crisp lettuce leaves and sprinkle the top with finely chopped peanuts. If fresh pineapple is used, it will be necessary to add a little sugar to it before combining it with the coconut. Canned pineapple is sweet enough and needs no extra sugar.

Orange Salad

Select solid seedless oranges for this salad. Peel them with a sharp knife, removing all the white pulp with the peel. Carefully remove each section from the peeled orange by cutting close to the membranes and lay them in a salad bowl on a bed of crisp watercress. If

it is possible to obtain some fresh green tarragon, add a few sprigs, which have been finely chopped. If green tarragon is not to be had, use tarragon vinegar to make the French Dressing (see Salad Dressings). Mix the French Dressing through the salad. Sprinkle with chopped Roasted Almonds (see Index) and serve.

Orange and Grapefruit Salad

Carefully peel 1 large orange and 1 small grapefruit. Use a small sharp knife taking care to remove all the white pulp with the peel. Remove the entire sections of orange and grapefruit by cutting close to the membrane sections and work from the outside to the center. Arrange crisp romaine leaves on salad plates and alternate the orange and grapefruit sections allowing about 6 or 8 sections for each portion. Garnish with 1 or 2 thin strips of canned pimiento. Serve with French Dressing. (See Index for Salad Dressing.)

Grapefruit and Pineapple Salad

Peel the grapefruit with a sharp knife, carefully removing the white pulp. Then remove the sections by cutting them away from the membrane and place in a cold salad bowl with an equal amount of cut up pineapple. If fresh pineapple is not available, use canned sliced pineapple. Add 8 or 10 mint cherries finely minced and mix with mayonnaise. Serve on crisp lettuce or chickory.

Cucumber and Pineapple Salad

Mix equal portions of finely diced cucumber and finely diced pineapple, about 1½ cups each, with ¼ cup chopped stuffed olives and ½ cup mayonnaise. Mix together and serve on shredded lettuce.

Stuffed Prune Salad

Ingredients include: 24 cooked prunes, one 3 oz. package of cream cheese, ½ cup cottage cheese, 1 cup chopped walnut meats, ½ teaspoon salt and ½ cup mayonnaise which has been diluted with strained lemon juice. Remove the stones from cooked prunes by making one incision with a small sharp knife. Mix prunes with cream and cottage cheese, chopped nuts and salt... add enough mayonnaise to moisten to obtain a light fluffy mixture and place 4 dressed prunes on a plate of shredded lettuce which has been slightly dressed with mayonnaise.

Pear and Pimiento Cheese Salad

Canned pears are to be used for this recipe, so place a can in the refrigerator to chill before making up the salad. Arrange 2 halves of pear (cut part downward) on a bed of crisp lettuce and cover the entire surface of the pear with riced Pimiento cheese. This is accomplished by pressing the Pimiento cheese through a ricer. Serve with French Dressing. (See Salad Dressings.)

SALAD DRESSINGS

16

It is a good plan to always have a quantity of Mayonnaise and French Dressing in the refrigerator. From these two basic dressings, many other varieties may be developed, and I know that you will find it more economical to make a quantity than to mix dressings every time a salad is served. Don't forget that the vitamins abound in fresh green leaves and vegetables, so plan them in your daily menus. A French Dressing should be made from pure olive oil...either Italian or French for perfect results. A very satisfactory Mayonnaise may be made with vegetable oil which is less expensive than olive oil.

French Dressing

Quantity Recipe:

1 cup olive oil
¼ cup vinegar
2 level teaspoons salt
1 level teaspoon pepper
1 level teaspoon paprika
½ teaspoon powdered sugar
½ teaspoon dry mustard
Few grains cayenne

Dissolve dry ingredients in vinegar, then add olive oil. Shake well before using.

Mayonnaise

Quantity Recipe:

4 egg yolks
1 quart salad oil
¾ cup vinegar
2 tablespoons lemon juice
1 teaspoon salt
1 teaspoon dry mustard
½ teaspoon white pepper
⅛ teaspoon cayenne

Have the ingredients and mixing utensils very cold before work begins. Put egg yolks into large mixing bowl; add seasonings and mix thoroughly. Beat in the lemon juice and add the oil, drop by drop.

When mixture thickens, add a few drops of vinegar, and then more oil. Continue this way until all the oil and vinegar is used. Beat well after each addition of oil. If the mayonnaise should separate while making it, get another bowl and 1 egg yolk and start beating the mixture into the fresh egg yolk. It will work out perfectly smooth.

Boiled Dressing

1 tablespoon flour
½ cup vinegar
1½ tablespoon sugar
1 teaspoon mustard
1 teaspoon salt
⅛ teaspoon cayenne
2 eggs
¾ cup milk
1 tablespoon butter

Mix and sift dry ingredients into top part of double boiler, add vinegar and beaten egg yolks. Stir until thoroughly mixed, add milk and cook over hot water until thick. Stir frequently to obtain a smooth mixture. Remove from hot water and add butter. Fold in beaten egg whites.

Sauce Vert

1 cup Mayonnaise
6 sprigs parsley
6 spinach leaves
6 green tarragon leaves
6 blades chives
1 small bunch watercress

Pound herbs in a mortar until reduced to a pulp. Force pulp through sieve and add 2 tablespoons strained pulp to Mayonnaise.

Thousand Island Dressing

Follow recipe for Russian Dressing (see Index). Just before serving add ½ cup whipped cream.

Pimiento Salad Dressing

½ cup Mayonnaise
¼ cup French Dressing (see Index)
2 tablespoons tomato catsup
1 tablespoon pimiento, finely minced
3 drops Tabasco sauce

Beat French Dressing into Mayonnaise, stir in tomato catsup, pimiento and Tabasco sauce.

Fruit Salad Dressing

1 egg
Pinch salt
1 tablespoon sugar
1 tablespoon cornstarch
1 cup canned pineapple juice
2 tablespoons lemon juice

Put slightly beaten egg, salt and sugar in a saucepan; add cornstarch which has been mixed with pineapple and lemon juice. Cook slowly until thickened. Chill and serve with any combination of fruit in a salad.

Chiffonade Salad Dressing

1 hard-boiled egg, finely chopped
1 tablespoon pimiento, finely chopped
½ cup French Dressing (see Index)
1 tablespoon green pepper, finely chopped

Stir finely chopped ingredients into the French Dressing and serve.

Sauce Tartare

½ cup Mayonnaise
½ teaspoon parsley
½ teaspoon chervil
½ teaspoon tarragon

½ teaspoon chives
½ teaspoon shallots
½ teaspoon capers
1 teaspoon vinegar pickle

Finely chop ingredients and mix into Mayonnaise. Keep in a cool place until needed.

Russian Dressing

1 cup Mayonnaise
1 tablespoon green pepper, finely minced
½ cup Chili sauce
4 stuffed olives, finely minced
1 teaspoon shallots, minced (optional)

Stir Chili sauce into Mayonnaise, add finely minced green pepper and olives. Keep in a cool place until needed.

Vinaigrette Sauce

1 cup French Dressing (see Index)
2 tablespoons vinegar pickle, finely chopped
1 teaspoon parsley, finely chopped
1 tablespoon capers, finely chopped
1 tablespoon chives, finely chopped

Stir finely chopped ingredients into French Dressing.

Epicurean Sauce

½ cup heavy cream
4 tablespoons Mayonnaise
2 tablespoons fresh grated horseradish
1 tablespoon tarragon vinegar
¼ teaspoon salt
Few grains cayenne
1 teaspoon English mustard

Beat cream until stiff, stir in the Mayonnaise, grated horseradish and dry ingredients which have been dissolved in the vinegar.

Roquefort Cheese Dressing

1 cup French Dressing (see Index)
¼ pound Roquefort cheese

Break cheese in small pieces using prongs of a fork (don't mash). Stir cheese into French Dressing.

Mayonnaise Figaro

1 cup mayonnaise
1 tablespoon finely chopped shallots, blanched
¼ cup Tomato Purée
Few grains cayenne

Prepare Tomato Purée by cooking one small can of tomatoes until reduced to one-half. Force pulp through sieve and simmer until thickness and desired quantity is obtained. Blanch finely chopped shallots by covering with boiling water, then drain. Gradually add Tomato Purée and blanched shallots to Mayonnaise, season with cayenne and stir until thoroughly mixed.

Sour Cream Dressing

1 cup Mayonnaise
½ cup thick sour cream

Beat sour cream into mayonnaise.

Horseradish Mayonnaise

½ cup Mayonnaise
¼ cup whipped cream
¼ cup grated horseradish
1 tablespoon vinegar
¼ teaspoon salt
¼ teaspoon paprika
Few grains cayenne

Combine grated horseradish, vinegar, salt, paprika and cayenne; stir it into Mayonnaise, and when well blended, fold in whipped cream.

EGGS

17

Plain Omelet, Poulard

Break the eggs in a wooden bowl and put in 1 tablespoon of milk for each egg. Beat well with a wooden fork and season with salt and pepper. Heat the omelet pan and melt a piece of butter that will cover the entire bottom of the pan and also the sides as the omelet rises in cooking, and it is just as important to have the sides of the pan buttered as the bottom. Pour in the beaten eggs and turn the pan over the heat so that the omelet browns evenly. Watch and regulate the heat as a high heat will burn the omelet before it is cooked. When the omelet is set, pour a little thick cream in the center, and with the rounded part of a tablespoon, smooth it out to the sides taking care not to bring the cream beyond the edge of the omelet. With a deft turn fold it over in the pan and then onto a hot platter. There is no economy in using substitutes, and the result will surely fall short of the mark; so in following this recipe, use the freshest eggs, butter and cream.

★

This omelet was created by Madame Poulard, who became world famous for making omelets. Madame Poulard prepared her specialty in her little hill-top Inn of Mont-St. Michel in the Normandy section of France.

Omelet, Cela

½ cup cooked chopped chicken
⅓ cup chopped mushrooms
2 tablespoons chopped shallots
4 eggs, separated
1 tablespoon grated Parmesan cheese
2 tablespoons butter
Cayenne pepper

Beat egg yolks until thick and lemon colored, then fold in beaten egg whites. Melt 1 tablespoon butter in a frying pan over medium-low heat. Turn the pan so the butter goes up the sides, this keeps the eggs from sticking. Pour in eggs. While eggs are cooking, sauté the chicken, mushrooms and shallots in 1 tablespoon butter for 5 minutes. Season with cayenne pepper. When eggs begin to set, pour sautéed mixture carefully onto one side of the omelet. Sprinkle with Parmesan cheese and fold the omelet. Remove to hot platter and sprinkle with finely grated Parmesan cheese.

Omelet au Fines Herbes

Follow directions contained in Plain Omelet, Poulard. While beating the eggs, add 1 tablespoon finely chopped parsley and 1 tablespoon finely chopped chives. This would be the correct amount of finely chopped herbs to add to a 4 egg omelet. Pour mixture into hot buttered frying pan and cook until lightly browned.

Shad Roe Omelet, Bercy

Cover shad roe with boiling, salted water and simmer 20 minutes. Drain, remove membrane and cut roe in pieces about the size of a small walnut. Prepare Sauce Bercy by cooking 1 cup of Tomato Sauce until quantity is reduced to ¾ of a cup, stir in 1 tablespoon beef extract and strain sauce through a fine sieve. Add roe to Sauce Bercy. Make a 6 egg omelet, and just before folding, add half the shad roe and sauce. Remove to hot platter and pour remaining roe and sauce around open edge of omelet. (See Index for Sauces.)

Creole Omelet

★

The chef, Escoffier, claimed to have had enough recipes *des oeufs* to cook eggs differently every day for twelve months. This recipe will give you a variation of the Omelet with Creole sauce to compete with the infamous French Chef, Escoffier.

Scald and skin 6 ripe tomatoes and chop them fine. Set aside. Slice and chop 2 onions, mince ½ clove of garlic. Add a heaping tablespoon of bread crumbs, which have been fried with a small pat of butter—until they are very brown and crispy. Then add the tomatoes and salt and pepper to taste. The Creole, also, always use a slight dash of cayenne. Let stew for at least 1 hour. Take 6 eggs, separate—beat the yolks to a cream and the whites of the eggs to a froth. Then beat them all together. Place 1 tablespoon of butter in a frying pan, and when it melts, add the omelet. Remember that the tomatoes and the eggs are in separeate pans. As the omelet becomes set, pour the well-done tomatoes on it, fold the omelet over and cook for 2 minutes longer. Roll into a dish and serve hot.

Omelet Argentine

Break 6 eggs in a bowl and beat with a wire whip or egg beater. Season with salt and pepper and strain the eggs into another bowl, add several bits of butter and beat again. Melt 2 tablespoons of clarified butter in a frying pan, and when it becomes hot, pour in the beaten eggs and stir lightly with a spoon. When the eggs begin to thicken, take a spoon or fork and gently scoop out a little of the center and bring it over to the edges. Do not disturb the bottom of the omelet while working from the center to the edges. Fill center of omelet with eggplant which has been peeled, cut into ¼-inch squares, sautéed in butter and enrichened with a little beef extract. Fold the omelet carefully having the edges meet. Serve with Tomato Sauce (see Index for Sauce).

Spanish Omelet

Make 1 cup of Creole Sauce (see Index on Sauces). Cook a 6 egg omelet in buttered pan until delicately browned. Just before folding, add half the Creole Sauce. Remove to hot platter and pour remaining sauce around omelet.

Omelet Soufflé

6 egg whites
4 egg yolks
2 tablespoons powdered sugar
1 tablespoon lemon juice

Beat yolks till thick and lemon colored, add powdered sugar and lemon juice. Fold stiffly beaten whites into yolks and pour mixture into a buttered baking dish. Sprinkle top with powdered sugar which has been mixed with a small quantity of cinnamon. Place in a moderate oven until lightly browned.

Eggs au Beurre Noir, (Black Butter)

4 eggs
1 tablespoon butter
Salt and pepper
1 tablespoon vinegar
1 teaspoon finely chopped chives
1½ tablespoons butter

Melt 1 tablespoon butter in small frying pan and cook eggs over low heat until set. Remove to hot plates, season with salt and pepper and sprinkle over with finely chopped chives. Add remaining butter to frying pan, let it turn brown, add vinegar, remove from heat and pour over eggs.

Eggs, Bercy

Butter small egg dishes. Break 2 eggs into each dish and place in moderate oven to cook, about 5 minutes. Garnish each dish with 1 broiled sausage, 1 chicken liver that has been dipped in flour and sautéed in butter and 2 tablespoons of Sauce Bercy. (See Index for Sauce.)

Eggs Aurora

Cut hard-boiled eggs in halves, lengthwise. Remove yolks and divide halved whites into 4 parts. Place these in a saucepan and season with salt, paprika and a very little nutmeg. Add enough thick Béchamel Sauce to cover, and also some finely minced chives. The correct proportion would be 1 teaspoon of minced chives to 1 cup of Béchamel Sauce. Use your own judgment, however, in regard to individual taste. Carefully mix all together taking care not to break the small pieces of egg whites and transfer to a baking dish. Rub the yolks through a wire sieve directly over the eggs and carefully brush the entire surface with Hazel-Nut Butter. Place in a hot oven to heat and serve immediately. (See Index for Béchamel Sauce and Hazel-Nut Butter.)

Coddled Eggs

Carefully place the eggs in a large saucepan and pour 1 quart of boiling water over them. The water will retain enough heat to cook the eggs in 8 or 10 minutes. The white will be perfectly coagulated, and the egg is much more palatable when cooked slowly and thoroughly instead of "boiled." It is the best way to cook eggs in the shell.

Eggs au Miroir, Provençal

Cut firm ripe tomatoes in halves, crosswise. Remove some of the seeds and carefully fry in olive oil. Cook only long enough to soften without losing the shape. Butter a baking dish and carefully transfer the halved tomatoes, sprinkle with finely chopped parsley which has been rubbed with garlic and a light sprinkling of fine buttered bread crumbs. Place in hot oven to brown about 10 minutes, and dot with a few pieces of butter during the cooking. Arrange 1 Miroired egg, as prepared in Eggs au Miroir, on each tomato and serve immediately.

Eggs au Miroir

Butter small egg casserole dishes and carefully drop 1 egg into each one. Place in hot oven and baste the yolk with very hot butter several times during the cooking. When eggs are set, remove from oven and serve immediately. Season with a very little salt and white pepper.

Scrambled Eggs with Fresh Tomato

Lightly beat the eggs and add 1 tablespoon of thin cream to every egg, salt and pepper to taste. Cut fresh tomatoes into quarters and stew them in a small saucepan until soft but not watery. Scramble the eggs, and just as they are forming, take a fork and lift the tomato pulp from the juice and add it to the eggs. Mix the tomato pulp through the eggs while they are cooking. Canned tomatoes may be substituted if fresh ones are not obtainable, but in either case, use only the tomato pulp and not the juice. Serve with triangles of toast.

Eggs Pastorella

A slice of mozzarella is put into cream, then flour, and then fried in olive oil. A fried egg is put over this fried piece of cheese, and over the egg put 1 slice of grilled ham. Arrange a few pieces of these eggs on a dish, adding over all a small quantity of fried, fresh mushrooms. Prepare quickly and serve immediately and very hot.

★

This recipe was offered by the winner of the 1924 Italian Chef's Exposition held in Rome. His name was Lanzi Francesco, chef of the Albergo Palazzo in Rome. The recipe he prepared was called, "Cold Lamb Tutenkhamun." For your curiosity, here is an idea of how you would prepare it, if you had the "gilded leaves!"

"Take a nice lamb saddle and roast it in a way so that it doesn't get too dry. When it is cold, the saddle has to be filleted. On the bone lay some Purée de Foie Gras, and then rearrange the fillets on the saddle, putting between them some Foie Gras Natural. Over the entire saddle goes brown Chaud-Froid sauce made with lamb itself.

The saddle is decorated with different kinds of vegetables, Truffles of Perigord and tongue. These decorations must be made all in dice, to resemble a mosaic. The saddle must be presented on a dish over which there ought to be a small sarcophagus with 4 mummies at the 4 corners. Decorate the whole dish with roses and gilded leaves."

Eggs Benedict

As this recipe calls for a Hollandaise Sauce, I would suggest making the sauce first, and then proceeding with the rest. (See Index for

Sauce.) Tear apart and toast an English muffin. Spread lightly with butter and place a slice of thin broiled ham on each half of muffin. The piece of ham is to be the same size as the muffin. Place a Poached Egg (see Techniques) on top of the ham and cover all with a liberal quantity of Hollandaise Sauce. Decorate the center at the very top with a piece of truffle cut in diamond shape or with a slice of mushroom.

Eggs Bombay

Poach 6 eggs (see Techniques). Arrange eggs on small circular pieces of buttered toast and cover each egg with 3 tablespoons of Curry Sauce made as follows: Melt 2 tablespoons butter, blend in 1½ tablespoons flour and 1 tablespoon of curry powder; gradually add 1 cup of hot White Stock and stir until boiling point is reached. Let boil 2 minutes, remove from heat and add 1 egg yolk slightly beaten with 2 tablespoons heavy cream. (See Index for Stock.)

Egg and Asparagus Timbale

2 eggs
Few grains pepper
Few grains salt
1 cup milk
1 cup cold asparagus

Beat eggs slightly; add seasonings and milk. Fill 6 small buttered timbale molds ¾ full with asparagus which has been cut into small pieces (asparagus tips are just right for this recipe) and cover with egg mixture. Place timbales in a pan of hot water. Bake in moderate oven (325°) until firm... about 30 minutes.

Egg Timbale, Arlequin

Sprinkle small buttered timbale molds with finely chopped beef tongue, truffles or mushrooms and parsley. Spread a thin layer of Chicken Forcemeat (see Glossary) over chopped tongue, truffles and parsley and break 1 egg into each mold. Place timbales in pan of hot water and cook in moderate oven until egg is cooked... about 10 minutes. Serve with Tomato Sauce (see Index on Sauces).

Plain Egg Timbale

2 tablespoons butter
2 tablespoons flour
1¼ cups milk
⅛ teaspoon pepper
⅛ teaspoon celery salt
Few grains cayenne pepper
6 eggs
½ teaspoon salt
(Optional) 2 tablespoons finely chopped parsley

Cream the butter, add flour, and gradually add scalded milk. Add seasonings and cook in top part of double boiler several minutes. Separate eggs, beat yolks until thick and lemon-colored. Add beaten yolks to milk sauce. Beat egg whites until stiff and dry, and fold into egg yolk and milk mixture. Parsley should be added to the mixture at this time. Turn mixture into buttered timbale molds, set in a pan of hot water (like baked custard) and bake in a moderate oven (325°) until firm.

Egg Nog (Orange)

½ cup orange juice
1 tablespoon lemon juice
1 teaspoon sugar
1 egg
Ice to cool
Few grains nutmeg

Dissolve sugar in fruit juices. Pour into blender containing cracked ice; add egg and blend very well. Strain into glass and top with a few grains of nutmeg.

CAKES & ICINGS

18

Butter Cakes

You will need the best ingredients suited for this purpose, like: Cake flour, fresh eggs, finely granulated sugar, fresh spices, nuts, butter or margarine, etc. Very successful cakes can be made with other shortenings instead of butter, but they do not taste quite so good.

Measure all ingredients accurately; the "cooking-school cup" holds one-half pint. Measure flour after once sifting, fill the cup with a spoon, and level off cup with a knife; do not pack the flour in cup.

Have pans ready and ingredients measured before beginning to mix the cake.

Have the heat in such a condition that the oven will be ready for use when the batter is mixed.

Be sure your egg beater is absolutely dry and clean before using.

Always work butter to a cream before adding any sugar to it. In cold weather, rinse the bowl with hot water and wipe dry before putting the butter into it.

The flour and milk should always be added alternately, beating hard after each addition.

The last motion in mixing a butter cake is to fold in the stiffly beaten egg whites.

Small and layer cakes call for a hotter oven than thick cakes. Do not attempt to bake cakes of varying thicknesses or of different mixtures at the same time. The heat of the oven can be regulated to only one mixture and one thickness of batter at a time.

Often you may know when a butter cake, that has not been disturbed during baking, is finished baking because it has separated from the sides of the pan.

A cake tester inserted in center of cake should come out without any particles adhering to it when cake is done.

The appearance of the cake, in connection with the time it has been in the oven, is the only safe guide to its baking.

A cake may be gently moved in the first and last quarters of time in baking; in the second and third quarters, the cell walls are not firm, and a jar of the oven will cause them to settle. The warm, expanded air, which makes the cake light, has already been evolved, and there is nothing present to lighten it again.

If the heat is too hot, lower the heat; protect the cake with paper or set a pan of hot water in the oven to cool it, but do not move the cake. Open the oven door a reasonable number of times, but shut it gently.

Never jar or move a cake in the oven before it is thoroughly baked, because this contracts the delicate, incompletely stiffened cell walls and will cause a "heavy" cake.

Old-Fashioned Strawberry Shortcake

2 cups flour
4 teaspoons baking powder
2 teaspoons sugar
½ teaspoon salt
3 tablespoons shortening
¾ cup milk
1 quart strawberries

Mix and sift dry ingredients. Rub in shortening and gradually add milk to make a soft dough. Smooth out and bake in a deep greased layer cake pan in a hot oven 20 to 25 minutes. Split, spread with sweet butter while hot and arrange whole berries on split under part. Put on top and pour crushed, sweetened berries over all.

Prize Devil's Food

½ cupful butter or substitute
2 cups light brown sugar
2 eggs
2¼ cupfuls cake flour
¼ teaspoonful salt
½ cupful sour milk or buttermilk
½ cupful boiling water
1 teaspoonful soda
1½ squares chocolate, melted, (or ½ cupful cocoa)
1 teaspoonful vanilla
1 teaspoonful baking powder

Cream shortening, add 1 cupful sugar gradually, creaming mixture thoroughly. Beat eggs until light. Add the other cupful of sugar to the eggs, mixing well. Add this egg mixture to the creamed shortening and sugar and beat hard. Sift flour once, measure, add baking powder, add salt and sift 3 times. Then add to the first mixture, alternating with the sour milk, beating batter hard after each addition of flour and milk. Into the boiling water, stir the soda and the melted chocolate or cocoa, and beat into the cake mixture. Add vanilla. Bake in three layers in a moderate oven (325°). Spread a white icing between the layers and on top and sides of cake. (See recipe for Fluffy Boiled Icing.)

Angel Food Cake

1 cupful egg whites (8 to 10 eggs)
¾ teaspoonful cream of tartar
1¼ cupfuls granulated sugar (sifted)
¾ teaspoonful vanilla extract
¼ teaspoonful almond extract
1 cupful cake flour,
sifted once, measured, and sifted 4 times
¼ teaspoonful salt

Pour the egg whites on a large platter or in a large bowl, add salt and beat until foamy. Add cream of tartar and continue beating until the eggs are stiff enough to hold up in peaks, but not dry. Fold in the sugar, 1 tablespoonful at a time. Add flavoring. Fold in the flour in the same manner as the sugar. Pour into an ungreased pan and bake in a very slow oven (275°) 50 to 60 minutes, increasing heat slightly when cake is almost done. Remove cake from oven and invert tin for 1 hour or until cake is cold. Remove cake from tin with a broad-bladed knife.

With good results, 4 tablespoons of cold water may be substituted with 2 egg whites. One-half of this recipe may be used to make a small Angel Cake, and the yolks which are left to make a Sponge Cake.

Sunshine Cake

8 eggs
½ teaspoon salt
1 cup sugar
¾ cup sifted pastry flour
½ teaspoon cream of tartar
1 teaspoon lemon extract
½ teaspoon almond extract

Separate eggs. Add salt to yolks and beat until thick and lemon colored. Add flavoring extracts to beaten yolks. Beat egg whites to a stiff froth, fold in sugar, then combine with beaten yolks. Fold in flour which has been sifted with cream of tartar. Bake in an ungreased tube pan in a moderate oven (325°) for 50 minutes.

Cinnamon Layer Cake

½ cup butter
1 cup sugar
2 eggs
½ cup milk
1¾ cups flour
2½ teaspoons baking powder
1 tablespoon cinnamon

Cream butter, add sugar and beaten eggs. Mix and sift dry ingredients and add to first mixture, alternately with milk. Pour into 2 buttered layer cake pans and bake in a moderate oven—20 to 25 minutes. When layers are cool, spread with Butter Cream icing:

Butter Cream Icing

½ cup sweet butter
2 cups powdered sugar
Few grains salt
1 egg yolk
½ teaspoon vanilla
Cream to smooth

Cream butter and sugar, add egg yolk, salt and vanilla. Smooth to proper consistency with cream.

Pineapple Up-side Down Cake

This cake can also be made with cooked, pitted prunes. It is baked in a large frying-pan.

Cut ½ cup of butter into small pieces and place in a cold frying pan. Add 1 cup of brown sugar and 1 can sliced pineapple (drained from juice). Arrange pineapple slices to cover bottom of frying pan. Cover with sponge batter made as follows: Beat 3 eggs until light, add 1 cup of sugar and 3 tablespoons of hot water. Mix and add 1 cup of flour which has been sifted with 2 teaspoons baking powder. Bake in moderate oven (350°) for 45 minutes. Remove cake while hot by inverting frying pan on cake plate.

Sponge Cake (6 Egg Yolks)

6 egg yolks
1 cup sugar
½ cup boiling water
1½ cups cake flour
½ teaspoon salt
2 teaspoons baking powder
1 teaspoon lemon extract

Beat egg yolks until light, thick and lemon colored; add sugar and beat well. Add boiling water, then sifted dry ingredients, beating thoroughly. Add flavoring which may be all lemon or half lemon and half almond. Pour batter into 2 paper-lined layer cake pans and bake in a moderate oven (375°) for 25 minutes. Put layers together with Vanilla Custard Filling:

Vanilla Custard Filling

4 egg yolks
¾ cup powdered sugar
¾ cup hot milk
1 teaspoon vanilla
1 cup sweet butter (creamed)

Beat egg yolks slightly and add powdered sugar. Stir hot milk in slowly and cook in top part of double boiler until boiling point is reached. Remove from water, add vanilla and gradually add butter which has been creamed. Stir until perfectly smooth.

Sponge Fruit Cake

4 eggs
1½ cups sugar
½ teaspoon salt
1 teaspoon flavoring extract

2 cups pastry flour
3 teaspoons baking powder
¾ cup boiling water
3 tablespoons candied pineapple, finely chopped
3 tablespoons candied citron, finely chopped
5 tablespoons candied cherries, finely chopped

Beat eggs until light, gradually add sugar and continue beating. Add salt and flavoring extract. Fold in pastry flour which has been sifted with baking powder, add boiling water, mix lightly and thoroughly, but do not beat the mixture. Fold in finely chopped fruit, pour into ungreased muffin tins and place at once in a hot oven (400°) to bake for 15 to 20 minutes.

Sour Cream Spice Cake

½ cup butter
2 cups brown sugar
3 egg yolks
2 cups pastry flour
¼ teaspoon salt
2 teaspoons ground cloves
2 teaspoons allspice
2 teaspoons cinnamon
1 teaspoon soda
1 cup sour cream
3 egg whites

Cream butter, gradually add brown sugar and cream again. Add yolks and beat thoroughly. Add dry ingredients which have been sifted together, alternately with sour cream. Fold in stiffly beaten egg whites and pour into a greased cake pan and bake in a moderate oven (350°) for 30 minutes.

Graham Cracker Cake

½ cup butter
¾ cup sugar
2 eggs
3¼ cups rolled and sifted graham crumbs
3 teaspoons baking powder
⅛ teaspoon salt

½ teaspoon cinnamon
1 cup milk

Cream the butter; beat in sugar and slightly beaten egg yolks. Roll the graham crackers (about 28 large ones) until crumbs are fine enough to pass through sieve. Then sift graham crumbs with baking powder, salt and cinnamon. Add cracker mixture to first mixture, alternately with milk. Beat egg whites very light and add to batter. Bake in shallow pans in moderate oven (350°) for 45 minutes. This cake is very nice when served with whipped cream.

Mocha Cake

1 cup sugar
2 cups cake flour
1 teaspoon baking powder
½ teaspoon soda
½ teaspoon salt
½ cup cocoa
⅓ cup melted butter
1½ cups sour milk or buttermilk

Sift and mix together sugar, flour, baking powder, soda, salt and cocoa. Add melted butter and sour milk and stir until thoroughly mixed. Bake in layers in moderate oven (375°) for 20 minutes.

Mocha Filling

1½ cups sugar
½ cup strong coffee
1 square chocolate (1 oz.)
⅛ teaspoon salt
2 egg whites

Boil sugar and coffee together until syrup spins a thread. Then pour the mixture into egg whites that have been stiffly beaten, beating constantly for 6 minutes. Add melted chocolate and salt; stir.

Mocha Cake (3 layer)
Pecan Pie
French Ice Cream

Mocha Butter Cream Icing

½ cup sweet butter
2 cups powdered sugar
4 tablespoons strong coffee
Few grains salt
1 square chocolate (1 oz.)
¼ teaspoon vanilla extract
Cream to smooth

Cream butter and gradually work in the sugar and coffee, vanilla and salt. Beat in the melted chocolate and smooth to proper consistency with cream.

Pound Cake

1¾ cups butter
2 cups sugar
8 eggs
⅛ teaspoon salt
3¾ cups cake flour
1 teaspoon baking powder
1 teaspoon mace or vanilla

Cream the butter and add the eggs, one at a time, without separating or beating. Sift the flour, measure, add the baking powder, salt and mace, if used, and sift again. Add the flour gradually and beat the batter hard. Turn into two greased and paper-lined (parchment or wax paper), brick-shaped pans, and bake 1 hour in oven set at 300° to 325°. Pound cake is not usually iced.

French Pancakes

½ cup flour
1 teaspoon baking powder
¼ teaspoon salt
1 egg
1 cup milk
¼ cup cream

Mix and sift flour, baking powder and salt. Add the egg that has been beaten with the milk and cream, and stir until perfectly smooth. Heat a frying pan which is about 8 inches in diameter, cover bottom and sides with butter, pour in just enough batter to cover bottom and cook until browned on both sides. Remove to hot plate, spread with jelly and roll. Sprinkle with powdered sugar.

Cheese Cake

Crust:

1 cup butter
1 cup sugar
1 egg
¼ cup milk
3 cups flour
½ teaspoon soda
1 teaspoon flavoring

Filling:

1½ cups cottage cheese (sieved)
½ cup sugar
3 tablespoons cream
Grated rind of 1 lemon
3 eggs
1 egg yolk (optional)

Cream butter; add sugar gradually and cream well together. Add unbeaten egg and beat thoroughly. Add milk, and when well-mixed, fold in flour which has been sifted with soda. Add flavoring. Roll out on floured wax paper to ¼-inch thickness and line pie or layer pan.

Filling: Mix together sieved cottage cheese, sugar, cream and grated lemon rind; then add well-beaten eggs. Fill lined pie or layer pan bake in a moderate oven (350°) about 35 minutes.

Apple Cake (German)

1 cup flour
1½ teaspoon baking powder
2 tablespoons sugar
½ teaspoon salt
2 tablespoons shortening
2 egg yolks

½ cup milk
2 apples
¼ cup sugar
½ teaspoon cinnamon
1 teaspoon grated lemon rind

Mix and sift together flour, baking powder, 2 tablespoons sugar and salt. Cut in shortening and add egg yolks which have been mixed with milk. Pour into shallow cake pan and top with apples which have been cut into eighths. Sprinkle top with sugar, cinnamon and lemon rind.

Jelly Roll

2 eggs
1 cup sugar
Grated rind of 1 lemon
1 tablespoon melted butter
⅓ cup hot water
1 cup cake flour
1½ teaspoons baking powder
⅛ teaspoon salt

Beat eggs until light and lemon colored. Add sugar gradually and grated lemon rind, melted butter and hot water. Sift pastry flour, baking powder and fold into first mixture. Line shallow pan with parchment or wax paper, turn in batter and bake in a moderate oven (350°) for 20 minutes. Turn out of pan at once onto a clean towel, cut off all four crisp edges, spread with jelly and roll lightly and quickly. Sprinkle with confectioner's sugar.

Chocolate Marshmallow Cream Roll

4 eggs, beaten light without separating
1 cup granulated sugar
1 cup cake flour
2 tablespoons milk
2 tablespoons cocoa
Pinch of salt
1 teaspoon baking powder
1 teaspoon vanilla

Gradually beat the sugar into the eggs, add the milk and vanilla, then fold in the flour, sifted with the baking powder, salt and cocoa. Turn into a baking pan 13½ × 8½ inches, lined with greased parchment or wax paper. Bake about 15 minutes in moderate oven at 350°. Turn onto a cloth or paper, trim off the crisp edges on the four sides, and when cooled somewhat, spread with Fluffy Boiled Icing for filling and roll like a Jelly Roll; roll with the cloth and let stand half an hour or longer. Spread Chocolate Confectioner's Icing (see Cakes and Icings) over the outside of the roll.

Chou-Paste for Éclairs and Cream Puffs

1 cupful boiling water
½ cupful butter or substitute
1 cupful cake flour
3 eggs

Set the water and shortening over the heat in a small saucepan; when boiling sift in the flour, cook and stir constantly until the mixture leaves the sides of the pan a smooth, compact mass. Turn into a mixing bowl, break in 1 egg and beat until the mixture is smooth; beat in the second egg, then the third egg. The eggs are added unbeaten. Shape (with 2 teaspoons) on a greased baking sheet in rounds for cream puffs; in strips 1 inch by 5 for eclairs. Bake in an oven (450°) about 25 minutes. When done, a cake lifted in the hand will feel light. With a sharp knife, make a cut in each puff large enough to admit Cream Filling, which can be forced in with a pastry bag and tube. Eclairs are sometimes covered with Chocolate Frosting (see Cakes and Icings for Filling and Frosting).

Fluffy Boiled Icing

Dissolve ¾ cupful of granulated sugar in ⅓ cupful of boiling water. Let boil until, when tested in cold water, a little of the syrup may be gathered into a soft ball. Pour the syrup in a fine stream on 2 beaten egg whites, beating the mixture constantly. Beat continually until cold or stiff enough to spread on a cake. If the mixture is cooked or beaten too hard, beat in lemon juice or water a few drops at a time. If it is not cooked enough (too thin), set the bowl of frosting over the heat in a pan of boiling water, and beat constantly until the icing thickens perceptibly. This icing is light and fluffy and will not harden as quickly as plain icing.

Chocolate Confectioner's Icing

Mix (about) 1¼ cupfuls of sifted confectioner's sugar with ¼ cupful of liquid-coffee, water, fruit juice, cream, or milk. With fruit juice add a teaspoonful of lemon juice. With other liquid a scant ½ teaspoon of vanilla or other extract. (Add 3 tablespoons cocoa for chocolate icing.)

Cream Filling for Cream Puffs

⅞ cup sugar
⅓ cup cake flour
⅛ teaspoon salt
2 eggs or 4 yolks
2 cups scalded milk
1 teaspoon vanilla or ½ teaspoon lemon extract

Mix dry ingredients, add eggs slightly beaten; add scalded milk. Cook 15 minutes in double boiler, stirring constantly until thickened, afterward stir occasionally; cool and flavor.

Chocolate Cream Filling

To the recipe for Cream Filling, add 1½ squares (1½ ounces) of melted chocolate to the milk when it is put on to scald; proceed as directed, but increasing the sugar to 1 cupful. Spread between layers of sponge cake.

Profiteroles au Chocolate

Profiteroles au Chocolate is a dessert composed of tiny Cream Puffs, filled with Vanilla Custard (see Custard) and covered with Chocolate Sauce. The Cream Puffs should be about the size of a large walnut, and four are served to a portion. Arrange three close together on a dessert plate and place the fourth one in the center on top of the others. Just before serving, pour chocolate sauce over top. (See

Chou-Paste recipe for Cream Puffs and Filling.) Chocolate Sauce: Melt 1 square of unsweetened chocolate (1 oz.), add 1 tablespoon butter and pour on gradually ⅓ cup of boiling water. Bring to boiling point and add 1 cup sugar and 2 tablespoons white corn syrup. Boil for 5 or 6 minutes. Cool slightly and add a few grains of salt and ½ teaspoon vanilla.

Chocolate Frosting

Cook 2¼ cupfuls granulated sugar in ¾ cup of boiling water, until it reaches 238°F., or it forms a soft ball when a little is put in cold water. Pour gradually over 3 stiffly beaten egg whites, beating constantly meanwhile. Add slowly 3 squares of melted chocolate, then, the vanilla, and beat until stiff enough to spread.

PIES

19

Boston Cream Pie

½ cup butter
1 cup sugar
2 eggs
1¾ cups flour
3 teaspoons baking powder
¼ teaspoon salt
½ cup milk
½ teaspoon vanilla

Cream butter, add sugar gradually and well-beaten eggs. Mix and sift dry ingredients together and add alternately with milk to first mixture. Bake in 2 layer cake pans in moderate oven about 20 minutes, or bake in one deep layer cake pan for 35 minutes. If deep pan is used, split cake for filling. Put Cream Filling between layers and spread top layer with Chocolate Frosting (see Cakes and Icings for Cream Filling and Chocolate Frosting).

Washington Cream Pie

2 eggs
1 cup flour
1½ teaspoons baking powder
½ teaspoon vanilla
¾ cup sugar
⅛ teaspoon salt
½ cup boiling milk

Separate eggs. Beat yolks until thick and lemon colored and add them to stiffly beaten whites. Sift dry ingredients together 3 times, and gradually add to beaten eggs. Add hot milk slowly, and vanilla. Bake in deep layer cake pan in moderate oven 35 minutes. When cool, split and put layers together with Cream Filling (see Cakes and Icings for Cream Filling). Sprinkle top with powdered sugar.

Butterscotch Pie

Pie Crust (single):

1 cup flour

¼ teaspoon salt
¼ cup shortening
3 tablespoons butter (cut into pieces)
3 tablespoons cold water

Butterscotch Filling:

1½ cups light brown sugar
1½ cups milk
2 tablespoons flour
3 tablespoons cornstarch
2 tablespoons white sugar
3 egg yolks
3 tablespoons butter
⅛ teaspoon salt
1 teaspoon vanilla

Meringue Top:

3 egg whites
4 tablespoon sugar

Make and bake pie crust first. Sift flour and salt, cut in shortening, butter and enough cold water to cut into a soft dough. Toss on slightly floured board, pat and roll out. Single crusts or shell should be laid over an inverted pie pan and baked in a moderately hot oven. Filling: Add milk to brown sugar and heat to boiling point. Add flour, cornstarch, and white sugar, which have been sifted together, and cook until thick. Add slightly beaten egg yolks and cook 1 minute longer. Remove from heat, stir in butter, salt and vanilla. Cool, fill baked pie crust, cover with meringue—made by beating egg whites until stiff, then folding in sugar. Place in hot oven or under broiler, heat 1 minute until meringue is lightly browned.

Pecan Pie

Follow directions for Butterscotch Pie. When preparing the filling, substitute 1½ cups water in place of the milk and add 1 tablespoon of rum instead of vanilla extract. Top with pecans.

Chocolate Cream Pie

Single Pie Crust:

1 cup flour
¼ teaspoon salt
¼ cup shortening
3 tablespoons cold water
3 tablespoons butter (cut into pieces)

Filling:

½ cup sugar
2 tablespoons cornstarch
2 tablespoons flour
2 squares grated chocolate
2 cups hot milk
2 eggs, slightly beaten
1 tablespoon butter
1 teaspoon vanilla

Topping:

½ pint cream

Make the pie crust first. Sift flour and salt, cut in shortening, butter and enough cold water to cut into a soft dough. Toss on slightly floured board, pat and roll out. Lay crust over an inverted pie pan and bake in a moderately hot oven. Filling: Sift together sugar, cornstarch and flour. Dissolve chocolate in hot milk and add it slowly to sifted dry ingredients. Add slightly beaten eggs and cook in top part of double boiler—20 minutes. Cool, pour into baked pie shell and top with whipped cream.

Apple Pie

3 cups sliced apples
½ cup sugar
⅛ teaspoon salt
¼ teaspoon cinnamon
1 tablespoon lemon juice
Grated rind of ½ lemon
1 tablespoon butter

Line pie plate with Pie Crust. Turn in apples and sprinkle with sugar, salt, cinnamon, lemon juice and lemon rind. Dot with small bits of butter. Put on top crust, pushing it toward the center. Press edges of dough together and trim. Bake in moderate oven (350°) for 50 minutes. (See Index for Pie Crust.)

Coconut Custard Pie

2 eggs
4 tablespoons sugar
2 cups milk
⅛ teaspoon salt
1 cup coconut
Few grains nutmeg

Stir sugar into eggs, and when well-mixed, add milk, salt, coconut and nutmeg. Stir until thoroughly mixed, then pour into well-lined pie plate and bake in moderate oven (350°) for 45 minutes. (See Index for Pie Crust.)

Cherry Pie

1 quart of cherries
2 cups of sugar
2 tablespoons cornstarch
¼ teaspoon cinnamon

Wash cherries, remove stems and pits. Turn into well-lined pie plate and sprinkle with cornstarch, sugar and cinnamon. Cover with crisscross strips of dough, which have been rolled ¼ inch thick and cut ½ inch wide. Bake in hot oven (450°) for 30 minutes.

Lemon Meringue Pie

¾ cup sugar
3 tablespoons cornstarch
2 tablespoons flour
1 teaspoon salt
1½ cups boiling water
4 tablespoons lemon juice
Grated rind of 1 lemon
2 egg yolks

Sift dry ingredients into top part of double boiler; add boiling water and cook until thick (about 20 minutes). Add slightly beaten egg yolks and cook 2 minutes longer. Remove from heat and add grated rind and lemon juice. When cool, fill baked pastry shell (See Index for

Pie Crust) and top with meringue—made by beating 2 egg whites until stiff, then folding in 4 tablespoons of sugar. Place in hot oven or under broiler heat until meringue is lightly browned.

Pumpkin Pie

2 cups stewed pumpkin
2 cups milk
1 cup brown sugar
2 eggs
½ teaspoon salt
1 teaspoon cinnamon
½ teaspoon ginger

Rub pumpkin through a sieve and mix it with milk, sugar, well-beaten eggs, salt and spices. Beat mixture for 2 minutes—then pour into well-lined pie plate and bake in moderate oven (350°) for 1 hour. (See Index for Pie Crust.)

Pineapple Pie (Canned Pineapple)

Basic Crust:

1½ cups flour
½ teaspoon salt
½ cup shortening
4 tablespoons cold water

Filling:

1½ tablespoons flour
1 tablespoon cornstarch
4 tablespoons sugar
2 cups grated pineapple and juice
¼ teaspoon salt
2 tablespoons lemon juice
1 tablespoon grated lemon rind

Sift flour and salt, cut in shortening. Add water, cutting into a soft dough. Toss onto a floured board, pat and roll out. (Double Crust.) Filling: Sift flour, cornstarch, sugar and salt; add to pineapple and juice and cook in top part of double boiler for 20 minutes. Then add lemon juice and grated lemon rind. When cool, pour into well-lined pie plate, cover with top crust and bake in a moderate oven (350°) for 45 minutes.

Rhubarb Meringue Pie

Filling:

2 cups rhubarb
3 egg yolks
1 cup sugar
2 tablespoons flour
¼ teaspoon salt

Meringue Top:

3 egg whites
6 tablespoons sugar

Wash rhubarb and cut in ½-inch pieces. Place rhubarb in colander and pour boiling water over and let drain. Beat egg yolks, and add sugar, flour, and salt, which have been sifted together. Stir rhubarb into mixture and pour into a well-lined pie plate and bake in a moderate oven (350°) for 45 minutes. When cool, cover with meringue—made by beating egg whites until stiff, then folding in sugar. Place in hot oven or under broiler heat until meringue is lightly browned. To make undercrust, cut Pie Crust recipe in half. (See Index for Pie Crust.)

Blackberry or Blueberry Pie

1 quart berries
1 cup sugar
1 tablespoon flour
⅛ teaspoon salt
½ teaspoon vinegar
1 tablespoon butter

Pick over and wash berries. Drain, sprinkle with sugar, flour, salt and vinegar. Turn into well-lined pie plate (deep) and dot with small bits of butter. Put on top crust and bake for 45 minutes in moderate oven. (See Index for Pie Crust.)

Puff Paste

Have ingredients cold, work rapidly, handle dough lightly and as little as possible. Butter must be washed for superior pastry, and this is accomplished by placing butter in a mixing bowl, holding it under cold running water and squeezing it with the hands until it is soft and waxy. Puff paste requires a moderately hot oven and should be baked on a tin sheet covered with a double thickness of unglazed, brown paper. Puff paste may be used for upper crusts of pies (never under crusts), patty shells, rissoles, vol-au-vents, bouchées and tarts. Sift flour once before measuring. A Pastry Blender is a good utensil for cutting shortening or butter into flour. It is composed of several flexible blades or wires connected to a handle. A good feature of the Pastry Blender is that it is light and stays cool while you are cutting in the shortening, which is essential for good pastry.

½ pound butter
½ pound pastry flour
Cold water (6 to 8 tablespoons)

Wash butter, squeeze and fold until all water is extracted. Cut 2 tablespoons butter into the flour, add cold water and knead the dough 5 minutes. Roll to ¼-inch thickness, keeping paste rectangular and corners square. Place remaining butter in center of lower half of dough, cover with upper half and fold right side under and left side over. Roll to ¼-inch thickness. Repeat this folding process 4 times. Put paste in cold bowl, cover over with a damp, not wet, cloth and chill in the refrigerator for at least 1 hour. Cut into desired shapes, place on papered baking sheet and bake in a hot oven (450°) for 5 minutes, reduce heat to moderate (375°) and bake about 30 minutes. (See Techniques.)

Flaky Pie Crust

Double Crust:

2 cups flour
½ teaspoon salt
Cold water (about 4 to 6 tablespoons)
⅓ cup shortening
⅓ cup butter (cut into pieces)

Sift flour and salt. Cut in shortening, butter and enough water to make a soft dough. Toss on slightly floured board, pat and roll out. Cut recipe in half for single crust or shell. Note: When making a double crust for 1 pie, wet the edge of the bottom crust just before putting on the upper crust in order to seal the crusts together.

Biscuit Dough (For Meat Pies)

1 cup flour
2 teaspoons baking powder
¼ teaspoon salt
1 tablespoon shortening
Cold milk (about 6 tablespoons)

Sift together flour, baking powder and salt. Cut in shortening and gradually add cold milk. Toss on slightly floured board, pat and roll to ¼-inch thickness.

GINGERBREADS, DOUGHNUTS, TOASTS & COOKIES

20

Dessert Gingerbread

½ cup butter
1 cup brown sugar
½ cup molasses
1 cup milk
1 egg
2½ cups flour
1 level teaspoon cinnamon
½ level teaspoon ginger
¼ level teaspoon each allspice, cloves and salt
1 level teaspoon each baking soda and baking powder

Cream butter, add sugar and beat until light and creamy. Add molasses, milk and egg. Mix and sift the dry ingredients together and add them to the first mixture. Beat all together for 2 or 3 minutes. Pour into a well-greased, shallow, square pan and bake in a moderate oven about 35 minutes. Serve with whipped cream or hot Chocolate Sauce:

Chocolate Sauce

Melt 2 squares of unsweetened chocolate over hot water. Add 2 tablespoons of melted butter, and when thoroughly blended, gradually add 1 cup of boiling water or milk. Stir constantly and add 1 cup of sugar. Bring to boiling point and let boil for 10 or 12 minutes. Remove from heat, cool, and flavor with 1 teaspoon of vanilla.

Soft Gingerbread

½ cup sugar
⅓ cup molasses
½ cup lard
2 eggs
¾ cup milk
2 cups flour
2 level teaspoons baking powder
1 scant teaspoon salt
½ level teaspoon baking soda
½ level teaspoon each of ginger, cloves and allspice

Beat eggs, and add molasses. Mix sugar and lard, then combine with eggs and molasses. Sift together 3 times: baking powder, flour, salt, soda and spices, and add milk, then combine with the first mixture and beat thoroughly. Bake in a moderate to hot oven (350° to 400°) about 20 minutes.

Drop Doughnuts

2 eggs
½ cup sugar
¾ teaspoon salt
½ teaspoon nutmeg
3 teaspoons baking powder
2 tablespoons melted shortening
⅓ cup milk
2 cups flour

Beat eggs until light; add sugar, salt, nutmeg, melted shortening and milk; add flour and baking powder which have been sifted together. Mix quickly and throughly. Drop by teaspoonfuls in deep hot oil and fry until brown. Get the dough off the spoon and into the oil as quickly as possible. The best way to do this is to dip the teaspoon in hot oil before taking up the dough. If you allow the dough to "pour" from the spoon into the oil, the result will be a long drawn out doughnut instead of a small round doughnut. Drain thoroughly and sprinkle with powdered sugar.

Doughnuts

3 tablespoons butter or substitute
¾ cup sugar
1 egg
¾ cup milk
3 cups flour
4 teaspoons baking powder
¾ teaspoon salt
1 teaspoon nutmeg

Cream butter; add sugar and beaten egg. Stir in milk, add dry ingredients that have been sifted together. Add additional flour (about ½ cup) to make dough stiff enough to roll. Roll out on slightly floured board to ¼-inch thickness. Cut out and fry in deep hot oil (370°) or hot enough to brown a piece of bread in 1 minute. Sprinkle with powdered sugar and cinnamon mixed together.

Baked Toast

3 eggs
3 cups milk
6 slices bread
Few grains salt

Beat eggs and milk together. Add salt. Dip each slice of bread in the beaten mixture and place in a well-buttered baking dish. Pour remaining mixture over the bread. Bake in a moderate oven until nicely browned. Dot with fresh butter and serve from the baking dish.

French Griddle Toast

3 eggs
1 cup milk
2 tablespoons sugar
¼ teaspoon salt
6 slices bread

Beat eggs slightly, add milk, sugar and salt. Strain through cheesecloth into shallow dish. Dip each slice until soft. Brown both sides on a hot, well-greased griddle. Remove to hot plate and sprinkle lightly with fine powdered sugar.

Cinnamon Toast

Remove crusts from thin slices of bread, and then cut the slices in halves, lengthwise. Toast in moderate oven—remove and spread with softened butter. Sprinkle with a mixture of 3 parts sugar to 1 part cinnamon. Return to oven to melt.

Maple Sugar Toast

Remove crusts from thin slices of bread. Toast in moderate oven—remove and spread lightly with softened butter and soft brown sugar. Return to the oven until the sugar melts. Serve each slice with 1 tablespoon of whipped cream.

Standard Sugar Cookies

1 cup butter
2 cups sugar
2 eggs, well-beaten
¼ cup cream
3¾ to 4 cups flour
2 teaspoons baking powder
1 teaspoon flavoring

Cream the butter and gradually add ½ of the sugar. Add the eggs and continue to beat until light and fluffy. Gradually beat in the remaining sugar. Mix and sift the dry ingredients and add them to the first mixture, alternating with the cream. Beat the dough well after each addition of flour as this will insure a smooth mixture. Add flavoring last or it may be added to the cream. Place the cookie dough in the refrigerator to chill for several hours or overnight. Roll the dough on a lightly floured board to about ⅛ of an inch in thickness... sprinkle dough with white or colored sugar, which should be gently pressed in with the rolling pin. Bake in a hot oven until browned... about 10 minutes. Cookies should be removed from cookie sheet while hot to prevent breaking.

Hermits

1 cup butter
3 cups brown sugar
4 tablespoons sour milk
4 eggs
2 teaspoons soda
6 cups cake flour
2 cups raisins
2 cups currants
1 cup nuts
1 teaspoon nutmeg
1 teaspoon cinnamon
A little grated orange peel

Cream the butter and add sugar gradually. Add the milk and eggs, well-beaten. Sift the soda with half of the flour, and add to the mixture, then, the fruit and nuts, which have been chopped and floured. Mix well. Sift the spices with the balance of the flour, and add to mixture. Drop by teaspoonfuls on greased tins, some distance apart and bake. These are delicious and will keep a long time.

Coconut Cookies

¼ cup butter
½ cup sugar
1 egg
1½ cups flour
3 teaspoons baking powder
¼ teaspoon salt
½ cup milk
½ teaspoon lemon extract
2 cups coconut

Cream the butter and gradually add the sugar and egg. Beat well for several minutes until thoroughly mixed. Add the milk and extract and the dry ingredients, which have been mixed together and sifted. Add the coconut and mix well. Drop by spoonfuls on buttered cookie sheet. Shape and flatten the tops with moistened knife. Bake in a moderate oven 15 minutes.

Sand Tarts

½ cup butter
1 cup brown sugar
1 egg
1⅓ cups flour
2 teaspoons baking powder
¼ teaspoon salt
½ cup sugar
¼ teaspoon cinnamon (for sprinkling)
1 egg white (for brushing)

Cream butter; add brown sugar and cream again. Add unbeaten egg and mix well. Fold in flour which has been mixed and sifted with baking powder and salt. Roll to ⅛-inch thickness and cut with cookie cutter. Brush over top with beaten egg white and sprinkle with sugar which has been mixed with cinnamon. Split Blanched Almonds may be placed on top. Bake in a moderate oven (375°) for 15 minutes. Blanched Almonds: Scald almonds for 2 minutes, plunge into cold water, drain and then rub off the skins with a soft towel.

Old Fashion Raisin Cookies

1 cup butter
3 cups sugar
1 cup sour cream
4 eggs
4 cups flour
1 teaspoon baking soda
1 teaspoon baking powder
¼ teaspoon salt
2 cups raisins

Cream the butter, add the sugar and the sour cream. Add the eggs, well-beaten. Mix and sift the flour, soda, baking powder and salt, add the raisins and add to first mixture. Drop by spoonfuls onto buttered cookie sheet and bake in a moderate oven for 15 minutes.

ICE CREAM & DESSERTS

21

Home made ice cream and frozen desserts are absolutely delicious. They are always refreshing and invigorating, and the ice cream freezer soon pays for itself. It is easy to familiarize oneself with the methods used to produce a variety of frozen desserts.

Flavor and texture improve by ripening several hours after freezing: When mixture is very firm, open the container, wipe off the cover and remove the dasher. Scrape ice cream from dasher and sides of container and pack down solidly. Cover with the lid and allow the ice cream to remain frozen for several hours.

Philadelphia Ice Cream (Vanilla)

You need 1 quart of thin cream, 1 cup of sugar, 1 tablespoon vanilla and ⅛ teaspoon salt. Scald ¼ of the cream, add sugar and stir until dissolved. Cool and add remainder of cream, vanilla and salt. Freeze. Makes 3 pints of ice cream.

Strawberry Ice Cream

Wash and crush 1 quart of strawberries and sweeten with 1 cup of sugar. Add to Philadelphia Ice Cream when mixture is half frozen. Freeze until firm.

Chocolate Ice Cream

Ingredients are: 1 quart of thin cream, 1 cup of sugar, 2 squares unsweetened chocolate, ⅔ cup hot water, 1 tablespoon vanilla and a few grains of salt. Melt chocolate, gradually dilute with hot water and add to cream. Then add sugar, vanilla and salt. Freeze.

Custard Ice Cream

Scald 1 quart of milk and 1 cup of cream. Beat 3 eggs and combine with ½ cup of sugar. Mix together 1 tablespoon of flour, ½ cup of sugar and ⅛ teaspoon of salt. Blend all ingredients with hot milk and cream and cook until thickened. When cool, add 1 tablespoon of vanilla. Freeze. Makes 2 quarts of ice cream.

Custard Ice Cream (Chocolate)

Melt 2 squares of unsweetened chocolate, add 2 tablespoons of sugar and 2 tablespoons of water. When thoroughly blended, combine it with the above hot Custard Ice Cream mixture. Cool and Freeze.

French Ice Cream

Scald 1 cup of milk and add it to 4 beaten egg yolks. Then add 1 cup of sugar, ⅛ teaspoon salt, 1 tablespoon vanilla and 1 quart of thick cream that has been whipped. Freeze.

Chocolate Sauce (For Ice Cream)

Melt 1 square of unsweetened chocolate, add 1 tablespoon of butter and pour on gradually ⅓ cup of boiling water. Bring to boiling point and add 1 cup of sugar and 2 tablespoons of white corn syrup. Boil for 5 or 6 minutes. Cool slightly and add a few grains of salt and ½ teaspoon of vanilla.

Butterscotch Sauce (For Ice Cream)

Mix 1 cup of brown sugar with 1 teaspoon of corn starch, add ¼ cup of water, 1 teaspoon of vinegar and 4 tablespoons of butter. Boil ingredients to soft stage (238°). Cool slightly and serve.

Junket Ice Cream (Gelatin)

Junket Ice Cream is an "uncooked" ice cream—meaning that the liquid is not cooked before freezing. It is very easy to make.

Junket Ice Cream is the most economical ice cream as it is creamier with less cream, and no eggs are used. 1 part cream to 4 parts milk is the general rule for making this ice cream. Condensed milk can be used in the proportion of 1 part condensed milk to 7 parts fresh milk:

Vanilla Junket Ice Cream

Makes 2 Quarts:

2 Junket Tablets
1 quart milk
½ pint cream
1 cup sugar
1 tablespoon vanilla
1 tablespoon cold water

Mix milk and cream together, and warm to lukewarm—not hot, then add sugar and vanilla. Dissolve Junket Tablets in the cold water, add to the milk, stir well a moment; then pour immediately into the freezer container and let stand in a warm room until firm—about 20 minutes. Place container in ice cream freezer and freeze.

Baked Alaska

A solidly frozen brick or fancy form of ice cream is needed for this recipe: Cover a bread board with a piece of parchment paper. Place a thin layer of sponge cake on the paper and then place the ice cream on the sponge cake. The sponge cake should extend about ½ inch beyond the ice cream. Cover completely with a thick coating of meringue—made by beating 4 egg whites and adding 6 tablespoons of sugar. This is enough meringue for 1 quart of ice cream. Brown quickly in a hot oven. Slip from paper onto a fancy serving plate and serve immediately.

Pistachio Parfait

A parfait is a rich, delicious dessert and should be served in a stemmed parfait glass. There is a white parfait and a yellow parfait, and from the basic recipe, many kinds may be made. This recipe calls for the white parfait base as follows: Boil ⅓ cup sugar with 4 tablespoons water until the syrup spins a thread when dropped from the tip of spoon. Remove from the heat and beat 2 egg whites until stiff. Add syrup slowly to the beaten egg whites and continue to beat until light and fluffy. Set in the freezer to chill while you beat ½ pint of cream until thick and flavor with 1½ teaspoons vanilla. Beat the chilled egg mixture into the whipped cream and add ½ teaspoon almond extract and ¼ cup finely chopped pistachio nuts. Fill fancy stemmed glasses and set in the freezer to chill.

Butterscotch Parfait

To ⅓ cup of brown sugar, add 1 tablespoon of butter. Stir over low heat until melted and boil for 1 minute. Then add ¼ cup water, stir and cook until butterscotch is melted. Beat 2 egg yolks in top of double boiler until light. Gradually add the butterscotch syrup to the egg yolks. Beat and cook over hot water until very light and fluffy, then place in the refrigerator to chill. While the butterscotch is in the refrigerator, beat ½ pint of cream until stiff, add a few grains of salt and flavor with 1½ teaspoons vanilla. Beat butterscotch mixture into whipped cream with a few turns of the egg beater. Fill parfait glasses with this mixture and place them in the refrigerator and freeze for 2 to 3 hours.

Maple Parfait

To ¼ cup maple syrup, add 1 tablespoon butter. Stir over low heat and let boil for 1 minute. Beat 2 egg yolks in top of double boiler and gradually add the hot maple syrup. Beat and cook over hot water until very light and fluffy, then pour the mixture over 2 egg whites that have been beaten stiff. Set in the refrigerator to chill. Beat ½ pint of cream until stiff, add a few grains of salt and 1 teaspoon of vanilla extract. Beat egg mixture into whipped cream and freeze for 3 hours. Decorate the top of the individual parfaits with bits of candied fruit arranged to form a design. For instance: Cut a candied cherry into 8 parts and arrange the pieces in daisy design. Fill in the center with finely chopped angelica, a licorice-flavord spice.

Marron Frappé

The small broken pieces of roasted marrons may be used for this recipe. Boil together the following mixture: 1 cup water, 1 cup sugar and 2 cups marrons, for 6 minutes. Drain and sieve marrons, reserving syrup. To the sieved marrons, add 1 cup of syrup which has been strained, and 1 pint of cream. Pour this mixture into the ice cream freezer and freeze. Serve in frappé glasses. Garnish with whipped cream and candied cherries.

Peach Melba à la Marron

Pack vanilla ice cream in the bottom of champagne glasses or ice cups. Arrange 1 whole peeled peach (Peel by blanching for 2 minutes in hot water—then soften peach by placing it in a mixture of 1 cup water, 1 cup sugar and 1 teaspoon vanilla; boil for 6 minutes.) in each glass on top of the layer of ice cream. Pour 1 tablespoon of Melba Sauce over each peach. Sprinkle with finely chopped pistachio nuts and top with a whole marron:

Melba Sauce

1 cup crushed raspberries
1 tablespoon lemon juice
¼ cup orange juice
1 cup water
1 cup sugar

Combine the sugar and water and boil for 6 minutes. Remove from heat. Place the raspberries in the hot syrup and steep until mixture cools completely. Strain, add the lemon and orange juices and serve.

Biscuit Tortoni

Whipped Cream, when frozen, becomes a dessert known as a mousse. A mousse can be greatly varied by the addition of different flavors and garnishes. Biscuit Tortoni is simple to make and a delight:

Pound and roll enough stale macaroons to make ¾ cup. Reserve ¼ cup of the rolled macaroons to sprinkle over the top of the dessert. Mix ½ cup of the rolled macaroons with ¾ cup thin cream, ¼ cup sugar and a few grains of salt. Stir until well-mixed and let soak for 1 hour. Then beat ½ pint of cream until thick and gradually beat the macaroon mixture into it. Flavor with ½ teaspoon vanilla and several drops of almond extract. Fill individual paper cases or a fancy mold with the mixture... cover the top with the reserved rolled macaroon crumbs and freeze. Now, just a word about freezing. A mousse does not have to be stirred during the freezing. Simply place in the refrigerator freezer and let stand for 2 or 3 hours.

Lemon Mousse

2 tablespoons cornstarch
1 cup milk
1 cup sugar
⅓ cup lemon juice
3 egg yolks
1 pint cream, whipped

Mix cornstarch with ¼ cup sugar. Add milk and cook in double boiler 15 minutes. Add egg yolks, remaining sugar and cook 1 minute. Add lemon juice and set aside until cold, then fold in whipped cream. Place in the refrigerator freezer for 3 hours.

Feuilles de Roses Cristallisées —Candy Rose Petals

Select 1 pound of the prettiest and nicest pink roses that have been freshly cut. Pick the petals one by one and drop them in water. Drain off the fluid and press the petals in your hands to bruise them gently. Set them in a sieve to drain.

Then take 1 pound of the best white sugar, add sufficient water to dissolve it and allow it to boil to a syrup. Clarify the syrup, and then drop in the rose petals. Allow the syrup to boil up 6 or 7 times. Remove from heat and allow to stand until the cooling sugar forms a coating around the petals. Then drain them off and set the petals apart on paper until they are perfectly dry. The rose petals will be crystallized and should be placed in paper lined boxes in a cool, dry spot. It is impossible to describe the taste.

The Creole also treats plums, oranges, orange blossoms, violets, ginger, and watermelon in the same way. This is where love of beauty crosses over to the side of economy.

Here is a simple recipe to Clarify sugar for Cristallisées:

The white of 1 egg and 1 pint of water is enough for 8 pounds of sugar. Beat the white of the egg to a froth in a dish with 1 cupful of water which should be added slowly to the egg during the beating process. Put the 8 pounds of sugar in a saucepan and dilute it with ½ the egg mixture. When it is thick, set it over the heat and allow it to boil up twice. Then skim it. Continue to add the egg by degrees until the scum on top is perfectly white. Add 1 cup of cold water to carry off any remaining scum. Take it from the heat and strain. The sugar can then be set aside for future use.

Pecan Pralines

Brown sugar is used for making this delicious candy. The ratio is 1 pound of sugar to ½ a pound of fresh pecans. Set the sugar to cook, and as it begins to boil, add the pecans, which should be freshly peeled and cut—some into small pieces and others into halves and quarters. 1 tablespoon of butter and 4 tablespoonfuls of water are enough to mix with the sugar and pecans before starting to boil. The water is sufficient to melt the sugar, and the butter prevents it from scorching.

Let it all boil together until it starts to bubble; while stirring constantly, take it off the stove. Ladle out with an ordinary kitchen spoon and drop the mixture into cakes on a moist marble slab or buttered plate. Each one should be a small cake about 5 inches across and ¼ of an inch thick. Allow them to dry out and lift them from the plate with a knife. If you have been careful to stir the mixture while it was boiling, you will have the most delicious "Pralines au Pacanes." They're marvelous.

Fruit Dumplings

For 12 pears, take 1 pound of flour, pile it on a bread board and make a hole in the center. In the hole, put a ½ pound of butter, 1 egg, 4 ounces of water and 2 pinches of salt. Work these ingredients together with your hands and spread the resulting dough out very thin with a roller. Cut a slice of dough and use each slice to cover a pear. The pears should be about half cooked before being covered with the paste. It is not necessary to peel the fruit, but, of course, a peeled pear is more appealing to the eye. After the pears are wrapped in the dough, brush them with egg yolk diluted with water.

This glazes the dumplings and gives them a nice brown color in the cooking. Place the dumplings in a large pie pan and put them in the oven to bake slowly for approximatley 30 minutes.

★

The Bourdelots, or fruit dumplings, of Normandy in France, are a specialty of that beautiful district, and can be made with apples, peaches or pears, like the recipe above.

Each little town in Normandy is famous for their individual thing—a fish dish, cheese, or a preparation of sausage. The creator of a new dish has the same chance of acquiring immortality as any of the Saints.

Fried Bananas, Cherry Sauce

Split the bananas in halves, lengthwise. Roll them in finely pulverized, stale macaroons, and then in flour. Deep-fry until they acquire a good color. Drain, and brush carefully with apricot marmalade or apricot jam. Arrange the entire quantity on an attractive, flat dish building from a wide base up to a point (pyramid shape). Dredge entire surface with freshly peeled and chopped pistachio nuts. The Cherry Sauce to be served separately:

Cherry Sauce

Melt 4 tablespoons of currant jelly in a saucepan and dilute it with 1 pint of syrup made as follows: Boil together for 6 minutes: 1 cup of water and 1 cup of sugar. Add syrup to melted currant jelly. Wash ½ cup candied cherries in hot water and add to syrup mixture.

Zabaione

This is a delicious Italian dessert and is also known as Sabayon. The Italians serve it in a stemmed glass, and as it is a very light and foamy dessert, it is always eaten with a spoon. The French use it as a sauce for various puddings and cakes. It is delicious when poured over a brioche and served as a dessert. The real Italian recipe calls for egg yolks only, but I like the French recipe better which calls for egg yolks and beaten egg whites. Put 8 egg yolks and 1 cup of sugar in the top part of a double boiler and whip with an egg beater until it becomes frothy. Do not have the boiling water in the lower part of double boiler touch the upper part; otherwise, the egg yolks will cook instead of becoming foamy. Now, add ½ cup of sherry or madeira wine and continue to beat until the Sabayon in very light and begins to thicken... then remove it at once from the hot water and pour it into the beaten whites of 8 eggs, beating constantly until blended.

Les Crêpes Caramello

Make a batter from the Crêpe Suzette recipe (see Crêpes) to make your crêpes. Use a crêpe maker or use a griddle to fry the razor-like pancakes. There are 6 crêpes to a set, and each one is covered with a different liqueur and ignited individually. First use Cointreau; second, Grande Marnier; then Benedictine, Chartreuse, Creme de Cocoa and Kirschwasser, followed in order. This is Caramello's variation of Crêpes Suzette, which he served after every luncheon:

★

Le Coq au Vin
Veal Kidneys

Caramello's restaurant, the Royale Résερve, was located on Cape Ferrat between Villefranche and Beaulieu in France. A réserve is a cafe popular along the Riviera, and there were hundreds along the rocky coast where the Maritime Alps drop into the Mediterranean. Les Crêpes were Caramello's specialty, but here are a couple of other of his recipes that deserve a brief mention:

Le Coq au Vin (Chicken with Wine)—once known as the national dish of Auvergne, and written in rough translation:

"Take the youngest chicken (place it in a casserole dish), but the very oldest bottle of red wine—a good glass is enough (about 6 ounces)—baste very often without stopping the ebullition (boiling process), close the pan hermetically, put in the oven at great heat (400°); in order to have the bottom of the inside form a glacé (icing, or layer of sauce), let it reduce. At the moment of serving, put in some butter to thicken the sauce. After having tasted it, put in the juice of a lemon."

If you will bear with me, I will give you his recipe for Le Rognon Caramello, or Veal Kidneys:

"Take a nice veal kidney, leaving a little grease on it, have it browned rapidly, in order to seal in the moisture. Take a little frying pan with Shallot Butter (see Prepared Butters), tarragon mustard, walnut sauce (Meat sauce), salt, pepper; cut the kidney in very thin slices and let it boil strongly—3 or 4 minutes in this sauce; pour some champagne on it, flame it, let it reduce and with the juice given in the pan, add parsley, chervil, rosemary and other spices; a little lemon juice. Cooking has to be done very quickly."

Dessert Waffles

Sift together 2 cups flour, 3 teaspoons baking powder, ½ teaspoon salt, a few gratings of nutmeg and 3 tablespoons of sugar. Add 1½ cups of milk gradually with 3 beaten egg yolks. Then add 4 tablespoons of melted butter and fold in 3 stiffly beaten egg whites. Have the waffle iron hot...brush over with melted butter and drop 1 tablespoon of batter in each section. Brown nicely on both sides and remove to hot plate and serve immediately with Maple Sugar Sauce:

Maple Sugar Sauce

Break ½ pound of soft maple sugar into small pieces and place in a sauce pan with ¾ cup of cream. Stir slowly until maple sugar is dissolved and boil gently for 5 or 6 minutes. Remove from heat and beat briskly for several minutes. Pour into warm pitcher and serve with the waffles. No butter is necessary with this sauce.

CUSTARDS, PUDDINGS & SAUCES

22

All custards are made from the same basic rule—allowing 1 egg to every cup of milk, plus flavoring and sugar. Various methods of cooking and combining ingredients will produce the different custards. If the whites and yolks of the eggs are separated and cooked over double boiler, you will have custard puddings or floating islands.

Basic Baked Custard

Beat 4 eggs slightly and add ½ cup sugar and ¼ teaspoon salt. Gradually add 1 quart of scalded milk and continue beating until thoroughly mixed. Pour into individual, uncovered molds or a large baking dish. Sprinkle grated nutmeg over the top and set in a pan of hot water. Bake in a moderate oven allowing 45 minutes for small molds and 1¼ hours for large baking dish.

Soft Custard

Follow above recipe for combining ingredients. Cook in double boiler stirring constantly until mixture coats the spoon. Strain and flavor with ½ teaspoon vanilla extract. If soft custard is cooked too long, it will curdle. Should this happen, place the pan in cold water and restore it by beating with an egg beater until perfectly smooth. This custard is a complete dessert, but may also be used as a sauce for puddings or cake.

Caramel Custard

In small saucepan, heat ½ cup of sugar at medium-low to brown for 5 minutes. When sugar begins to melt, stir constantly to prevent it from burning. After an additional 5 minutes, when sugar has browned, carefully add ¼ cup of boiling water. Remove from heat and stir until dissolved. You now have a caramelized sugar known as caramel. Put 1 tablespoon of caramel into each individual custard mold and pour the Basic Baked Custard mixture slowly over it. Bake the uncovered molds in moderate oven for 45 minutes. When the custard is turned out (invert a saucer over the top of a mold and quickly turn it over), there will be a coating of caramel sauce over the custard.

Orange Custard

½ cup sugar
3 tablespoons cornstarch
Few grains salt
2 cups milk
2 egg yolks
½ teaspoon almond extract
3 oranges
⅓ cup sugar
2 egg whites

Mix together sugar, cornstarch and salt. Add milk and cook in top part of a double boiler until thick... about 20 minutes. Add beaten egg yolks and cook 1 minute longer. Remove from heat and add almond extract. Cut oranges in half and carefully remove the sections with a small, sharp knife. Place diced orange in the bottom of a shallow baking dish. Pour custard over fruit and cover with meringue—made by beating egg whites until stiff, then folding in ⅓ cup of sugar. Place in a moderate oven to brown. Serve cold.

Baked French Custard

Heat 1 pint of thin cream in a double boiler. Beat 3 egg whites until stiff and add 3 tablespoons of sugar, a pinch of salt and ½ teaspoon of vanilla. Add beaten egg whites to cream and beat with an egg beater. Turn into buttered custard cups... set in a pan of hot water and bake in moderate oven until firm. Chill thoroughly. Remove from cups and serve with Creamy Lemon Sauce or Chocolate Sauce. (See Lemon and Chocolate for Sauces.)

Orange Sabayon Sauce

2 egg yolks
¼ cup sugar
½ cup strained orange juice
½ cup orange pulp (free from seed and membrane)
⅓ cup hot water

Beat yolks until thick, add sugar, juice, pulp and hot water. Cook over hot water until thickened. Serve hot.

Soft Sauce

½ cup sugar
1 tablespoon cornstarch
⅛ teaspoon salt
1 cup water
1 tablespoon butter
1 teaspoon vanilla

Mix sugar, cornstarch and salt. Add water and cook until mixture thickens. Remove from heat, add butter and vanilla. Serve hot.

Creamy Lemon Sauce

¼ cup butter
½ cup powdered sugar
Grated rind from ½ lemon
1 tablespoon lemon juice

Cream the butter, add sugar gradually while beating constantly. Then add grated lemon rind and—drop by drop, add the lemon juice. Heat over hot water, beat thoroughly and serve as a warm liquid sauce.

Floating Island

Arrange soft custard in individual glass dishes. Beat 2 egg whites until stiff and add 4 tablespoons of granulated sugar and 2 tablespoons of strained lemon juice. Drop from tablespoon onto soft custard and decorate the top with currant or apple jelly.

Old-Fashioned Rice Pudding

Wash ½ cup of rice in cold water and remove any discolored grains. Also wash ½ cup seedless raisins. Mix rice and raisins with 1 quart of milk, ½ cup sugar, ¼ teaspoon salt and ¼ teaspoon mace. Pour into a buttered pudding dish that will just hold its quantity—about 1 quart, and bake 4 hours in a slow oven (250°). Fold every 20 minutes during first hour of baking to prevent rice from settling on the bottom of the dish. Do not put a small quantity of pudding in a large dish because the milk will evaporate too quickly, and there will be quite a space between the top of the pudding and brim of dish. For appearance, this is to be avoided.

Plum Pudding

Plum pudding, the cornerstone of the British Isles, consists of ¾ pound bread crumbs, 1½ pounds raisins, ½ pound of currants, ½ pound mixed candied peels, ¾ pound suet, 8 fresh eggs and 1 wineglassful of brandy.

Wash and clean the raisins, clean the currants thoroughly, shred the candied peels and mince the suet very finely. Rub the bread crumbs through a sieve. Mix all together, beat the eggs and add to the mixture. Then stir in the brandy. Press the mixture into a greased basin or deep pie dish until it is flush with the top. Remember that the basin must be exactly full. Tie a scalded, floured cloth over the top and boil for 5 or 6 hours. Plum pudding is usually made 4 weeks before it is required, and reboiled at least 2 hours before being eaten. When you are ready to serve it and it has had the second boiling of 2 hours, turn it out onto a hot dish, pour brandy over it and ignite the brandy.

Serve with a Brandy Sauce: This sauce is made from a Sweet White Sauce, and the ingredients are: ½ pint of milk, 1 tablespoon butter and 1 tablespoon of flour, the same quantity of powdered sugar, and pinch of salt. Melt the butter in a pan, stir in the flour and cook well without browning. Add the milk and stir until it boils; then allow it to simmer for 2 or 3 minutes. Add the sugar and a good pinch of salt. Add brandy to taste.

Yorkshire Pudding

★

You will find this pudding all over England: In homes, castles, hotels, taverns and hovels. Yorkshire Pudding is the English cousin of the Corn Fritter, which we serve wtih Chicken à la Maryland.

The ingredients are: 2 cupfuls of flour, 2 eggs, 1 pint of milk and salt. The preparation is simple: Sieve the flour into a basin or deep pie dish, add a pinch of salt, make a hollow in the center and add the unbeated eggs and a little of the milk. Mix the flour in gradually from all sides, adding more milk by degrees. When about half the milk has been added and the flour is well-mixed, beat well, preferably with a wooden spoon, until perfectly light and smooth, then gradually stir in the rest of the milk. Allow this batter to stand about 40 minutes, then pour it into a flat tin pan containing a little boiling fat. Bake in a moderate oven for 40 minutes.

Cottage Pudding

¼ cup butter
¾ cup sugar
1 egg
½ teaspoon vanilla
¼ teaspoon salt
½ cup milk
1½ cups pastry flour
2 teaspoons baking powder

Cream butter; add sugar gradually and stir in beaten egg. Add vanilla and salt, then add milk alternately with flour that has been sifted with baking powder. Bake in buttered cake pan in moderate oven for 35 minutes. If individual size is desired, bake in cup cake pans for 20 minutes. Serve with sauce.

Coffee Delicious à la Andre

1 Junket Tablet
1 tablespoon water
½ cup plain brewed coffee
1½ cups milk
¼ cup chopped figs
¼ cup chopped nuts
¼ cup chopped marachino cherries

First prepare the fruit and nuts and put into the bottom of dessert glasses. Next, dissolve the Junket tablet in water and set aside. Put milk and coffee into a sauce pan and heat until mixture is lukewarm, not hot. Now, add the dissolved Junket mixture to the milk and coffee and stir until thoroughly blended. Pour mixture, immediately, into the waiting dessert glasses and let stand in a warm room, undisturbed until firm—about 20 minutes. When firmly set, put the dessert glasses in the refrigerator and leave until serving time. Serve with whipped cream.

Date Whip

Soak 1 tablespoon gelatin in ¼ cup cold water for 5 to 10 minutes; dissolve over hot water. Add ¼ cup lemon juice and fold mixture into 1 cup finely chopped dates. Set aside until it reaches the thickness of molasses. Beat 4 egg whites stiff and fold in ½ cup sugar; then fold in date mixture. Turn into molds and chill. Serve with Soft Custard. (See Custard.)

Apple Snow

Steam quartered apples until soft enough to rub through a sieve. For every 1 cup of apple pulp, allow 3 egg whites. Beat the egg whites stiff and fold in ½ cup of sugar, 1 tablespoon of strained lemon juice and the cup of apple pulp.

Pile lightly in a glass dish or individual glasses and serve with Boiled Custard: Beat 3 egg yolks slightly; add ¼ cup sugar and a pinch of salt. Add 2 cups of scalded milk very gradually and cook in a double boiler until the custard thickens. Stir it during the cooking to keep it perfectly smooth. Strain, flavor with ½ teaspoon vanilla and set aside to chill.

Pineapple Jelly Dessert

Soak 2 tablespoons of gelatin in ¼ cup of cold water for 5 minutes, then add 2 cups of boiling water and stir until dissolved; Add ½ cup of sugar, and when the sugar is dissolved, add 1 cup of pineapple juice, 2 tablespoons strained lemon juice and 2 tablespoons strained orange juice. Pour into fancy molds (dip them in cold water first) and chill. Serve with whipped cream.

MENUS

String Bean Salad
Boiled Cod
Anchovy Sauce
Fried Mushrooms
Noodles, Alfredo

Lettuce Salad
Ragoût of Beef,
Bourgeoise

Whole Wheat Muffins
New England Boiled Dinner
Vanilla Ice Cream
Butterscotch Sauce

Salad
Veal Chops à la Zingara
Boiled Parisian Potatoes
Spinach
Apple Snow

Lettuce Salad
Creamed Cod
Glazed Carrots
French Pancakes with
Orange Sauce

Lettuce Salad
Baked Fillet of Bass
Hollandaise Potatoes
Green Beans
Lemon Pie

Pineapple and Cucumber Salad
Meat Loaf
Cauliflower au Gratin
Browned Parisian Potatoes
French Ice Cream

Pear and Pimiento Cheese Salad
Shad Roe à la Newburg
Cold Slaw

Salmagundi Salad
Minestroné à la Genovese
French Bread

Waldorf Salad
Filet Mignon à la Stanley
Hollandaise Potatoes
Caramel Custard

Salad
Lamb Chops, Soubise
Noodles, Alfredo
String Beans
Sand Tarts

Rice
Chicken Chop Suey
Glazed Onions

Salad
Ham Mousse
Epicurean Sauce
Baked Beans
Spoon Bread

Hawaiian Salad
Broiled Salmon, Fine Herbes
Spinach
Rice
Coconut Custard

Salad
Fried Oyster à la Newburg
Potatoes au Gratin

Fruit Salad
Broiled Chicken
Maître d'Hôtel Butter
O'Brien Potatoes
Cauliflower, Sauce Mornay

Filet Mignon
Sauce Béarnaise
String Beans
Baked Potato
Apple Pie

Salad
Fried Oyster à la Newburg
Potatoes au Gratin

Purée of Tomato Soup
Lobster Creole
Cold Slaw
Rice

Lettuce Salad
Cream of Onion Soup
Liver Creole

Salad
Pork Chops, Florentine
Pasta
Orange Custard

Beet Soup
Roasted Short Ribs
Raisin Sauce
Brussels Sprouts
Special Baked Potato
Washington Cream Pie

Seafood Cocktail
Salad
Fried Oysters, Rector
Glazed Onions

Orange Salad
Broiled Squab
Maître d'Hôtel Butter
Potatoes au Gratin
Spinach en Casserole

Salad, Chiffonade Dressing
Veal, Parapluie
Carrots and Parsnips
Potatoes au Gratin
Pumpkin Pie

Seafood Cocktail
Tomato Bouillon
Crabmeat Creole
Cold Slaw

Mushroom Stems
Baked Cod Espagnole
Rice

Orange Salad
Trout, Sauté Meunière
Parisian Potatoes
Peas

Waldorf Salad
Fried Chicken
Creamed Gravy
Special Baked Potatoes
Corn Soufflé

Fresh Squeezed Orange Juice
Eggs Bombay
Coffee

Seafood Cocktail
Salad
Oyster Stew
Crackers
Basic Custard

String Bean Salad
Scallops à la Stites
Special Baked Potatoes
Rhubarb Meringue Pie

Chicken and Fruit Salad
Baked Haddock
Savory Stuffing
Fried Egg Plant

Orange Salad
Chicken Fricassee
Boiled Parisian Potatoes
Broccoli

Salad
Crackers
New England Fish Chowder

Tomato Surprise Salad
Soufflé

Lamb Stew
Dumplings
French Ice Cream

Orange Salad
Crabmeat à la Mornay
Special Baked Potato
Fried Mushrooms

Salad
Chicken Sauté à la Rector
Asparagus
Potatoes Anna

Steamed Halibut
Babcock Sauce
String Beans
Parisian Potatoes
Orange Custard

Lettuce Salad
Baked Haddock, Italienne
Hollandaise Potatoes
Braised Lettuce

Jellied Tomato Bouillon
Spanish Omelet
Potatoes O'Brien
Coffee

Lettuce Salad
Baked Halibut Creole
Stuffed Baked Tomatoes

Orange Salad
Chateaubriand, Maître d'Hôtel
Zucchini
Special Baked Potato
Fried Mushrooms
French Vanilla Ice Cream

Cold Slaw
Lobster à la Newburg
Baked Potato
Cheesecake

Filet Mignon
Sauce Béarnaise
String Beans
Baked Potato
Apple Pie

Tomato Aspic
Clams Casino
Green Corn, Rector
Special Baked Potatoes

Seafood Cocktail
Bismark Salad
Broiled Oyster
on Toast

Asparagus Salad
Veal Cutlets
Sauce Figaro
Braised Endive
Cheesecake

Lettuce Salad
Boiled Chicken St. Simeon
Rice
Zucchini

Fruit Salad
Broiled Chicken
Maître d'Hôtel Butter
O'Brien Potatoes
Cauliflower, Sauce Mornay

Salad
Ham Mousse
Epicurean Sauce
Baked Beans
Spoon Bread

Lettuce Salad
Fillet of Beef
Mushroom Sauce
Carrots Vichy
Boiled Parisian Potato
Philadelphia Ice Cream

Hawaiian Salad
Fillet of Sole
Tartare Sauce
Rice
Plain Custard

Roast Leg of Lamb
Mint Sauce
Kidney Beans en Casserole
Potatoes Bayonne
Rice Pudding

Orange Salad
Chicken à la King
Spinach en Casserole
Special Baked Potato

Stuffed Celery
Roast Duck
Danish Stuffing
Sauce Bigarade
Home Style Beets
Blueberry Pie

Salad
Breaded Pork Chops
Sauce Piquante
Rice
Green Beans

WEIGHTS & MEASURES

LIQUID MEASURES

1 gallon	4 quarts	
1 quart	2 pints	
1 1/16 quart (Am.)	4 1/4 cups	litre
1 pint	16 fl. oz.	456.0 ml.
1/2 pint	8 fl. oz.	227.0 ml.
1 cup	8 fl. oz.	227.0 ml.
3/4 cup	6 fl. oz.	171.0 ml.
2/3 cup	5 1/3 fl. oz.	152.0 ml.
1/2 cup	4 fl. oz.	114.0 ml.
1/3 cup	2 2/3 fl. oz.	76.0 ml.
1/4 cup	2 fl. oz.	57.0 ml.
	1 fl. oz.	28.5 ml.
1 Tablespoon	3 teaspoons	15.0 ml.
1 Teaspoon		5.0 ml.

DRY MEASURES

2 lb. (generous)	32 oz.	1.00 kilo
1 1/2 lb. (generous)	24 oz.	0.75 kilo
1 lb. (generous)	16 oz.	0.50 kilo
8 oz.	227 grams	0.25 kilo
7 oz.	200 grams	
6 oz.	170 grams	
5 oz.	142 grams	
4 oz.	114 grams	
3 oz.	85 grams	
2 oz.	57 grams	
1 oz.	28 grams	

OVEN TEMPERATURES

	F°	C°
Low	200–225	93–107
Very slow	250–275	121–135
Slow	300	149
Moderately slow	325	163
Moderate	350	177
Moderately hot	375	190
Hot	400–425	204–218
Very hot	450–500	232–260

TOOLS

TOOLS FOR COOKING:

4 Saucepans (large and small)
with lids
2 Frying pans (large and small)
with lids
1 Double boiler
1 Dessert mold
Strainers (fine and coarse)
Colander
Steamer (optional)
Toaster
Griddle
Waffle iron
Deep-fat fryer
Electric frying pan (optional)
Coffee Maker
Roasting pan with rack
2 Small loaf pans
Cake pans (round and square)
Soufflé dish
Casserole dish with lid
6 Custard (timbale) cups
Cookie sheet
Cookie rack for cooling
Pie pan
2 Whisks
1 Soup tureen
1 Marmite (clay pot)
Chafing dish (fondue-like skillet)
Scallop dishes (optional)

TOOLS FOR PREPARATION:

Mixing bowls
Measuring cups
Measuring spoons
Knives (2 paring knives,
1 cook's knife and sharpener)
Cleaver
Cutting board

(continued)

Grater
Flour sifter
Rolling pin
Pastry blender
Biscuit cutters
Potato Ricer (optional)
Vegetable peeler
Egg slicer
Egg beater
Electric mixer (optional)
Electric blender (optional)
Scales (optional)
Ice cream freezer
Icing tubes (optional)
Juicer
Mortar and pestle (optional)
Funnel
Spatula
Wooden spoons
Tongs (optional)
Poultry lacing pin
 and thread
Sieve
Cheesecloth
Cocktail glasses

BOUQUET OF HERBS

The Bouquet of Herbs is a combination of different herbs which are tied in muslin or cheesecloth and dropped in with boiling meat for seasoning. For fish you would use a group of herbs such as parsley, thyme, and a bay leaf. With other meats you would use parsley, cloves, peppercorns, and lemon peel. Any other spices that you desire to use to change the seasoning could be added at this time.

SOUP BUNCH

A Soup Bunch is used as a flavoring for boiled meat. It contains celery, parsley, garlic, and a bay leaf, which are tied together and dropped in the water along with the meat.

(continued)

LARDING

1.
This is a method of preparing meat to keep it tender and moist while cooking. First, prepare your lard, which can be cut from the solid fat of bacon. Cut the bacon in strips. The size of the bacon strip will be determined by your needle size. Use the smaller needles for small game birds or small cuts of meat and the large needles for roasts and larger cuts of meat.

2.
When you have finished preparing the larding fat, place it firmly in the needle so that it will stay in the needle as you are pulling it though the meat.

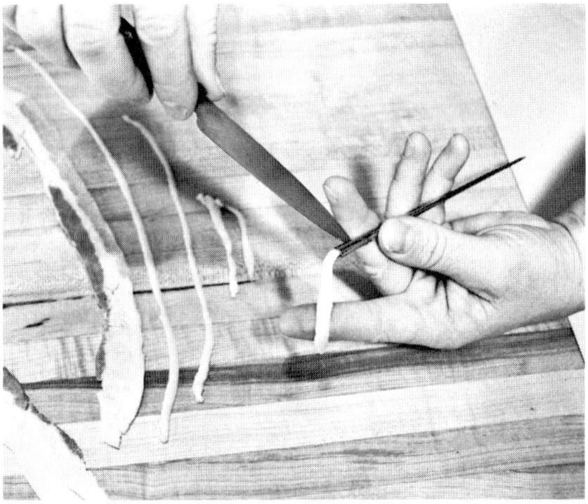

3.
Now push your needle through the meat.

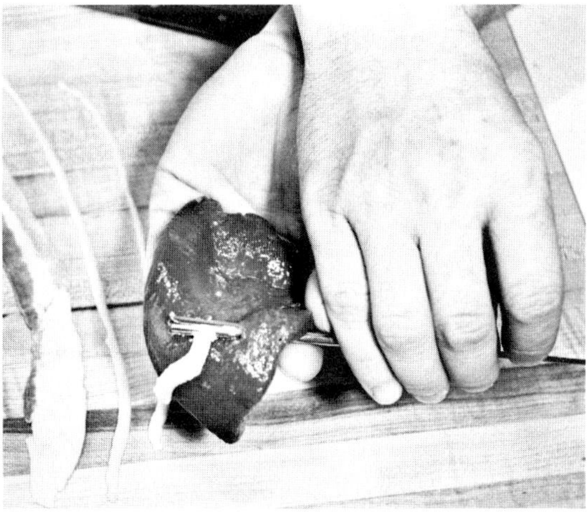

4.
As the larding is pulled through the meat, prepare to remove it from the needle.

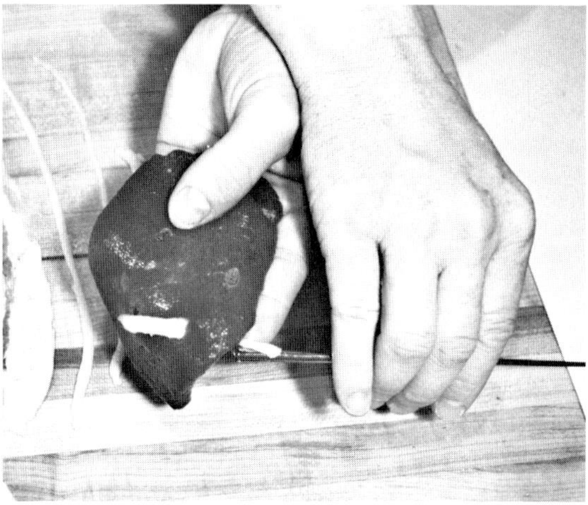

5.
If you have cut your strips short enough, you will not have to trim them. Just use your thumb and forefinger to grasp the larding strip and pull it out of the needle. Otherwise, you should trim the larding strips with scissors.

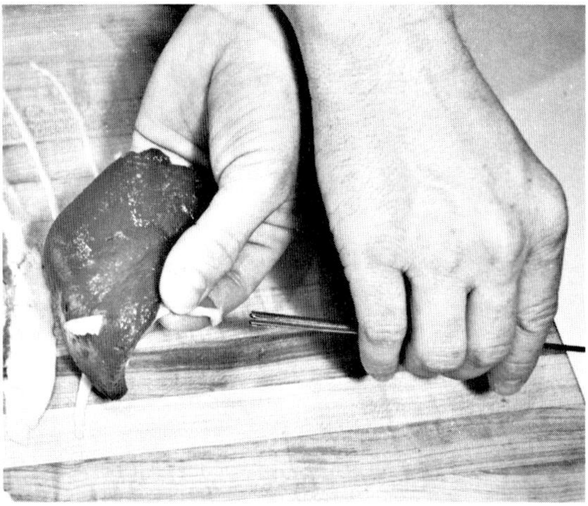

6.
This is a quick illustration of the method of larding. If you were preparing this for display at the table, I would suggest that you create a design with your larding technique. Here you see the finished piece of larded liver. The fowl on the right has been Barded, which is a form of larding. The two bacon strips crossed over the breastbone help protect it from the heat while roasting. The bacon should be tied with string and removed before serving.

POACHED EGGS

1.
To poach eggs, you need 1 quart of water to which 1 tablespoon of vinegar has been added. Bring to a boil, then reduce heat to simmer. Break your eggs as close to the hot water as possible and as quickly as possible.

2.
When the eggs are in the water agitate the water gently to keep the eggs from sticking to the bottom of the pan.

3.
Let the eggs simmer for 3 to 4 minutes.

4.
With a skimmer, remove the poached eggs from the hot water and place them into ice cold water. This will stop the cooking process and will insure perfectly coagulated yolks.

5.
Now trim any unformed egg whites from the poached eggs and set on a towel to dry. The poached eggs can be used right away or refrigerated for a couple of days before use.

PUFF PASTE

1.
This is a fine pastry dough used as a crust for a variety of pastries. See Glossary for specific pastry. To begin, select ½ pound of quality butter. Hold the butter under cold running water and squeeze it until is is soft and waxy. Fold the butter—extracting all the water.

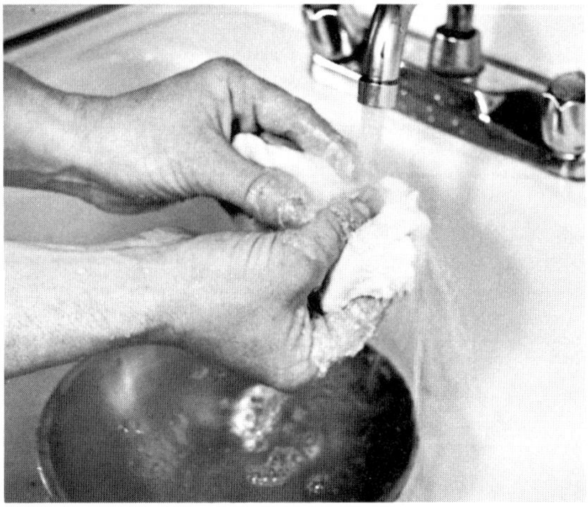

2.
In addition to the butter, you will need ½ pound of pastry flour, and 6 to 8 tablespoons cold water. The flour should be sifted once. Don't forget your rolling pin and pastry board.

3.
Cut 2 tablespoons from the butter and add this—plus the water—to the flour.

4.
Knead the dough for 5 minutes.

5.
Roll out the dough to ¼-inch thickness, keeping the dough rectangular in shape.

6.
Place the butter in the center of the lower half.

7.
Fold the upper half down to cover the butter.

8.
Gently press the edges of the dough together and then press the butter down slightly to prepare for the next step.

9.
Fold the left side over and the right side under. You can also fold both sides up toward you, folding the right side and then the left. As long as the dough is folded in thirds, either method is fine. Roll out again and repeat this process 4 times. First, fold the upper half over the lower half (without the butter this time) and fold the left side over and the right side under. Roll out.

10.
Put Puff Paste in an earthen bowl, cover with a damp towel and let stand in the refrigerator for at least 1 hour. Roll out and cut into desired shapes.

NOTES

INDEX

C

D

E

G

H

Q

R

XYZ